UNITIES AND DIVERSITIES IN CHINESE RELIGION

Also by Robert P. Weller

POWER AND PROTEST IN THE COUNTRYSIDE:
Studies of Rural Unrest in Asia, Europe, and Latin America
(edited with Scott Guggenheim)

Unities and Diversities in Chinese Religion

Robert P. Weller

University of Washington Press
Seattle

Library of Congress Cataloging-in-Publication Data
Weller, Robert P. (Robert Paul), 1953–
Unities and diversities in Chinese religion.
Bibliography: p.
Includes index.
1. Taiwan—Religion.   2. Ghosts—Taiwan.   I. Title.
BL1975.W45   1987   306'.6'0951   86–9085
ISBN 0–295–96397–2

Contents

List of Maps, Tables, Figures and Plates

Maps

Tables

Figures

Plates

Acknowledgements

This book owes its existence to a great many people. I am particularly grateful to the people of Sanxia, whose hospitality and generosity made my research possible. It is impossible to mention everyone who helped by name, but I want to thank especially Zheng Youcai, Huang Yuanlong and Wang Hongzhi, who opened many doors for me; Liu Bingzhen and his entire family, who looked after me; and the staffs of the Changfu Yan and Cede Si, who always helped me with patience and care. Guo Shuhua served as my assistant, and her help made the scope of the research possible. The Institute of Ethnology at the Academia Sinica provided me with an institutional home, and its faculty was an important source of intellectual stimulation.

Emily Martin advised the dissertation research on which much of the book is based. She, Stevan Harrell and Alice Ingerson generously read and commented on the entire manuscript. I am very grateful for their time and effort. I also want to thank Virginia Dominguez, Scott Guggenheim, Susan Naquin, Kathleen Ryan, Brackette Williams, and the members of the faculty seminar on Marxism and Society at Duke University for their comments on parts of the manuscript. My general intellectual debt to Maurice Freedman, Arthur Wolf, and C. K. Yang should be clear from the pages that follow.

The research for this book took place in Sanxia over twenty months between 1976 and 1979, funded by a Wenner-Gren Foundation Grant-in-Aid, a Social Science Research Council International Doctoral Fellowship, and National Science Foundation Grant for Improvement of Doctoral Dissertation Research No. BNS 77–09617. The conclusions and other findings of this book, of course, are my own, and not necessarily those of the funding agencies.

ROBERT P. WELLER

1   Introduction

On my first morning of fieldwork in Taiwan, as I wondered where to begin, my next-door neighbor announced that a ritual was in progress, and led me by the arm to a nearby Buddhist temple. As it turned out, little would happen until the afternoon, and in the lull I asked my new neighbor to show me around the temple. According to my neighbor, all three huge, golden Buddhas that dominated the main room were Hut Co, the Buddha Patriarch. This seemed typical of popular religion in Taiwan; temples often have multiple images of a single deity on their main altars. These images looked a little different from the usual popular deities – they wore robes instead of traditional Chinese dress, and they were bigger than most images in popular temples – but these differences seemed like minor Buddhist variations on a common Taiwanese theme.

Next my neighbor identified the two colorful images that flanked either side of the main altar as the temple door gods (*mng-sin*). One was red, the other was white, and both had the colorful dress and threatening posture typical of door gods found in all popular temples. They were statues instead of the more usual paintings on the temple doors, but this again seemed like a minor Buddhist variation.

Finally, I learned the proper procedure for worship. Just as in any non-Buddhist temple, the supplicant should offer incense first to the Emperor of Heaven (Thi: Kong) in a large incense pot that stands outside the main doors of the temple, then to the gods on the main altar, and finally to the secondary deities like the door gods. None of this information surprised me; all of it fits the extensive literature on popular religion in Taiwan.

The surprises came the next day, when I put the same questions to two nuns who lived in the temple. First, the main gods were not Hut Co. In fact, they were not gods (*sin*) at all, but a Buddha (Sakyamuni) and two associated Bodhisattvas. I pointed out that the three images looked identical, but the nuns showed me slight iconographic differences. Second, the 'door gods' also got new identities. One nun explained that the red-faced statue represented Kuan Kong, one of the most important deities in the popular beliefs; I could see the strong resemblance. She seemed to be claiming that Buddhism was so powerful that even the major deities of the popular religion became merely devoted door gods in a Buddhist temple. My surprise

1

increased when the second nun interrupted, saying that because I had come to study religion, I should learn who the 'door gods' *really* were. In fact, the two images were not door gods at all, but the Protectors of the Dharma (Hufa Shen), two Bodhisattvas (not mere gods at all) who protect the faith. Finally, I learned that even the Emperor of Heaven had lost his place at the top of the cosmology. The nuns held that incense should go first to the Buddhas, and only afterwards to mere gods like the Emperor of Heaven.

These new interpretations no longer seemed like simple variations on the popular tradition, but instead called the entire popular cosmology into question. The popular cosmology closely parallels the secular political hierarchy. People will explain that the Emperor of Heaven is like President Jiang, that Co Su Kong (the main deity in Sanxia, the area I studied) is like a governor, that the Earth God (Tho Te Kong) is like a police officer, and so on. Did Buddhist interpretations challenge that political metaphor? If so, what were the implications for political and ideological unity in a complex society like China?

I was especially puzzled as to how my neighbor and the nuns could maintain their apparently very different interpretations so easily while worshipping in the same temple. These questions about unity and diversity, interpretation and reinterpretation, set the tone for the research that followed. This book examines Chinese religion in Taiwan as a whole, covering both the popular religious traditions and the established traditions like Buddhism, Taoism and the state cult. How far can we say that more than one religious tradition exists in China? How do people use and interpret religion in different situations? How far does religion unify this complex society, and how far does it instead divide one group from another? What are the political implications of religious unity and diversity?

Unity or Diversity

Debates about unity or diversity have been central in recent studies of religion in complex societies. C. K. Yang (1961, p. 276), for example, holds that the elite and the common people in China shared their most central religious concepts.

> Even taking into account the relative difference in the belief in magic and miracles, the Confucians did not constitute a group separate from the general current of religious life of traditional

Chinese society. They shared with the rest of the population a basic system of religious beliefs in Heaven, fate, and other supernatural concepts. More important was the interflow of religious ideas between the Confucians and the general population.

Maurice Freedman (1974, p. 20), who cited Yang approvingly, writes that Chinese religion shows an order 'of a kind that should allow us . . . to trace ruling principles of ideas across a vast field of apparently heterogeneous beliefs, and ruling principles of form and organization in an equally enormous terrain of varied action and association'. He goes on to justify this search for unity behind apparent diversity:

> It is reasonable to assume (I think) that a country of China's extent and political cohesion would demonstrate a large measure of agreement on religious assumptions among all its people. And, more important, one might predict from first principles that a society so differentiated by social status and power would develop a religious system that allowed differences in beliefs and rites to complement one another – or, to put the point more provocatively, that allowed religious similarity to be expressed as though it were religious difference. (Freedman, 1974, p. 38)

Although Freedman never developed this argument in detail, it rests on the assumption that the diversity of Chinese religion stems from various transformations of a basic structural unity.[1] He writes, for example, that apparently diverse ideas may be 'reflections, perhaps misshapen reflections, or idiomatic translations of one another' (1974, p. 21), and that differences between elite and popular understandings of geomancy are a 'neat transformation' (1969, p. 10). Certain basic themes do underlie much of Chinese religion. A strong parallel between the supernatural hierarchy and the secular political hierarchy, for example, penetrates much of Chinese society at all levels (see Chapter 2). Yet the search for underlying unities can be misleading if it simply dismisses diversities like the alternate interpretations of Buddhist iconography that I encountered in my first two days of fieldwork. The chapters that follow discuss many similar examples of fundamental diversity in detail. The religious diversity of complex societies like India, China or Europe is striking, and it demands explanation beyond reduction to a structural unity.[2]

Freedman's presentation of his ideas about Chinese religious unity met with some disagreement. Robert Smith, for example, replied to Freedman that 'this society may have treated religious differences as though they were religious similarities' (1974, p. 341). Arthur Wolf also disagreed with Freedman. Wolf expects people with different perspectives on Chinese society to hold different sets of beliefs, and he thus sees 'a vast gulf between the religion of the elite and that of the peasantry' (1974a, p. 9). Wolf (1974a, p. 9) thus emphasizes diversity over unity:

> We should begin by reconstructing the beliefs of people who viewed the Chinese landscape from different perspectives . . . The fact that an idea was shared by people with such very different perspectives would suggest to me that it was relatively insignificant or that it was easily invested with very different meanings.

Some studies from other parts of the world also suggest that complex societies support diversity within their religions. For sixteenth- and seventeenth-century England, for example, Thomas (1971, pp. 159–66) argues that formal religion had only a precarious hold on much of the population, in spite of the ongoing religious controversies among the elite. Most of the population maintained its own set of traditional interpretations, largely independent from arguments about Christian orthodoxy. In a study of a modern Spanish valley, Christian (1972) argues that there are three major structures of interaction between people and God. For most people, saints are divine intermediaries who can act in the world, and who can help on the road to salvation. For older priests with local roots, the Church and its priests mediate people's relation to saints, who in turn mediate with God. Both structures are hierarchical, and are close enough to each other to allow peaceful coexistence. More recently, a younger group of priests has challenged these structures, stressing individual, personal relationships with God, and promoting community action as a means to personal spiritual satisfaction (Christian, 1972, pp. 180–7). All of this variation exists within the rural community, and it extends even to the basic structures of worship.[3]

Thus some people stress the unity of religion in complex societies: different groups may use different methods of expression, but the entire society shares the fundamental meanings of the religion. Others, however, emphasize its diversity: different groups have different life experiences, and the fundamental meanings of the religion must vary according to each group's position in the society. There are convincing arguments for both unity and diversity in religion, and in culture more generally. Both the unity and the diversity hypotheses suggest that there is a shared body of culture (or at least religion), but they differ in the social group with which they associate it. One view associates culture with society as a whole, while the other associates culture with groups within the society. Phrased in this form, the two hypotheses cannot be reconciled (as the Freedman/Wolf debate seems to require): culture is unified if one focuses on the whole society, and diverse if one focuses on the groups within it. A solution is possible, however, by adopting a more flexible and less traditional view of culture, which does not automatically associate a predetermined set of beliefs with a particular, bounded group.

Culture and Work

Edward Sapir (1934, p. 200) was an early proponent of a more flexible view of culture:

> Culture, as it is ordinarily constructed by the anthropologist, is a more or less mechanical sum of the more striking or picturesque generalized patterns of behavior which he has either abstracted for himself out of the sum total of his observations or has had abstracted for him by his informants in verbal communication . . . No matter how accurate their individual itemization, their integrations into suggested structures are uniformly fallacious and unreal.

He concludes that culture is 'not something given but something to be gradually and gropingly discovered' by members of a society (1934, p. 205). Culture is thus not an entity to be located at the level of either whole societies or of classes (or other groups) within them; culture is instead *made* by people experiencing the real constraints of both society and class.

People create their culture (including their religion) within the constraints of their society as a whole, and of their own position within that society. These constraints produce both a fundamental unity (where the general social constraints are active) and a fundamental diversity (where the individual or group constraints are active).[4] Certain meanings are indeed shared, while others are shaped by particular experiences. It is not possible to provide a catch-all characterization of religion in a complex society as unified or diverse. Instead the variation (or lack of it) relates to the varying social relations of the people involved.

E. P. Thompson's studies of class and consciousness explore one path toward a more flexible and historical view of culture.

> By class I understand an historical phenemenon, unifying a number of disparate and seemingly unconnected events, both in the raw material of experience and in consciousness. I emphasize that it is an *historical* phenomenon. I do not see class as a 'structure', nor even as a 'category', but as something which in fact happens (and can be shown to have happened) in human relationships. (Thompson, 1963, p. 9)

While this study is not primarily about class, it makes a similar point: people make their ideas and ideologies within the changing constraints of social organization. There is no need to choose between unity and diversity, or between opposed elite and peasant ideologies. All these processes become clearer by examining how they really occur in the experiences of people in particular social positions.

Raymond Williams has developed a similar approach, which sees culture and ideology as a kind of work. The production of meanings in culture is a concrete social process just as crucial to the society as the production of material commodities. He writes that

> The limiting condition within 'ideology' as a concept, from its beginning in Destutt, was the tendency to limit processes of meaning and valuation to formed, separable 'ideas' or 'theories'. To attempt to take these back to 'a world of sensations' or, on the other hand, to a 'practical consciousness' or a 'material social process' which has been so defined as to exclude these fundamental signifying processes, or to make them essentially secondary, is the persistent thread of error. For the practical link between 'ideas' and 'theories' and the 'production of real life' are all in this material social process of signification itself, (Williams, 1977, p. 70)

Meaning, in other words, cannot be isolated from social process. This view of culture as a kind of work leads to an emphasis on active interpretation, rather than seeing culture as a code of predetermined meanings. Throughout this book, I shall be concerned with the constant interpretation and reinterpretation of religious practice. Religion is not simply a mental object for members of the appropriate class or society to decode. It is instead a process of making meaning out of a set of symbols and practices, based on experience of a particular set of social relations.

People make meanings (as they work) in social organizations. Some meanings are in fact very institutionalized; the Church is the final interpreter and promoter of Catholicism; the imperial government controlled the state cult in China, and so on. Institutions promote their systems of thought and reserve the right to impose 'correct' interpretations of them. Institutions tend to promote self-consciously organized, explicit systems of thought – ideologies. They ideologize thought because promoting a set of ideas requires making them explicit, and because imposing an interpretation requires a self-conscious organization of those ideas. The ideas that most institutions promote generally support the social status quo, simply because major institutions that fundamentally oppose the power structure are not likely to survive long. If they do survive, they usually create a new power structure, which they support by ideologizing their ideas.

Much culture, however, is neither strongly institutionalized nor strongly ideologized. It exists instead as a process of pragmatic interpretation and reinterpretation. I take the term pragmatic from sociolinguists like Hymes (1974) and Silverstein (1976) who distinguish between two crucial functions of language: (1) a referential function in which factual information is communicated, and (2) a pragmatic function in which social situations are defined and manipulated. Most native speakers, for example, hold no explicit, self-conscious theories about their language, and they do not learn what it means through any formal institution. Language, like common sense, is instead taken for granted as part of daily social interaction. Williams contrasts this kind of pragmatic interpretation, which he sees organized into 'structures of feeling', with more ideologized thought: 'structures of feeling can be defined as social experiences *in solution*, as distinct from other social semantic formations which have been *precipitated* and are more evidently and more immediately available' (Williams 1977, pp. 133–4). Pragmatic interpretations (those in solution) are less explicitly worked out than precipitated ideologies; they are also less tied to specific institutions, and more to everyday social relations. Yet both ideologized and pragmatic interpretations remain processes of making meaning, not predetermined codes for thought.[5]

These processes, as they have shaped religion in Taiwan over the last century, form the core of this study.

Styles of Interpretation

This new viewpoint changes the focus of the unity/diversity debate, because it no longer asks simply whether the culture of a group is unified or diverse. Instead, a series of new questions should clarify both the unities and the diversities in Chinese or any other culture: when do ideologies precipitate out of pragmatic interpretations? how can we characterize the differences between more and less ideologized interpretations? what types of social experiences support particular styles of interpretation, and how do those experiences relate to the political economy and its institutions?

Max Weber (1951) is the most important social theorist who applied a general theory about the development of particular types of consciousness specifically to Chinese material. 'Traditional' religion, according to Weber, fills popular needs for meaning and assurance by providing an enchanted world where every object is filled with supernatural qualities. Under certain historical conditions, however, a particular status group may begin to question traditional religious assumptions self-consciously. The result is a 'rational' religion that abstracts the supernatural from the natural world, and that uses the supernatural as a basis for an ethical code. Traditional and rational religion thus partially resemble pragmatic and ideologized interpretation, as defined above.

Geertz (1964b, p. 172) has summarized Weber's distinction between traditional and rational:

Traditional religions consist of a multitude of very concretely defined and only loosely ordered sacred entities, an untidy collection of fussy ritual acts and vivid animistic images which are able to involve themselves in an independent, segmental, and immediate manner with almost any sort of actual event . . . Rationalized religions, on the other hand, are more abstract, more logically coherent, and more generally phrased. The problems of meaning, which in traditional systems are expressed only implicitly and fragmentally, here get inclusive formulations and evoke comprehensive attitudes. They become conceptualized as universal and inherent qualities of human existence as such, rather than being seen as inseparable aspects of this or that specific event.

In his discussion of China, Weber opposes the traditional 'magic garden' of Taoism to the rational 'disenchanted' world of Confucianism (Weber, 1951, pp. 226–7). There are many specific problems in Weber's analysis of China (see Metzger, 1977), but the most serious problem for understanding unity and diversity in religion lies in his characterization of popular and elite beliefs. On the traditional side, he conflates Taoist and popular beliefs despite the important differences between them (see Chapter 4). He also includes diviners, geomancers and other experts in five-phase theory as part of traditional religion, although this theory was an important part of elite education (see Chapter 6). On the elite side, he overemphasizes the unity and dominance of the Confucian tradition, and underestimates the importance of Buddhism, Taoism, the state cult and five-phase theory. Elite ability to manipulate the popular religion was also important in China, especially at the local level. Thus he oversimplifies the distinction between a rational elite religion (Confucianism) and a magical popular religion (Taoism) on at least two counts: (1) he combines traditions that are in fact significantly different (e.g., Taoism and geomancy), and (2) he underestimates the importance of access to more than one tradition (e.g., for local elites, see Chapter 2). In addition, Weber does not allow for flexible interpretation and reinterpretation; his analysis of China tends to treat meaning as a given, rather than as a process of work. In spite of the problems in Weber's specific application of his distinctions, his work suggests several possibilities for analysis of Chinese religious traditions. Are some traditions more systematized than others? more rationalized? more associated with elites? Where, in other words, does the distinction between pragmatic and ideologized interpretation apply in Chinese religion?

Other scholars make distinctions reminiscent of Weber's. Basil Bernstein (1970, 1972), for instance, suggests a relationship between the form of language and the social experiences of its speakers. The working class, which he characterizes by 'restricted social relationships based on communalized roles' (Bernstein, 1972, p. 166), tends to speak in a restricted code – they use extensive metaphoric and condensed language that is meaningful only when a lot of common knowledge can be assumed, and only when tied to a particular social context. Borrowing loosely from Weber, restricted codes are more traditional (more inseparable from established social experience), and elaborated codes are more rational (explicit and context-free).

Some studies of Western political ideologies make a similar distinction. Converse (1964), for example, characterizes elite beliefs as more abstract and more logically coherent than the more context-bound ideas of most people. Mann (1970), in a review of the literature, concurs wih Converse, and adds that workers usually express dissident values only where the issue is concrete and relevant to their lives. These works thus also point to a distinction between context-bound ideas and more explicitly developed ideas abstracted from any immediate social context.

Finally, the Soviet psychologist A. R. Luria (1976[1974]) contrasts the 'graphic-functional' (concrete and situational) thought of illiterate Uzbeki peasants, with the more abstract and discursive thought of individuals who worked on collective farms and who had a little formal education. The works of these authors are not strictly comparable; Weber is concerned with religion and the development of capitalism, Bernstein with language and education, Converse with political ideology, and Luria with cognitive development. Yet their similar conclusions suggest that all are addressing common underlying issues. All address the relation between thought and social experience, and all distinguish a more context-bound kind of thought from a more explicit kind of thought, which has been systematized and abstracted out of any specific social context.

All also suffer from treating their distinctions as two separate structures of thought, rather than as two flexible styles of interpretation, to which everyone may have (at least potential) access. Converse (1964, p. 211) himself backs off from a claim that elite ideologies are more objective and logical, and Luria's informants were probably using a style of interpretation appropriate only to particular social contexts. Labov (1969) has criticized readings of Bernstein that consider middle class English superior to Black English, and Bernstein himself insists that both codes have the potential to express any ideas. It is not clear exactly what force words like rational or logical are supposed to have in these contexts, and I will not use them. The important difference between ideologized and pragmatic styles of interpretation lies in their relation to immediate social context, not in their inherent rationality.

I also reject the notion that only certain people are capable of certain styles of interpretation. Pragmatic and ideologized interpretations characterize everyone, and are constantly developing into and out of each other. When I argue below that elites tended to develop more ideologized religious interpretations, I do not mean to imply that others are incapable of ideologized interpretations, or that structured ideologies are more rational than pragmatic interpretations.

Pragmatic and ideologized interpretations are two ways of giving meaning to experience, not two structured codes of thought. The distinction between the two clarifies the social basis of different interpretations. The chapters that follow emphasize the flexibility of interpretation as people remake their religion in changing social conditions. They also expand on the distinction between pragmatic and ideologized styles of interpretation by introducing new, cross-cutting distinctions.

Freedman praised what he considered a dormant sociological tradition that took a very broad view of Chinese religion, and that included DeGroot (1897), Granet (1975 [1922]) and Yang (1961).[6] I am indebted to all these works, and build on them here both ethnographically and theoretically.[7] I concentrate on religion within a single township in Taiwan, sacrificing some of the wide scope of the other studies for a more detailed ethnographic understanding. My scale is small by the standards of those works, but it is much larger than the scale of most anthropological studies of Taiwan. I approach these problems of unity and diversity primarily by analyzing a single ritual, the ghost-feeding ceremony (Universal Salvation festival, Pho To), from different points of view. Either Buddhists or Taoists can perform this major annual community ritual that attracts all classes of people. The argument throughout concentrates on diversities in style of interpretation, on flexibility in interpretation as social conditions change, and on the social roots and political implications of unity and diversity for Taiwanese religion. Although I concentrate on northern Taiwan, these concerns are also directly relevant to the study of late imperial and Republican China, and more broadly to the problems of ideology in any complex society.

Sanxia Township

The traditional anthropological emphasis on popular religion in Taiwan results in part from limiting ethnography to single villages. Villages usually lack just the kinds of informants who are essential for a broader understanding of religion: politicians, wealthy businessmen, college graduates and religious specialists. By concentrating on the town of Sanxia and its rural environs, I had available a range of informants and religious understandings much wider than is available to traditional village studies. I worked with people from a wide range of classes, occupations and educational backgrounds, attempting to establish the relation between religion and various sociological and historical influences on individual experience.[8]

Sanxia Township consists primarily of the drainage basin of the Sanxia River, located at the southern end of the Taibei Basin.[9] Outside of the valleys created by the Sanxia River and its major tributary, the Hengxi, Sanxia is mountainous and sparsely populated. It includes a major town of about twenty thousand (also called Sanxia), with several dozen villages scattered in the valleys.

Like many rural areas in Taiwan, Sanxia Township now has many small factories that offer employment to many of its residents. Many others commute to factories in larger towns nearby or in Taibei. The valley areas of the township double-crop wet rice. The more mountainous areas produce tea and tangerines. The mountains are also an important source of coal.

Most of the early Chinese settlers in Sanxia originally came from Anxi County in Quanzhou Prefecture of Fujian Province. They brought with them the most important local god in Anxi, Co Su Kong. Sanxia first erected a temple to Co Su Kong in 1769, and it remains the ritual center of the township and some of the surrounding areas. Settlers from Meizhou (also in Fujian) were second in importance after the Anxi people, and they built a temple to their primary deity, Ma Co. Both temples are losing their identification with people from different areas of the mainland, and are now oriented more toward contemporary geographic communities (see Chapter 2).

The Chinese ceded Taiwan to Japan in 1895. Sanxia was one of the centers of spotty resistance to the Japanese in northern Taiwan. The Japanese took revenge by burning the Co Su Kong temple (along with much of the rest of Sanxia), although some residents managed to save the primary image of the god by removing it to an outlying village. The Japanese generally discouraged Taiwanese religious expressions for two reasons. First, they feared the congregations of people that large rituals create. Secondly, they wanted to promote Japanese Buddhism as a tool for the cultural unification of their planned pan-Asian empire. Buddhism was the most appropriate religion for this purpose because it was important in Japan, and because it existed in various forms in many of the nations of East and Southeast Asia. Chapters 3 and 5 expand on this period of Sanxia's history.

The Japanese defeat in 1945 and the arrival of the Nationalist government brought political turmoil to Taiwan, but (after a few difficult years) it also ended most of the religious repression. The residents of Sanxia survived the turmoil relatively unscathed. Those who held local power during the Japanese period remained important local figures. Sanxia's first township head under the Nationalists soon took charge of a major reconstruction of the Co Su Kong temple, and this grandiose project was still in progress while I lived in Sanxia thirty years later.

After 1945, many Buddhist and Taoist clergy, including the Taoist Heavenly Master and several renowned Buddhist monks and nuns, moved to Taiwan from the mainland. The Buddhist influence has been especially strong in Taiwan because the immigrant clergy set up numerous schools; the young Buddhist monks and nuns of Taiwan are thus more firmly versed in Chinese Buddhist orthodoxy than were their local predecessors (see Chapter 4). Several young nuns in Sanxia have been educated in these new schools, and a monk who immigrated from the mainland after the civil war has also established a temple there.[10]

One portion of my research centered on a settlement in the Sanxia valley, providing an opportunity to examine the popular religious tradition within a small community. This settlement, called Kiu Kiong Kiou, consisted of only forty-one households while I was there, and is part of a larger administrative unit called Zhongpu Li. Kiu Kiong Kiou was settled late in Sanxia's history, in the mid-nineteenth century, when the economy was becoming commercialized and little land was available. Most of the residents have always been manual laborers; most are employed today in construction or in nearby factories. There is rapid population turnover as old residents move toward the town of Sanxia or toward Taibei, and more rural people move in as they abandon farm for factory. As in nearby Ploughshare (Harrell 1974b, 1982), there are no lineages, probably due to the late settlement and lack of land in the area.

Kiu Kiong Kiou is a small, clearly defined community, and I could therefore interview every household in depth. Much of my research, however, took place outside Kiu Kiong Kiou, because the settlement does not represent the range of religious variation in Sanxia as a whole. Most people are poor, and no one could be considered very wealthy. Only one person had attended college. There are no Taoists, although there is a small Buddhist temple. As a result, I spent much time surveying all the temples in Sanxia Township, talking to religious specialists, and interviewing a wider range of informants than was available in Kiu Kiong Kiou. Toward the end of my stay, I also used a questionnaire that included items about the frequency of worship at various temples in Sanxia, and about participation in various types of rituals.[11] It included both open-ended and multiple-choice questions about the efficacy, meaning and importance of particular religious acts. I interviewed 122 respondents with a wide variety of backgrounds. The sample was not random, and I will use the results primarily as a supplement to other kinds of data.

Feeding the Ghosts

On the first day of the seventh lunar month (usually sometime in August), during the most oppressive period of Taiwan's muggy summers, all souls suffering in the underworld are released to enjoy a month of freedom.[12] During a series of small rituals throughout the month, and in one climactic ritual on the fifteenth of the month, the living provide the unfortunate souls with spiritual solace in the sermons of Buddhist and Taoist priests, and with material help in offerings of everything from baths to food to cigarettes. Everyone joins in this climactic ghost-feeding ritual. Specialists of all kinds take part, the entire spectrum of the community population prepares offerings, and low-level government officials help organize the ceremony. In late imperial times, even the local scholar–officials took part in the ritual (Gordon-Cumming, 1900, p. 219, Wieger, 1913, p. 433). At least superficially, the ghost-feeding ritual is one of the unities of Taiwanese religion. This section is a glimpse of the most obviously shared part of the ritual – its physical performance. It begins to suggest the various ways that different kinds of participants experience and interpret the ritual, relying primarily on my attendance at various ghost-feeding ceremonies in 1976, 1977 and 1978, on historical evidence about the ritual, and on interviews with participants. The succeeding chapters expand and interrelate the points of view of the major kinds of participants – the majority of ordinary worshippers, the religious specialists and the secular elite – clarifying how they understand and use the ritual, how it relates to pragmatic and ideologized styles of interpretation, and how it connects to social organization.[13]

The Popular Viewpoint

The Co Su Kong temple, which is the ritual center for Sanxia Township and some of the surrounding areas, organizes the primary performance of the ghost-feeding ritual. Planning for the ceremony begins several weeks before the actual performance. The temple management, which is tied to one of Sanxia's political factions, calls a meeting of all the village heads (*li tiu:*) – elected officials at the bottom of the political hierarchy. The temple announces the schedule of events for the ceremonies of the fourteenth and fifteenth, and it instructs the village heads to organize their constituents' offerings at the various altars that will be set up in the town. Discussion at the meeting demonstrates clearly the political importance of religion. Chapter 2 examines one such meeting in detail, including some bitter debates provoked by a pro-government faction's suggested changes in the ritual.[14]

On the day of the ceremony, representative village heads set up five altars at appointed places in Sanxia town. Four of the altars represent the Four Great Pillars (*si tua thiau*), a geographical division of the Sanxia valley into four units. The details of each altar are subject to the whim of the person in charge. Some have images of gods, others have scrolls of calligraphy; all have incense pots for the gods and offerings of fruit and candy. In front of each altar a row of tables stretches out for perhaps twenty meters to hold the offerings for the ghosts. A fifth altar occupies the Zhong Shan Tang (Sun Yat-sen Hall), an official community center.

The evening of the lunar fourteenth sees the first major ritual that involves both the general public and the priests – the Release of the Water Lanterns (*pang cui tieng*). Each water lantern is a little red and white paper house on a bamboo base, about one cubic foot in size. Sanxia uses eight of them – one for each of the Four Great Pillars that represent the Sanxia valley, one for the incense pot master who represents the whole community, and one for each of his three assistants. A lit candle flickers through the paper walls of each water lantern. Several dozen people, including the officiating priests, parade out from the temple. Some carry signs that announce the festival, others carry torches, and still others hold the water lanterns. They march up and down the main streets of the town, and then as many as can fit board a truck to more distant areas of the Sanxia valley.[15] The parade winds up at the shore of a river. Here the priests conduct a quick ceremony to invoke the gods of the water, and to invite the drowned ghosts to the next day's ceremony. The people then gently release the lanterns into the water, where they drift downstream, signaling to the ghosts of the river that a feast is being prepared in their honor.

The bustle increases throughout the next day. Everyone must

prepare food for their offerings to a whole host of spirits in addition to the ghosts. Like most feast days, the fifteenth of the seventh month includes worship of the Earth God, the ancestors, and the Lord of the Foundations (Te Ki Co). Chapter 2 will examine these beings, their offerings, and their relations to the ghosts. Many families also prepare huge feasts for the living. Festive meals always follow major rituals. Often only the family takes part, but some people (often businessmen or politicians) may provide feasts for up to several hundred guests. Ghost rituals and huge feasts were traditionally scattered throughout the seventh month, and people with connections to maintain might attend feasts every few days during the month. Chapter 2 discusses the social implications of this pattern of feasting.

Late in the afternoon of the fifteenth, the ghosts get their specific worship. Ghosts are always worshipped outside – at the altars set up in town, or in front of the house, or both. Ghosts normally eat fully prepared food, just like the ancestors or the living. In the seventh month, they also receive raw and cooked rice, raw noodles, unopened cans of food, unpeeled fruit (especially lichees and longans), rice wine and beer, various types of cakes, a platter of cooked, uncut meats (*sieng le*), cigarettes, and sometimes wash basins and towels.[16] Offerings at home or for smaller ceremonies elsewhere are slightly less elaborate, but include as a minimum a meat offering and individual sticks of incense stuck into each plate. By late afternoon, the enormous tables at the five temporary altars set up in the town are totally covered with offerings, and incense smoke obscures the front of each altar.

The priests (whether Buddhist or Taoist) spend most of the late afternoon performing their rituals on a temporary altar that stands in the temple plaza. People are free to watch, but they generally do not know, or care about, the details of what the priests are doing. The climax of the ceremony, from the point of view of the people watching, comes near the end when the chief priest tosses buns, crackers, candy and rice into the watching crowd. This is ostensibly for the ghosts, but the living anxiously push and shove to catch the food for good luck. When I saw this ritual at the Co Su Kong temple, the crowd was relatively small – several dozen people – but at other ceremonies I witnessed and have heard described, the crowds were much larger and made violent attempts to get the thrown food. After the ritual, people burn paper spirit money to transfer it to the ghosts in the supernatural world. These bonfires are set along the shore of the river, because they are too large to allow in built-up areas.[17]

In the late nineteenth and early twentieth centuries, people made their offerings in a very different way.

> In front of the temple, in addition to the Pho To altar [to be discussed in the next section], they also build a *ko pi:* [lonely ghost frame] in order to present the 'lonely ghost rice' and other offerings . . . The *ko pi:* is about three to six meters high, six meters wide, and it is covered with wooden boards to make a platform of about ten or twenty mats [six to twelve square meters]. The goods offered by every household totally cover the 'frame' . . . A bamboo pole over three meters high is raised in the center of the *ko pi:*, and from its top are hung gold medals and three large, red, triangular flags. (Wu, 1975, p. 23)

After the priests had finished their rituals, mobs of young men would storm the *ko pi:*. They trampled over each other to take the ghosts' offerings for themselves (*chiu: ko*, 'robbing the lonely ghosts'). Injuries were common, and deaths were not unknown at these annual semi-riots. The change from this organized violence to the modern form, where an often elderly and generally good natured crowd elbows and shoves to grab the food thrown to the ghosts, forms a key to the pragmatic interpretation of ghosts in the popular tradition. Chapter 3 examines how the treatment of ghosts at the festival has changed, even though the food, incense and other offerings have not. The unchanged symbolic structure of offerings sets the parameters for possible meanings of ghosts, but real performances in the changing material conditions of Taiwan influence the particular interpretations people make.

The ghost festival itself exists both in the contexts of its actual performances, and in its contrast to other rituals for other types of beings. Chapters 2 and 3 examine popular ritual in detail. Chapter 2 emphasizes the piecemeal, pragmatic character of popular interpretations behind our usual understanding of the gods, ghosts and ancestors of the popular religious tradition. Chapter 3 follows changes in the popular interpretation of the Universal Salvation in Taiwan as the political economy has changed over the last century.

Specialist Viewpoints

Religious specialists of all kinds share this ritual with ordinary worshippers; they help people organize their offerings, and they conduct the rituals that form the core of the festival. The priests carry out their rituals throughout most of the lunar fourteenth and fifteenth. Few laymen watch them intone their rituals, and even those who do have no way to understand the mumbled texts. For the priests, however, each ritual has an important function, as explained in the text itself, and in the priests' professional training. Their access to the ritual texts, to traditions of textual interpretation, and to a wide body of other rituals gives specialists their own independent views of the ghost festival.

Either Buddhists or Taoists can do the ritual, but at Sanxia's Co Su Kong temple a third kind of specialist, locally called 'black-headed' priests (*o thau sai kong*), always feeds the ghosts. Black-headed priests in Sanxia specialize in funeral ritual, and use primarily Buddhist texts.[18] No matter what kind of specialist takes charge, however, the visible performances of the ritual are nearly identical (see Plate 1.1). There is thus a superficial unity across types of specialists: Chapter 4 examines the actual unities and diversities in their interpretations of the ritual, and the social conditions that influence those interpretations.

The priests construct a series of altars at which they conduct their rituals. These altars are equally the backdrop for popular participation in the ritual, but in general, only the priests can provide very detailed interpretations of them. Just in front of the temple, the priests raise three bamboo poles (*tieng ko*) about seven meters high. One carries seven lanterns, another holds a single lantern, and the third holds a banner calling down the Protectors of the Dharma (a pair of Bodhisattvas who will control the ghosts). The lanterns signal the ghosts to congregate for the ritual offerings. At their foot stands a little bamboo and paper hut that serves as a washroom for the ghosts to cleanse themselves before the ritual. Its two doors are carefully marked 'men' and 'women', to help keep things orderly.

A number of larger bamboo and paper structures stand directly in front of the temple. Two human-sized images guard the temple doors, and thus the purity of the temple. The Earth God rides his tiger on the left, and the Mountain God rides his lion on the right. Both are brightly colored, with fearsome faces. The priests also hang a purifying charm over the entrance for further protection.

A black paper 'mountain' stands in the middle of the temple plaza. Various paper deities stand on the mountain to oversee the events. These include Kuan Im (the Bodhisattva of Mercy), the Protectors of the Dharma again, the Earth God, the Mountain God, and some characters from historical fiction – Monkey, Tripitaka, and their companions on the trip to India for Buddhist scriptures are especially popular. In the center of the mountain, overseeing the entire field of ghosts, stands Tai Su Ia, the blue-faced, red-tongued, demonic transformation of Kuan Im. Some temples attract so many ghosts (by raising their lanterns on especially high poles) that a human-sized image of Tai Su Ia replaces the paper mountain; he guards the temple gates and keeps the ghosts under control (see Plate 1.2). Two paper houses flank the mountain; they resemble the houses burnt for the dead at funerals. The house at the stage-left side of the temple (the superior side) is the more ornate. It is reserved for the ghosts of literati and officials, who would not want to mix with less sophisticated ghosts. The door is appropriately labelled 'Hanlin Academy' – the highest institution of learning in traditional China.[19] The house at the inferior, stage-right side is less pretentious; it will shelter the ordinary ghosts.

Inside the temple itself, the specialists set up more altars for rituals that will attract little public attention. They mark off a new ritual space by unrolling and hanging a series of scrolls depicting their deities. This temple within a temple reduces the usual temple deities to spectators, and places its own special deities in the position of honor. These inner altars are nearly identical, no matter what kind of specialist conducts the ritual. Buddhists and Taoists may nevertheless understand their altars in different ways. Chapter 4 returns to these altars, to the rituals conducted in them, and to the unities and diversities in specialist interpretations of them.

The climax for priests and laymen alike occurs when they feed the ghosts on the afternoon of the fifteenth. As the altar tables fill with food and the streets of Sanxia fill with people, the priests make a round of the five altars, inviting the lonely ghosts to follow them back to the temple to enjoy the impending feast. Meanwhile, the two paper houses and the god mountain in the temple plaza have been turned around to face the temple. A new altar has been constructed just in front of the temple, and sacks of raw rice are placed along the temple doors. The new altar consists of a table of offerings and ritual equipment, and seats for the musicians and the five priests involved. This is the 'Pho To altar' mentioned in the quote in the previous section.

As the priests return from their parade, they stop briefly in front of the paper houses, but soon mount the altar, Nonspecialists have only a vague idea of what the subsequent performance means: the costumes worn by the priests are colorful and rarely seen, the chief priest sits in a meditational posture, and he performs a long series of complex hand movements (mudras) while reciting religious texts to music; the two- or three-hour performance multiplies the amount of food offered so that it will suffice to feed the hordes of hungry ghosts who have come. Specialist interpretations of the ritual differ systematically from most people's understandings. Chapter 4 ties the specialists' more systematized, ideologized interpretations of Buddhism and Taoism to the institutionalized social relations of the people involved, and contrasts them with the more piecemeal interpretations of the popular tradition.

Elite Viewpoints

The immediately visible participation of the modern elite in the Universal Salvation festival differs little from the participation of the general population. Sanxia's elite – the most educated and the most powerful citizens – contribute to the ritual, attend the ceremonies, and worship the ghosts, much like the rest of the lay population. Unified participation, however, need not imply unified interpretations, and Chapter 5 shows systematic elite reinterpretations of shared rituals.

The various governments of Taiwan have been attempting to discourage or manipulate the festival for at least a century, but they have been only partially successful. In late imperial times, for example, the government pressed its attempt to control the festival by making an alternative ghost worship part of its official state cult. The current government in Taiwan is trying to discourage the ghost festival entirely. Most major community temples now conduct their ceremonies on the fifteenth of the month, at the government's request. This campaign has been partially successful. Most people in Sanxia now worship on the same day, and all the feasts thus occur simultaneously, making it impossible to attract as many guests as previously. Within each area, however, smaller temples continue to stagger their ceremonies throughout the seventh month. Reciprocal feasting in Sanxia still follows the older pattern in the first lunar month, when Co Su Kong celebrates his birthday. Thus, rotating feasts (and their high costs, which the government finds so objectionable) still occur, but on a smaller scale than before.

Chapter 5 will thus address two related issues: (1) the nature of elite interpretations of religion, and the ways those interpretations require expansion of the pragmatic/ideologized distinction; and

(2) the successes and failures of the elite attempt to bend religion to its political purposes (illustrated both by the traditional state cult and by elite reinterpretations of the popular ceremony).

The ghost-feeding ritual is one starting point for an analysis of religious unity and diversity in Taiwan. The ritual is widely shared across groups, and traditionally across China. Yet specific understandings of ghosts vary from one group or informant to another. The chapters that follow will introduce some informants who fear the ghosts, others who pity them, and still others who do not believe in them. Some people worship to propitiate the ghosts who might otherwise make them sick; others worship just to impress their neighbors, who might otherwise think them poverty stricken; still others worship because it is fun. Some people disapprove of the ritual because it is expensive; others approve because it is the custom to worship ghosts in the seventh month. Everyone, for all the variation, takes part. The chapters that follow analyze how people shape these ideas in varying social conditions to create different styles of interpretation.

2 Ancestors and Gods, Family and Politics

The popular beliefs are the least ideologized part of Taiwanese religion. Although some aspects of popular beliefs are consciously systematized and explicit, they form at best a partial ideology in comparison to Buddhism, Taoism or the state cult. One of the primary goals of this chapter and the next will be to show how much of the popular beliefs exists only in pragmatic, context-bound interpretation. This holds for all aspects of the beliefs, but especially strongly for the ghosts, whom I address in Chapter 3. A second goal of these chapters is to ask why only certain aspects of popular ritual precipitate into a partial ideology, while many others remain in solution. In general, I will argue that ideologies occur where the ritual changes little across social contexts and over time, and especially where many different groups (including the state and local elites) reinforce popular interpretations of rituals. Pragmatic interpretation remains more likely instead where the contexts in which a ritual is interpreted have changed rapidly, and where elites try to discourage those interpretations.

Many anthropologists who study Taiwan now generally agree that the popular pantheon consists of three primary types of beings – gods, ghosts, and ancestors – which closely reflect the social world (Feuchtwang, 1974a; Jordan, 1972; Wolf, 1974b). Wolf (1974b, p. 175), for example, writes:

> The conception of the supernatural found in Sanhsia [Sanxia] is thus a detailed reflection of the social landscape of traditional China as viewed from a small village. Prominent in this landscape were first the mandarins, representing the emperor and the empire; second the family and the lineage; and third, the more heterogeneous category of the stranger and the outsider, the bandit and the beggar. The mandarins became the gods; the senior members of the line and the lineage, the ancestors; while the stranger was preserved in the form of the dangerous and despised ghosts.

This parallel between the social and supernatural worlds is the most ideologized part of the popular worship. It rests in part on explicit informant statements, and in part on an implicitly structural argument that builds meaning out of a code of symbolic contrasts: a three-way structure of symbols encodes the structure of society. Wolf (following the explicitly structuralist analysis in Feuchtwang, 1974a) sees this symbolic structure in a set of ritual dichotomies:

> Gods are contrasted with ghosts and ancestors; ghosts are contrasted with gods and ancestors; and ancestors are contrasted with gods and ghosts. For example, gods are offered uncooked (or whole) food, ghosts and ancestors are offered cooked food; ghosts are worshipped outside homes and temples, gods and ancestors are worshipped inside; ancestors are given an even number of incense sticks, ghosts and gods are given an odd number of sticks. (Wolf, 1974a, p. 7)

According to this type of analysis, ghosts are meaningful because of their structural relationship to gods on the one hand, and to ancestors on the other; the variable details of specific social contexts are not taken into account.[20] Many recent studies of Chinese religion have been influenced by structuralism, although the theoretical apparatus is consistent and explicit only for some (e.g., Baity, 1975; Feuchtwang, 1974a, 1974b). Freedman's (1974, p. 21) assertion that the religious ideas and forms of the various levels of Chinese society are basically 'reflections, perhaps misshapen reflections, or idiomatic translations of one another', also assumes an underlying structural code.

People do indeed understand incense, food, and the other ritual media partially in relation to an abstract code of symbolic contrasts, and it is no accident that the structure of the ritual media meshes with informants' explicit comparisons of ancestors, gods and ghosts to kinsmen, bureaucrats and outsiders. The ritual media are one of the experiences that remain consistent and widely shared across all contexts of worship, and the simplicity of their three-way structure lets them remain broadly relevant even to changing social experience. Religious specialists further encourage consistent use of the ritual media.

Yet a concentration on structural codes and explicit, ideologized statements does not account for the full range and flexibility of people's interpretations; it does not address pragmatic interpretation in social context. Wolf (1974a, p. 8) himself recognizes this when he insists that 'the study of Chinese religion must begin with the social and economic history of particular communities'. A full clarification of the Universal Salvation rites, or any other aspect of Taiwanese popular religion, thus requires exploration of both the ideologized (including the structure of ritual media) and the pragmatic interpretations of the cosmology. The ghosts of the festival communicate social messages partly through their structural contrast to ancestors (as marginal to kinship) and gods (as marginal to politics), and partly through the political and economic contexts in which they appear. The more pragmatic interpretations occur largely where the material experience of kinship and community is quite variable, and where local elites and specialists do not share popular pragmatic interpretations of that experience.

This chapter addresses the popular tradition as a whole, concentrating especially on its most respectable objects of worship – the gods and ancestors. It will examine the structural codes of symbols that help to define these beings in contrast to ghosts, and to create a partially ideologized interpretation of family and community. It will also address the more variable social conditions that gods and ancestors can index, building on the insights of Wolf and other anthropologists of Taiwan, but with special emphasis on the pragmatic flexibility of interpretation, even when it departs from more ideologized interpretations. After this analysis of the popular tradition, Chapter 3 can return to actual interpretations of the Universal Salvation rites.[21]

Ancestors, Kinsmen and Domestic Worship

Ancestors are the key actors in the relation betwen kinship and ritual, although the analysis of the domestic cult will also have to consider rituals besides ancestor worship.[22] These rituals do not simply reflect a kinship system, but instead relate to contradictions within the kinship system and changes of the system over time. The domestic cult ideologizes ancestors into a model of kinship. Each aspect of the cult reiterates family solidarity and filial piety – the aspects of kinship that informants state explicitly most often. These features are, in fact, one of the most unified aspects of Taiwanese religion. Yet actual realizations of domestic worship also allow pragmatic interpretations of less ideal aspects of kinship.

Ideally in Taiwan, each family is the momentary expression of an eternal patriline, and each line forms a solidary unit, independent of all other patrilines. Even though marriage invariably compromises the ideal, families and patrilineages are nevertheless important components of productive and social relations. Families carefully manage their human and natural resources to create a communal, often diversified, economy (see, for example, Cohen, 1976). Lineages, where they exist, often center on communally-owned plots of land (Pasternak, 1969; Potter, 1970). The income from this land frequently goes to support lineage ritual; to the upkeep of the elaborate halls that lineages and their segments construct; to the education of promising lineage children; and to the welfare of needy members. When this critical mass of land disappears (through sale or land reform, for example), the lineage organization itself usually weakens (see Gallin and Gallin, 1982, for example).

When informants interpret ancestor worship, they emphasize precisely this idealized patriline, whose living representatives form a united family responsible for worshipping past generations and creating future generations. Both ancestor worship and procreation are filial acts of gratitude toward parents and other (ideally patrilineal) forebears. Family solidarity and filial piety toward the patriline form the most ideologized treatments of domestic worship; they are its most explicit, consciously thought out and easily expressed features. Yet when we move beyond descriptive statements to actual performance of domestic ritual, the major themes of solidarity and filial piety are compromised by ties to the social position of the family and to the tensions within the family. The following analysis of the rituals emphasizes first the ideology of solidarity and filial piety, but then also addresses how variation in wealth, competition between brothers, tensions among households related by marriage, and the difficult position of a bride in her husband's family create pragmatic countercurrents to the ideology.

Filial Piety and Family Solidarity

The center of the domestic cult is an altar (*ang ke touq*) that dominates the main room of nearly every household in Sanxia. All domestic altars hold an incense pot at the stage-left side (the position of honor) for the gods, and the ancestor tablets with their incense pot at the stage-right side. Most of the altars have a backdrop depicting some of the more popular deities. The newer, more prestigious backdrops are painted on glass in bright colors and glitter. Some households may add one or more carved god images on the stage-left side, each with its own incense pot. Varying amounts of religious miscellanea, including written charms and souvenirs of visits to temples, also often decorate the altar. Domestic altars are very public – many are visible from the street, and guests usually sit in front of them. They represent the solidarity of the family and its filial piety to the outside world and to the family members themselves. The physical presence of the altar also represents the family as a well-knit, integrated unit. A house with two altars contains two families; a household with no altar usually considers itself part of another family, and will return there for important rituals.

The ideology of family solidarity disguises one of the basic tensions internal to Taiwanese families – the tension between brothers. Brothers inherit equal portions of the estate, but they may choose to divide the estate before their father's death, after his death, or not at all. The pressure to divide varies with the economic interests of the family (see Cohen, 1976, p. 216–25), but it often begins with the death of the father as, for example, a childless younger brother resents his income going toward the education of an older brother's child, or as he wants to declare his economic independence from his father. Domestic altars hide these tensions because they cannot react to them. They represent only ancestors, not the living. This situation changes only when the family divides formally, and each branch establishes its own altar.

Family division may take place gradually. Separation of pooled economic resources may occur first, then the new families may begin to cook at separate stoves. The religious center of the family is usually the last to divide. This is partly because new altars are expensive, but also because the shared domestic altar is the most public display of family integrity. Altars maintain the pretence of solidarity even after brothers have effectively divided. New altars again claim solidarity for their new families, but they are also evidence of past divisions. Domestic altars thus support explicit, ideologized statements about family solidarity, covering up less desirable realities like the eventual break-up of extended families. Family solidarity is more successfully ideologized than the tension between brothers because families do not want their problems exposed in public, and because the older generation (which controls the altar) nearly always opposes division.

In strong lineages, the ancestor tablets themselves affirm the ideologized picture of the Chinese family as a patrilineal, virilocal kinship unit that commemorates its immediate patrilineal forebears (and their wives) with ancestor tablets. The lineage of such a family may also own an ancestral hall housing the tablets of more distant forebears. If a family must worship ancestors of another surname (as a result, for example, of an uxorilocal marriage), they will not place the tablets on the lineage or domestic altars; people with the wrong surname are relegated to dark corners of back rooms, where they will not detract from the appearance of patrilineal unity that the altars create. The communal halls of Qinan Village (Ahern, 1973) provide an extreme case of the ideologized patrilineal model. Each of Qinan's four lineages shares a common altar, as if the lineage were an enormous extended family; as a rule there are no separate household altars. Tablets for ancestors with other surnames, which often become important in uxorilocal marriages and adoptions, are not permitted on these altars. The tablets ideologize surname solidarity especially where a strong lineage leadership promotes that view, as in Qinan.

Various acts of worship reaffirm solidarity and filial piety – the explicit, ideologized interpretations of the domestic cult. Worship at the domestic altar, for example, takes place every day for most families in Sanxia (84 per cent of the sample interviewed, see Table 2.1). A representative of the family, usually one of the older women, burns three sticks of incense there. One stick goes in the ancestors' incense pot, another is for the gods, and the third goes outside the front door. Informants explain worship inside as filial respect toward the ancestors of the family. This use of incense treats the family as solidary, and ignores internal tensions until the eternally solidary family has split into two or more new, eternally solidary families.

Not everyone in Taiwan takes part in the domestic cult to the same extent. The distinctive roles of the elite and religious specialists in this cult, for example, will be discussed separately in the chapters that follow. Age, however, also affects how much people worship. In general, the old worship more than the young. This may always have been true in China, and it is no great surprise in modern Taiwan where the young have been exposed systematically to a Western education. Yet there is no significant difference between young and old in the extent of their daily worship at the domestic altar, excluding other kinds of worship (see Table 2.2).[23] Daily worship of ancestors is one of the most widespread ritual acts in Taiwan.

People also commemorate the death days of their closer ancestors.

Table 2.1   Frequency of Performance for Selected Rituals

	Done	Not done
1. Daily worship at domestic altar	103	20
2. 1st and 15th (2nd and 16th)	115	8
3. New Year	111	12
4. Universal Salvation	115	8
5. Thau ge/be ge	112	11
6. Thi: Kong's birthday	110	13
7. Kuan Im's birthday	64	58
8. Kim Bo's birthday	21	101
9. Dividing the incense (*kua hiu:*)	54	69
10. Gathering the frights (*siu kia:*)	77	46
11. Pacifying the year demon (*an thai sui*)	67	56
12. Worshipping the peck (*an tau*)	52	70
13. Covering the soul (*kham hun*)	40	83
14. Pacifying the womb spirit (*an thai sin*)	31	92

Note: Kim Bo is a deity almost unknown in Sanxia, and was added to the questionnaire as a check on the quality of the answers.

The number of these will vary; some families may remember only one or two death days, while others may commemorate more than a dozen every year. The ancestors get more than incense on these occasions. Their descendants serve them full meals, complete with bowls and chopsticks, rice and noodles, and some of their favorite dishes. In this context, people treat ancestors almost as if they were still living kinsmen. The family eats the food after the ancestors have finished. Ancestors who are no longer remembered as individuals are worshipped as a group in the same way on the ninth day of the ninth lunar month. Ancestors also receive offerings during major festivals for the gods (discussed in the following section). The domestic ancestral cult thus comes to life both in daily worship and on numerous special occasions throughout the year, reminding people of filial piety, as everyone constantly explains in Taiwan.

Funerals also closely involve kinship and family life, marking the ideology of solidarity and filial piety. Mourning dress is one of the most important expressions of the boundaries and internal structure of families. The various colors and types of cloth make fine distinctions among the descendants of the deceased. Color, for example, codes how many generations separate the mourner from the de-

Table 2.2   Relation Between Age and Frequency of Worship

	Done by self	Done in family	Not done
Daily worship[a] All<45	32	32	12
All≥45	25	14	18
All other worship[b] All<45	202	396	390
All≥45	244	149	218

[a.] $\chi^2 = 1.98$, n.s.
[b.] $\chi^2 = 80.1$, $p < 0.001$

ceased. People of generational rank equal or higher than the deceased, as well as very close friends, wear white. Affines also wear white, but with distinctive hats showing how they are linked to the deceased (Wolf, 1970). Affines are also specially marked at funerals (and at weddings) by the deferential ritual behavior they command (Ahern, 1974). Sons and unmarried daughters of the deceased wear a coarse, undyed burlap called *mua: po*, grandsons wear a finer cloth called *te-a po*, their children wear blue cloth and so on (Wolf, 1970). Combinations of colors represent unusual kin relationships. Mourning dress shows explicitly who owes a debt of filial piety (and who thus also has a claim to inherit): white robes deny the debt, while undyed or colored robes acknowledge it.

Families enter the domestic cult most fully at the lunar New Year. Most people have a long vacation at this time, and if at all possible, they return home. The entire family worships the ancestors at the New Year, although not with the pomp of elite families. In contrast to most of the major ritual events of the year, the feast on New Year's Eve is purely a family event; one does not ordinarily invite guests. The lunar New Year is the clearest expression of the social and ritual position of the family, and informants often cite it as a celebration of family solidarity and wholeness.

Worship of gods can also express kin relations. The Stove God (Cau Kun), while not especially important in Sanxia, is the most obvious example. Every household has its own Stove God. He appears in most households as a piece of red paper with his name written on it, pasted over the stove. Other parts of China use a multicolored print of him instead. Just before the new lunar year, the Stove God returns to the heavens to report to the highest deity, Thi: Kong, on the family's activities. His departure occurs when each family burns his image or his name, thus transporting him to the spirit world (Wolf, 1974b, p. 133). A new image pasted over the stove marks his return, some days later. The Stove God, like the stove itself, is closely tied to the family as a social unit.

Domestic worship of other gods occurs, for most families, on the first and fifteenth of every lunar month (that is, at the new moon and the full moon). Businesses usually stay open on the first and fifteenth to take advantage of the extra activity, so businessmen conduct these rituals instead on the lunar second and sixteenth. Even families who do not worship every day ordinarily carry out these rituals (93 per cent of the sample interviewed). The Earth God (Tho Te Kong) is associated with neighborhoods, and receives offerings in front of the household altar or, for some, at his local temple. The offerings include three sticks of incense, gold spirit money (*hok kim* and *kua kim*), and three kinds of cooked but uncut meat (*sieng le*). Afterwards, people set up a table at the door with its own candles and incense pot. They cut up and fully prepare the meat from the Earth God ritual, and offer it again accompanied by cooked rice. Most people explain that this portion of the ritual, called *kho kun* (rewarding the troops), is for the spirit soldiers who guard the town of Sanxia. The food, with its spiritual essence now removed, is then eaten in a dinner much more elaborate than usual. Many people, mostly older women, worship in each of the major temples in their area on these days. Individuals conduct most of the rituals, but they are not acting simply as individuals; they are representing their families.

Ancestors and the Problems of Kinship

Ancestor altars, daily worship, mourning dress, and many other ritual acts help reinforce the partial kinship ideology that stresses filial piety and family solidarity. This ideology is widely shared across classes and consistent over time in Taiwan. Literature and education further reinforce it. Real kinship, however, may not always match the ideology – children may be unfilial, families always divide, and relations among kinsmen (especially between brothers and between affines) may be inherently tense. These problems often do not mesh with the ideology, and tend to appear in popular worship only in some contexts. People tend to leave them as pragmatic interpretations, dealing with them in context, but not generalizing broadly about them.

Some ancestor altars, for example, compromise family solidarity by worshipping tablets of many surnames. The altars in several Sanxia villages differ strongly from Qinan's solidary altars, although they are only a few kilometers apart. Ploughshare Village (Harrell, 1976), for example, has no lineages. Most of the population are landless laborers, and the lack of potential communal land makes it difficult to support lineages (Harrell, 1982, pp. 117–28). Here, where lineage ties are weak and people are poor, ties through marriage become an especially important social resource, and village endogamy increases. Commemorating nonagnatic relatives on the domestic altar is one way to help cement those ties, and Ploughshare has a large number of altars that commemorate more than one surname. Kiu Kiong Kiou is very similar to Ploughshare. Residents of both villages settled late in Sanxia's history in areas where little rice land was available. The people are relatively mobile, there are no lineages, and uxorilocal marriages are common. Over half of the altars in Kiu Kiong Kiou worship two or more surnames; altars with three or even four surnames are not rare.

The difference between the altars in a village like Qinan and in one like Ploughshare or Kiu Kiong Kiou relates as much to varying social context as to an abstract symbolic code or an ideology of solidarity; altars indirectly index wealth and local economic ties. There is always a tension between a lineage and its affines in Taiwan, because affines threaten and interfere with the unity of the patriline, even while they provide the line with valuable allies. Villages like Qinan disguise this tension on their altars because their strong lineages allow more independence from affines, and because a strong lineage leadership can promote ritual solidarity. Ploughshare and Kiu Kiong Kiou rely more heavily on their affines, and they have no lineage leadership; the result shows clearly on their altars (see also Weller, 1984). All these villagers share a partial ideology of family solidarity and filial piety, but the particular conditions of some villages also promote a pragmatic countercurrent, especially where lack of lineages leads to a stronger position for the problematic affines.

Altars can also depart from the ideology as contextual expressions of wealth. Wealthy families buy large, expensive and ornately carved altar tables, complemented by gaudy, glittering backdrops. In poor households, however, the domestic altar may simply be a decoratively painted shelf attached to one wall. Although solidarity and filial piety are uppermost in people's minds, every altar also reveals the wealth of its family. Domestic religion from the beginning ties pragmatically into the external social relations of the family, even though most domestic ritual itself is directed at an internal family audience.

Funerals can also question the ideology, especially where patrilineal family solidarity is in question. One funeral in Kiu Kiong Kiou, for example, was dominated by young men and women dressed in the blue cloth of great-grandchildren. They were the daughter's daughter's children of the deceased. This flaunted rejection of patriliny resulted from successive uxorilocal marriages. It could occur very easily in a village like Kiu Kiong Kiou, where people may worship relatives of three or four surnames; it would be very unusual in a village with strong lineages. The meaning of mourning dress, as of ancestor tablets, relates to lineage strength, and thus also to wealth and local social relations.

Mourning dress can also show the divided loyalties of a virilocally married woman. Wolf's (1970, pp. 202–3) informants disagreed about what kind of dress such a woman should wear for her natal parents:

> Whereas some people are willing to accept the fact that a married daughter belongs to her husband and prescribe *te-a-po* as the proper mourning dress, others claim that a married daughter's head is still theirs and prescribe a headdress of *mua:-po*. Still others compromise by prescribing a headdress of *mua:-po* with a patch of *te-a-po* 'to show that the woman is married.'

Wolf (1970, p. 203) gives other examples of disagreement over correct mourning dress, and concludes that 'the only way to avoid variation in mourning dress without imposing an arbitrary code would be to resolve the conflicts that it reflects'. When people actually attend funerals, of course, they must commit themselves to one or another of the variant possibilities. The alternative they choose is a statement about family loyalties and about property rights; controversial choices may lead to arguments (Wolf, 1970, p. 205). Funeral dress relates to the local importance of lineages and to the contradictory loyalties of a wife, as well as to its more explicitly ideologized expression of filial piety and family solidarity.

The descendants always hire a professional to bury the coffin according to the divinatory system called geomancy (*hong sui* or *te li*), which allows the deceased to funnel good (or bad) influences from the landscape into his or her descendants (see Chapter 6 and Appendix A). Ideologically, geomancy unifies the family by dividing the patrilineal descendants of the deceased (who benefit or suffer from the geomantic influence) from all other relatives (who are unaffected). Yet pragmatically, geomancy also expresses dissension within the ranks of the descendants; it is especially sensitive to competition among brothers. Some graves help or harm all descendants equally, while others are sited to affect each branch of the family differently. Geomancy thus provides a flexible idiom with which to express various social relations (see also Freedman, 1966, ch. 5).

Weddings: An Example

The ideology of filial piety and solidarity that informants use to explain their kinship ritual is not sufficient. Understanding the ritual also requires exploring pragmatic interpretations based on problematic aspects of kinship. These are not explicitly developed like the ideology; they are more bound to particular realizations of rituals where, for example, the tensions between affines, between brothers, or between a daughter-in-law and her husband's family come to the forefront. Weddings provide a clear example of both ideologized and pragmatic interpretations, because they intend to develop new links of filial piety and family solidarity, while at the same time they create a new set of troublesome affines and a potentially threatening daughter-in-law. Relations between affines are friendly and reciprocal, yet simultaneously formal and tense; the bride is a welcome new member of her husband's household, yet simultaneously a dangerous threat who is tied to outsiders. These rites are complex and contradictory because they speak directly about the problematic ties they create and they involve direct practical contact with the new affines; the affinal problem is unavoidable.

The major message of the ceremony (described fully in Suzuki 1978[1934] or Cohen, 1976, ch. 6) fits the ideology. It illustrates the apparently unequivocal transfer of the bride from her natal family to her husband's family. This begins on the day of betrothal when the groom's mother places a ring on the hand of her future daughter-in-law. It continues on the wedding day when the bride is transferred to her husband's house in a typical rite of passage; she and her dowry are ritually cleansed; now in a liminal state, she is ritually transferred to a waiting taxi; she undergoes the supernaturally dangerous journey to her husband's house; she is ritually cleansed again; and she is finally reintegrated into her husband's family by worshipping the gods and by worshipping his ancestors (Freedman, 1967, pp. 265–8). Several stages of the ceremony also include hopes that the bride will soon bear sons.

Several traditional manuals explain how the rituals ought to be performed, and they describe the etiquette of these rituals in detail. Lü (1975[1880], pp. 106–71), for example, includes extensive discussion of the proper form for invitations, the places everyone should take at the ceremonies, and the proper order of the rites. He never departs from a prescription for idealized kinship; he does not address the contradictions that the marriage creates. These ritual manuals were written by the traditional elite, and they ideologize kinship consistently.

All this represents the ideal, benevolent aspect of the bride – the new mother who will guarantee continuation of the line. The rites, however, also contain a pragmatic counterpoint that indicates the more dangerous aspects of the bride as an outsider who may break up the family. The specifics of this counterpoint vary from place to place; they are not as standardized as the ideologized rite of passage, nor are they approved by the marriage manuals. Each example shows the pragmatic complexities of kinship in action, as future affines negotiate over their coming rights and roles: (1) When the groom's mother puts the ring on the bride's finger, the bride may bend her second joint to prevent her mother-in-law from getting the ring all the way on. If the bride succeeds, her mother-in-law will not dominate her in the future (Ahern, 1974, p. 283; Wolf, 1972, p. 125). (2) Freedman (1967, p. 268) reports a belief that whoever enters the wedding chamber first – the bride or the groom – will dominate the relationship. (3) There is another belief that the groom must place his robe over his wife's in order to be dominant in the future (Freedman, 1967, pp. 268–9; Lin, 1948, p. 44; Suzuki, 1978[1934], p. 197). (4) If the bride steps on the groom's shoes on the wedding night, she will dominate (Suzuki, 1978[1934], p. 197). Some other unofficial rituals indicate the continuing ties of the bride to her natal family: (1) during a feast at the bride's house, the groom is served a soft-boiled egg. Breaking the yolk indicates breaking the bride's natal ties. Brides' mothers are sometimes said to hard-boil the eggs, thus retaining their ties with their daughters (Wolf, 1972, p. 135). (2) 'It is said of one area that when the girl leaves her natal home she drops a lock on the ground which is then attached half open to the door to signify that while she has been sent away the house is not completely closed to her' (Freedman, 1967, p. 271). This counterpoint shows what the major theme of the wedding disguises – the bride is not fully detached from her natal family, and she thus creates a threat to the solidarity of her husband's family. Where affines are socially unimportant, this counterpoint of pragmatic kinship may not be as strong. When brides marry into the powerful Hong Kong Teng lineage, for example, their brothers do not give ambiguous messages about leaving the door unlocked, but instead give the bridal sedan chair an unambiguous kick out of her natal household (Watson, 1981, p. 600).

Weddings also address a second problem in marriage – the benefits and threats of an alliance between two groups. Before the wedding, the two families about to be united engage in a complex dialogue of gifts and countergifts. Although the ritual presets the occasions for giving and the approximate content of the gifts, the two sets of affines must negotiate the quality and quantity of each gift, and their negotiations in such applied kinship often become tense and acrimonious (Fei, 1939, p. 43; Gallin, 1966, p. 179; Wolf 1972, pp. 119–24). These gifts are thus simultaneous acts of friendly reciprocity and battles for prestige and profit; they illustrate the problems in the long-term relationship to come – an idealized alliance superimposed on a practical manipulation of the tie. Suzuki (1978[1934], p. 173) gives a ritual example of this combined reciprocity and conflict: the groom's family includes in the bridewealth several symbols of its prosperity (including a chicken, a duck and dried longan fruit); these must be returned to the groom's family immediately, or else the bride's family is thought to be trying to steal the prosperity of their future affines. Gift exchanges thus publicize the reciprocity of the idealized affine tie, yet the actual tensions of affinal kinship can compromise ideal weddings through acrimonious negotiation and through symbolism that recognizes the threat in the new bride.

Weddings also involve the affines of the senior generation: the mother's brother and father's mother's brother of the groom must sit at the table of honor at the marriage feast, along with the bride's father or brother. In addition, grooms in some areas had their mother's brothers brought to the wedding in a sedan chair (Chiu, 1966, p. 8), and in other places they worshipped at the ancestral altars of their mother's father and their father's mother's father on the day before the marriage (Cohen, 1976, p. 153). These are all displays of ideologized kinship.

Once again, however, the problems of marriage come into play unofficially. Ahern (1974, pp. 292–3) cites several examples of prestige battles involving the treatment of affines at marriage and other ritual feasts. In one case, for instance, a mother's brother did not get along with his sister's son, so he sent his young son to a feast instead of coming himself. The sister's son reciprocated by not giving the boy the seat of highest honor, and the boy countered by taking food reserved for the guest of honor (Ahern, 1974, p. 293). Ritual feasts show the life-long dilemma of affinal relationships: affines are honored guests, yet at the same time they are interfering meddlers.

Watson's (1981) analysis of the Hong Kong Teng again shows how the existence of a powerful lineage, where affines are not socially important to most people, may discourage pragmatic interpretation of kinship at weddings. Male affines do not attend wedding feasts, and female affines are not placed in seats of honor. Even here, however, the practical results of negotiation over marriage payments lead to differences between rich and poor within the lineage, and compromise the idealized unity of the lineage. Watson (1981, p. 609) states:

> In relation to the ideology of fraternal unity, affinity was seen by the Teng as a divisive force. It was divisive not only because ties to affines could lead to potentially disruptive contacts with outsiders, but also because affinity highlighted economic and social differences within the lineage. In Ha Tsuen [the Teng village] the uniform set of marriage rites denied that there were differences between agnates, while marriage payments and affinal behavior highlighted and enhanced these differences.

Wedding ritual thus presents both an idealized family, and simultaneously interacts with the real strains of domestic kinship. Affines exchange gifts and attend feasts as friendly, equal, and independent allies; yet both the exchanges and the feasts reflect real underlying tensions between relatives by marriage. Ritual transfer of the bride to the groom's house shows her to be fully integrated into her husband's lineage; yet many secondary rituals show the underlying tension in her lack of full loyalty to her new lineage, and her remaining ties to her natal family.

The domestic cult and its explicit messages about family solidarity are so widely shared because people at all levels of the society experience the primary importance of the family defined through worship. Yet the full pragmatic interpretation of the domestic cult goes beyond solidarity and filial piety by indexing other social relations, including wealth (in the quality of the altar, and indirectly in the limitation of nonpatrilineal relatives' tablets on the altar or wearing mourning dress), the competition between brothers (especially in geomancy), the tension between affines (in gift exchanges and ritual feasts), and the conflicting loyalties of a wife (in wedding ritual and mourning dress). The cult offers a pragmatic interpretation closely tied to real experiences of family solidarity, and of the tensions that lie beneath that solidarity. Pragmatic interpretations occur especially strongly where the real experience of kinship offers challenges to the ideology (as when affines are powerful) and where there is no mechanism (like a lineage elite) to promote a particular interpretation.

Gods, Bureaucrats and Community Temples

Just as people explicitly explain the ancestral cult as based on solidarity and filial piety, informants at all levels of society explain god worship as a metaphor for politics. Gods are bureaucrats who rule communities. Just as does ancestor worship, however, gods tie into many of the changes and contradictions in local politics. Pragmatic interpretations of gods go beyond fixed political hierarchies to reflect heterodox power, ethnicity, regional opposition to national control, and local political maneuvering. This section begins with the more explicitly recognized and clearly ideologized relation between gods and communities, and moves on to the more flexible realization of god worship.

Temple and Community

Temples provide an important method to express changing community allegiances and boundaries.

The individuality of a village is inseparable from the particular configuration of gods who guide its policy, and its conflicts with other villages necessarily entail conflicts between the divinities that each side is able to muster. Accordingly, alliances between men and gods are a common idiom in which historical events are recounted. (Jordan, 1972, p. 42)

There are four main types of temples in Sanxia: Earth God temples (*tho te biou*), temples for major popular deities, Buddhist 'vegetarian halls' (*chai tng*), and ghost temples (*iu ieng kong biou*). Table 2.3 shows frequency of worship at a selection of Sanxia's major temples.

Table 2.3   Frequency of Worship for Selected Temples

	Daily	1/15 or 2/16	Occasionally	Never
Tho Te Kong	12	19	57	12
Co Su Kong	6	23	60	12
Ma Co	1	20	61	19
En Cu Kong	0	0	77	24
Siong Te Kong	1	8	33	59
Sian Kong	0	3	58	41
Iu Ieng Kong	0	0	42	58

Earth God temples tie closely to neighborhoods. Each god governs a small community, and moving into a new community means worshipping a new Earth God. Their areas are mutually exclusive: no one worships at more than one Earth God temple.[24] The boundaries of the area they govern closely follow social divisions, and do not always coincide with administrative boundaries. Changes in community structure or in community alliances can result in building new Earth God temples that reflect the new social situation (see Wang, 1974, Ahern, 1973, pp. 64–6). Many neighborhoods in rural Taiwan have recently built new Earth God temples or renovated old ones. These communities are advertising their wealth, competing with other nearby communities, and, at least apparently, showing their loyalty to Taiwanese traditions in the face of government attempts to discourage large expenses on popular religion (see also Ahern, 1981a).

Zhongpu Village, for example, has two shiny new Earth God temples, one at each end of the village. Although Zhongpu is barely large enough to meet the 200-household minimum for an official administrative village (*li*), it nevertheless includes two separate communities – Kiu Kiong Kiou and Tiong Pho. Relations between the two communities had been getting worse, and when the village head began to renovate the temple in his neighborhood, Kiu Kiong Kiou, saying that he wanted to make a more impressive symbol for the whole community, the people of Tiong Pho responded by renovating their own temple. The village head's claim to be uniting the entire village was read as an attempt to strengthen his part of the administrative village at the expense of the other part.

Responsibility for worship of the Earth God may accompany a plaque that circulates daily among the households of the community. The cyclic path of this plaque thus traces the boundaries of a socially defined neighbourhood. Earth Gods govern neighborhoods, but unlike earthly bureaucrats, the boundaries of their territories alter flexibly as social relations on the ground change.

People worship more often at Earth God temples than at any other kind of temple. These temples vary in size from simple roadside shrines to small buildings capable of holding up to about a dozen people. Unlike most of the temples to higher ranking gods, Earth God temples rarely have special keepers (*biou kong*) in charge of them. There are also several iconographic markers of their lower status: door gods, for example, are not permitted on Earth God temples, and Earth Gods often wear the costume of local gentry, rather than the official court dress of most of the higher gods.

Temples to the popular gods are most important in the large-scale organization of the community. In Sanxia, the largest and most spectacular of these is the temple dedicated to Co Su Kong (see Plate 2.1). According to the official temple history (QSZS), Co Su Kong was a military figure in the Song Dynasty who, fleeing south with the defeated dynasty, established himself as a Buddhist monk in Anxi County of Fujian Province (the place of origin for most of Sanxia's inhabitants).

The Co Su Kong temple in Sanxia was completed in 1769. It was destroyed and rebuilt after an earthquake in 1822. When the Japanese began their fifty-year occupation of Taiwan in 1895, Sanxia was one of the few pockets of resistance in northern Taiwan. The temple was an organizing center for the resistance, and the Japanese burnt it down in retribution. It was rebuilt again in 1899. The Japanese departed in 1945, and Sanxia began to collect funds for yet another reconstruction of the temple, this time on a much more grandiose scale than ever before.

It is difficult to clarify the details of the history of this period, because it saw major political upheavals in Taiwan, and it is not easy to discuss the period with informants, even now. The ambitious temple reconstruction project was apparently in part a reaction to religious repression towards the end of the Japanese occupation, and in part an attempt by one of Sanxia's political factions to substitute the temple, as an informal power base, for the official power they had lost. Reconstruction of the temple still continues, more than thirty years after it began. The extraordinarily ornate wood and stone carving is all being done by hand, and the temple has become an important center for the few craftsmen capable of doing this kind of work. The temple is one of the most impressive in Taiwan, but the slowness and the expense of the project have angered many residents.

The temple was originally the center of worship for all of Sanxia, and parts of the neighboring towns of Shulin, Dingpu, Yingge and their hinterlands. Dingpu now has its own temple to Co Su Kong, and parts of Shulin have now joined local cults (Wang, 1974). Nevertheless, the catchment area of the temple still exceeds the political boundaries of Sanxia township.

The Co Su Kong temple is the scene of Sanxia's most important rituals. The biggest ritual takes place in the first lunar month of each year, to celebrate Co Su Kong's birthday. Everyone in the temple's catchment area makes offerings, and there are numerous feasts in the weeks before and after the birthday. On the day of the birthday itself, enormous crowds gather to worship and to admire the gaudily decorated pigs offered to Co Su Kong. The mob of onlookers, the peddlers lining the main street, and an occasional lion or tiger dance combine to block traffic throughout the town. This festival is the major event of the year in Sanxia, and even people who have left for Taibei or other areas usually give at least monetary support.

The organization of this ritual clarifies the central role of the temple in defining the larger social community of Sanxia. For the birthday celebration, the temple divides Sanxia into seven 'inner shares' and twelve 'outer shares'. The outer shares are the communities outside the basic area of Sanxia and Yingge (the next township to the north) that take part in the ritual. The seven inner shares are much more important, and their representatives are responsible for administration of the temple. With one exception, surname defines these seven shares. Five of the shares are for the five most populous surnames, one is for people of miscellaneous surname, and the exceptional share consists of people from a small area called Zhongzhuang. The god's image was supposedly stored in Zhongzhuang before the original temple was built, and these people were thus granted the privilege of constituting their own share.[25]

In addition to appointing people to the temple committee, each share is responsible on a rotating schedule for raising pigs to offer to Co Su Kong on his birthday. Thus, the opportunity to kill a pig for Co Su Kong comes to each family only once every seven years. The twelve families who raise the most obese pigs each year have the privilege of offering them in front of the temple on the morning of Co Su Kong's birthday.

Each year, the temple chooses a *lo cu* (incense pot master) and three assistants (*hu lo cu*). The *lo cu* is reponsible for the annual birthday celebration for Co Su Kong; he is the religious representative of Sanxia as a whole. The temple chooses a new *lo cu* each year by divination, and thus, technically, anyone is eligible. In fact, however, only a few people who are wealthy enough to shoulder the burden of subsidizing the ritual will submit their names.

Sanxia also devotes several weeks at this time to special worship of Co Su Kong in each individual community. This begins in the 'outer shares', then moves to the villages of the Hengxi valley, followed by Yingge, and finally the Sanxia valley. Images are taken from the temple and paraded out in sedan chairs to the area involved, accompanied by traditional music and sometimes also by men dressed in ten-foot tall costumes representing low-ranking deities. On reaching his destination, still more offerings (including a *kho kun* offering for his troops), more operas, and, of course, more feasts greet Co Su Kong (see Harrell, 1982, p. 189 for a map of the rotation).

The ghost-feeding ritual, the Universal Salvation rite described at the end of the preceding chapter, is the temple's second most important festival. This ritual organizes a smaller area than the celebration of Co Su Kong's birthday; it involves only the Sanxia River valley. In contrast to the organization by surnames for the birthday ritual, the ghost-feeding organization is entirely geographical. Only the inner Sanxia valley is involved – the very center of the temple's catchment area (see Map 2.1). The villages of this area combine into the 'four great pillars' (*si tua thiau*), each of which is theoretically responsible for a different aspect of the event: (1) the *cu hue*, chairman of the committee, is responsible for money collection and accounting; (2) the *cu tua:*, chairman of the altars, is responsible for preparation of the altars and hiring an opera troupe; (3) the *cu ciou*, chairman of the *ciou*, is responsible for the ceremony itself; and (4) the *cu pho*,

Map 2.1   Rotation for the Universal Salvation Festival

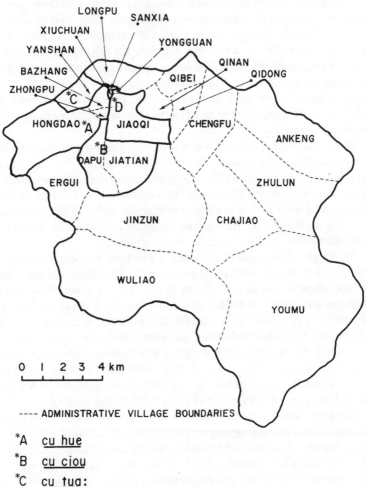

---- ADMINISTRATIVE VILLAGE BOUNDARIES

*A   <u>cu hue</u>
*B   <u>cu ciou</u>
*C   <u>cu tua:</u>
*D   <u>cu pho</u>

chairman of the Pho To (ghost-feeding ritual), is responsible for the offerings. As the titles indicate, the same organization would be used if Sanxia were to hold a *ciou*, a major ceremony to be discussed below. Each 'great pillar' consists of two or three administrative villages, and a few of the largest villages are divided into two or three neighborhoods for this purpose, to make the distribution more equitable. Within each 'pillar' responsibility rotates annually from one section to the next. When a section, which usually consists of an administrative village, includes more than one social community, the communities share responsibility, but make a symbolic expression of their separate identities. For example, when Zhongpu Village was the representative for its 'pillar', the village head set up a single altar, but the members of the two constituent communities kept their offerings separate: Kiu Kiong Kiou kept its offerings at the rear of the altar table, and Tiong Pho kept its at the front. The ghost-feeding offerings thus clearly mark both the administrative and social territories within the Sanxia valley.

The division of labor among the four pillars, however, is only theoretical. The actual responsibility of the village head in charge of each pillar is to set up an altar in an appointed place in the town of Sanxia, and to make sure the people of his village bring offerings on the day of the ceremony. The man responsible for organizing that year's birthday offering for Co Su Kong (the *lo cu*) also sets up an altar to represent the entire area. This altar always stands in the Zhong Shan Tang, a government sponsored meeting hall that exists in every town.

Large religious ceremonies like the Universal Salvation rites are expensive. Voluntary donations fund most ritual functions of the temple, including the festive birthday celebration for Co Su Kong. The ghost-feeding ritual, however, is unique. The village heads collect a tax from every household; in return they give as receipts paper charms (*hu-a*) printed by the temple. The rate varies from year to year. In 1978 it was set at NT$50 (about US $1.40) for every household. Unlike real taxes, of course, the temple cannot force everyone to pay this fee. Nevertheless, nearly every family contributes. By assuming the power to tax, the temple again takes a manifestly political role.

The Co Su Kong temple thus organizes the community in several ways. The birthday celebration divides Sanxia by surname for its broadest organization, and by geographical area in the rotating feasts held by each community. The cycle of feasts distinguishes the three main geographic sections of the temple catchment area (Yingge, the Hengxi valley and the Sanxia valley), and also distinguishes the smaller communities within each section. The Universal Salvation festival organizes only the Sanxia valley, dividing it into four geographically defined regions, which are in turn broken up into smaller geographical units.

A number of other rituals also take place at the Co Su Kong temple, although none have such important roles in community organization. The *pai to*, for example, involves continuous recital of sutras for a week in the tenth lunar month. This is for the benefit of people who have purchased a *tau* (peck measure) filled with raw rice and various symbolic paraphernalia for good luck and long life. Several hundred of these *tau* are placed on the temple altar during the ritual, and afterwards the family eats the rice (see Baity, 1975, for a fuller description).

Four Taoist priests alternate the responsibility of performing *po un* (repairing the fate) rituals for people each morning. On the first and fifteenth of each lunar month, which are the most popular days for this ritual, all four are present. This rotation was set up recently because several of the priests had been squabbling over customers. The ritual itself involves the priest reading a petition to Co Su Kong on behalf of his client, and then stamping some article of the client's clothing with Co Su Kong's seal. Although the temple takes a cut of the profits, the only real relationship is between the Taoist and his client.

Sanxia's temple dedicated to the goddess Ma Co follows the Co Su Kong temple in importance. Like many of the smaller temples in Sanxia, the Ma Co temple has a small local clientele, most of whom consider it secondary to the Co Su Kong temple. The annual celebration for Ma Co's birthday is smaller than that for Co Su Kong. The Ma Co temple performs neither the *pai to* nor the ghost-feeding, but the man formerly in charge could perform *po un* rituals and various types of divination. Tan Kim-thian, an ambitious village head, has recently replaced this man as official head of the temple. Tan is a retired businessman, and a member of the Nationalist Party. His political loyalties, his election to village office, his take-over of the Ma Co temple, and his availability as an expert to lead families through funeral ritual suggest that he has a two-pronged strategy to create a political base. Tan is working along ordinary political lines (through Party and office), and also along religious lines (by becoming a religious authority in charge of a major temple). Tan needs to make the Ma Co temple more prominent, to expand its clientele and thus his own power base. He is planning to rebuild it on a larger scale, and will solicit funds as he gets permission from the government.

The third most important temple in Sanxia, and the last that I will mention separately here is in a rural area called Peq-ke, and is dedicated to En Cu Kong (more commonly called Kuan Kong). This is one of three temples in northern Taiwan built by a coal mine owner to express his thanks to Kuan Kong for helping him to rise from poor pedlar to wealthy capitalist. It is one of the newer temples in Sanxia. Shortly after his death, a special altar was built for the founder, and many people now worship him at this temple or at his grave. The three En Cu Kong temples are not entirely ordinary, because they are the centers for a special cult whose members are vegetarians. Members are easily distinguished by the blue robes they wear at temple rituals.

In the past, temples to Kuan Kong were sometimes considered Confucian and made part of the state cult. While the state religion no longer exists (except in a token annual ritual for Confucius), this temple apparently claims to inherit its prestige. Like a temple to Confucius, its doors have 108 raised yellow bumps on a red background instead of door gods. Furthermore, the birthday ritual is clearly modelled on the one that takes place each year at Taibei's temple to Confucius.

To most people, however, it is just an ordinary temple with two unexplained restrictions: one never offers meat nor burns paper spirit money.[26] The temple offers the same range of rituals as the Co Su Kong temple, and its *po un* is considered especially efficacious. The people of Sanxia clearly see this temple as less important than the Co Su Kong temple. It is similar in its functions to the Ma Co temple or any of the other temples to popular deities. Outside of Sanxia, however, the temple has a reputation as a tourist attraction, partly because of its association with its two sister temples and the fame of its cult, and partly because of its beautiful setting.

There are sixteen other temples in the Sanxia area dedicated to popular deities and large enough to employ a temple keeper. All have birthday celebrations (although none compare to Co Su Kong's), many have *pai to*, and a few have people who can *po un*. To my knowledge, only one has a Universal Salvation festival. Two of them also have regular spirit medium (*tang-ki*) sessions. These temples (including the Ma Co and En Cu Kong temples) divide the area into rough and overlapping geographical segments. The popularity of each relates both to its reputation and to the convenience of access to it. Only the Co Su Kong temple serves a large and unified community.

In addition, there are five Buddhist vegetarian halls (*chai tng*) in the Sanxia area. Three of these house ordained Buddhist monks or nuns; the fourth has a large number of male and female lay Buddhists belonging to the Xian Tian sect. This last temple is located, along with several other temples, on top of Longevity Mountain, which is another of Sanxia's better-known scenic areas. One old man there is a famous fortune-teller, and the temple also supports a sutra singing group that can be hired out to chant at funerals.

Another of these temples is in Kiu Kiong Kiou itself. It houses three nuns and, unlike many vegetarian halls, has close ties with the people of the area. The main reason for this is that the nun in charge grew up there, her family still lives there, and she thus has many close ties with the people of Kiu Kiong Kiou.

A Pure Land monk, who came over from the mainland after the Communist victory, runs one of the others. He is primarily concerned with Buddhist education, and runs periodic study groups in various sutras. Because he is unable to speak Hokkien, he appeals primarily to young intellectuals, who feel comfortable speaking Mandarin. The last *chai tng* is isolated far up in the mountains of Sanxia. The monk at this temple belongs to the Chan (Zen) sect, and his primary ties are to the intelligentsia of Taibei. He has little contact with the people of Sanxia. Both of these last two temples typify the new influx of mainland Buddhism into Taiwan after 1949.

Vegetarian halls offer one service not found in other types of temples: they will take responsibility for worship of the tablets of deceased relatives (see Baity, 1975). Some (although not in Sanxia) also store ashes from cremations. There is an annual service for these souls that includes a ghost-feeding ritual. They also celebrate the ghost-feeding ritual in the seventh lunar month, along with the birthdays of certain Buddhist deities, especially Sakyamuni and Kuan Im. Many will also do *po un* rituals.

With the exception of the Buddhist temples, worship of gods ties very closely to the social boundaries of communities, and to local politics: the Co Su Kong temple can call a meeting of local elected officials, it can collect taxes, it served as a base for political mobilization against the Japanese, and both it and the Ma Co temple currently serve as bases for local political groups. The gods thus lend themselves to an ideology that emphasizes the close ties that bind together community, politics and religion.

Sangren (1979, ch. 6) has discussed the relation between the religious, economic and administrative regions. Temple areas for gods higher than the Earth God differ from the discrete administrative regions: like economic regions, temple areas have fuzzy boundaries, and some neighborhoods may be loyal to more than one territory. The extent of a temple's area depends in part on its reputation for efficacy, but also on its economic situation. Temple areas resemble economic regions in part because they are economic enterprises. The temple must make enough money to support itself and its staff.

This is no problem for a major community temple like the Co Su Kong temple, but Sanxia's many smaller temples rely on attracting a steady clientele that will invest in the temple, buy incense and spirit money to burn, or purchase minor ritual services. Areas that are too sparsely settled cannot support a temple, even if they are unified communities. Areas with little community solidarity may support several temples, especially where they are convenient to major roads and a potential tourist trade. Map 2.2 shows, for example, that very few temples occur in the more inaccessible parts of Sanxia. On the other hand, temples may concentrate along main roads where they can attract members of other communities. Three temples with no real community following, for example, depend primarily on weekend tourists from Taibei, Sanxia, and the surrounding towns. These three temples (Map 2.2, numbers 12–14) cluster on Longevity Mountain; they require an invigorating, but not especially taxing, climb up from the side of the major road connecting Sanxia and Taibei. The Co Su Kong temple itself is trying to take advantage of the growing tourist and pilgrimage trade to attract income. Temples thus reflect both local community solidarity and opportunities to generate income from non-residents.

The striking parallels between gods and traditional bureaucrats add to the ideologized connection between temples and communities. The many analogies between gods and bureaucrats have been discussed often (e.g., Feuchtwang, 1974a; Jordan, 1972; Wolf 1974b). Temple architecture provides one of the clearest analogies. Temples are explicitly modelled on yamens, the traditional residences of government officials. Traditional sumptuary laws limited use of the colorfully decorated and sharply curved roof typical of temples to the houses of official degree-holders. Temple architecture also distinguishes the relative rank of various gods by the amount of roof decoration or by the type of door gods. The Earth God, for example, is too low to merit any door gods at all, and his roof has few decorations. The Co Su Kong temple, on the other hand, has four bronze guardians at its doors, and the roof is covered with dragons, phoenixes and other traditional motifs.

Iconography also underlines the political, bureaucratic ideology of gods. Most gods sit in a dignified posture, wearing the robes of

Map 2.2   Major Temples of Sanxia

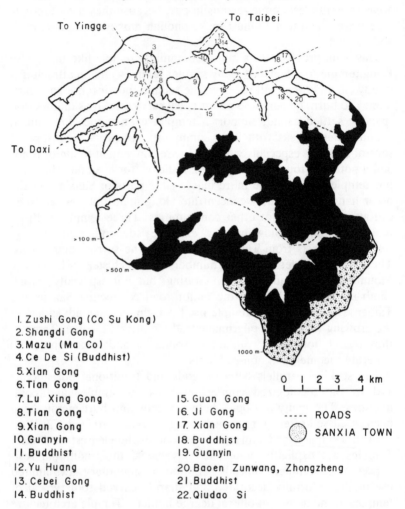

1. Zushi Gong (Co Su Kong)
2. Shangdi Gong
3. Mazu (Ma Co)
4. Ce De Si (Buddhist)
5. Xian Gong
6. Tian Gong
7. Lu Xing Gong
8. Tian Gong
9. Xian Gong
10. Guanyin
11. Buddhist
12. Yu Huang
13. Cebei Gong
14. Buddhist
15. Guan Gong
16. Ji Gong
17. Xian Gong
18. Buddhist
19. Guanyin
20. Baoen Zunwang, Zhongzheng
21. Buddhist
22. Qiudao Si

----- ROADS
SANXIA TOWN

traditional civil or military officials. The bureaucratic iconography is most explicit for the City God, who rules in every administrative capital, and who is always depicted with a full panoply of scribes, runners, guards and all the other necessities of managing a magistrate's office.

People's behavior toward gods provides still more evidence for the bureaucratic analogy. People make important requests to both secular and heavenly bureaucrats by hiring an appropriate expert to write a formal petition. Petitions to the gods work in exactly the same ways as documents intended for the secular government (Ahern, 1981b, ch. 2). Even in ordinary acts of worship, people must identify themselves with full name, address and birthday to allow the god to locate their file properly. Acts of respect toward gods are similar to acts of respect toward secular superiors (Ahern 1981b, ch. 3). Finally, a superior official must appoint (*hong*) gods to office. If gods fail to perform their duties properly they can be removed from office, just like secular officials.

Many informants also make an explicit analogy between the gods and the government. The Jade Emperor, they say, is like President Jiang, Co Su Kong is like a governor, the Earth God is like a policeman, and so on. The detailed parallel between the religious and secular bureaucracies meant that the popular pantheon could not easily question the general system of bureaucratic authority.[27] One could replace a particular god, just as one could replace a particular magistrate (though not easily in either case) by taking drastic action. Yet the system as a whole would remain intact in both cases. The celestial bureaucracy confirmed the secular political hierarchy as an inevitable, natural order.

The analogies that unite deities, yamens and local elites into a social and symbolic whole are central to Chinese religion. Both elites and common people share an experience of the ritual importance of community, which makes the connection between gods and communities easy to ideologize. Yet local communities and politics can take many different, sometimes problematic forms. The state played down these problems, ideologizing the analogy further by amplifying the bureaucratic details of the Heavenly pantheon, and by stressing each temple's proper place in an administrative hierarchy that culminated in the divine Jade Emperor and the secular Emperor, the Son of Heaven (see Chapter 5). The popular religion, however, often treated the pantheon more pragmatically, adjusting and manipulating it in relation to the local political economy. The rest of this chapter analyzes the less ideologized relation of the gods to the changes and contradictions of local social relations.

Goddesses

Many deities do not fit the model of a secular magistrate. For example, Kuan Kong, who is one of the most important gods in

Taiwan, is a military figure. Yet the bureaucratic model can easily expand to fit cases like Kuan Kong; traditional China had parallel military and civil hierarchies, and both were important for the analogy between the secular and supernatural hierarchies.

Goddesses are a much more troublesome discrepancy. Several of the most important deities in Taiwan are female, and they are thus completely detached from the bureaucratic hierarchy. There are three primary goddesses in Taiwan: (1) Ma Co is the object of a major cult, and her temples are often community-based like those of the 'magistrate' deities. She is particularly known for saving seafarers in distress. (2) Cu Si: Nia:-nia: (Goddess Who Aids Birth) usually holds a baby; women worship her to guarantee the birth of a son, or for help in labor generally. (3) Kuan Im was originally Buddhist. Like Cu Si: Nia:-nia:, images sometimes depict her holding a baby and helping in childbirth; like Ma Co (with whom she is sometimes confused in Taiwan), she is famous especially for helping people in desperate straits. Each goddess emphasizes the nurturing and reproductive roles of women. Taiwanese religion thus has a female undercurrent that stresses compassion and birth, rather than the bureaucratic order of the male deities (Sangren, 1979, pp. 371–5). This female undercurrent relates back to the idealized role of a woman in her family: it stresses her role as nurturing, lineage-reproducing mother.

This cosmology idealizes the political system and the position of women in the family. Yet a few goddesses stray from their idealized kin roles. The most important of these is the Eternal Venerable Mother (Wu-sheng Lao-mu). The Venerable Mother is the chief deity in some of the major heterodox sects, including the White Lotus and its offshoots, which rebelled frequently during the last dynasty (Naquin, 1976), and in the Religion of Unity (Yi Guan Dao), which is currently outlawed in Taiwan (Jordan, 1982). Her infinite compassion makes her similar to a Bodhisattva like Kuan Im, while her creation of the world and control over all heaven and earth make her superior to anything in the orthodox, male-dominated cosmology.

These female deities can become a metaphor for unofficial power. They are especially popular among women in Taiwan. They can be seen as the nurturing counterpart of the male deities, but as the Venerable Mother shows, they also have the potential to oppose the gods and their bureaucracy. People rarely ideologize this aspect of the pantheon, largely because it conflicts with the male-centered bureaucracy that the state and most community temples provide. Female deities make the cosmology a much more flexible index of social relations than the male gods alone suggest. They allow the cosmology to fit the experience of women, and of potentially rebellious groups.

Gods and Ethnicity

Traditional religious ideology associated gods with the units of the administrative hierarchy, but specific localities often reinterpreted gods and temples according to the particular social relations of the area. In Taiwan, there has been a steady change from an association of temples with ethnic groups (people with a common point of origin on the mainland), to an association with geographical areas. This has accompanied the decreasing importance of this kind of ethnicity in Taiwan. The Japanese stopped the ethnic battles over land and water rights in the nineteenth century, and many young people today do not know their ancestors' place of origin.

Co Su Kong is the patron of people from Anxi County in Fujian, from which the ancestors of most of Sanxia's residents emigrated. The Co Su Kong temple was originally an ethnic temple, serving only people with Anxi origins. As place of origin in the mainland lost its significance for the Taiwanese, however, the organizational base of the temple changed from ethnic group to geographical area.[28] The division of Sanxia by surname is a remnant of the time when the temple was less concerned with Sanxia as a geographic entity, and more concerned with Anxi origins as the basis for social alliances. The Universal Salvation is strictly geographically organized because the arrangement is more recent than the seven surname-shares; it was created when the temple was already more geographically oriented. This change is typical of temples in Taiwan. Wang Shih-ch'ing (1974), for example, has described the same process for Shulin, a township near Sanxia.

The Ma Co temple has a similar history. It originally represented Sanxia residents with ancestors from Meizhou, also in Fujian Province. Like the Co Su Kong temple, the Ma Co temple has a seven-share rotation based on surname for its annual birthday celebration. The people involved all have Meizhou ancestry, and do not take part in the birthday celebration for Co Su Kong. These people are a small minority of the population of Sanxia, however, and Ma

Co's birthday is not a major event. Aside from the birthday celebration, the Ma Co temple is now simply a small local temple with no
particular ethnic affiliations. Even the Meizhou residents now consider Co Su Kong their most important deity.

The most important ethnic distinction in Taiwan today is between
the original Chinese inhabitants, and the mainlanders who arrived
after 1945, and who soon dominated the political and economic
structures of power. Religion is again a part of this new system of
social relations. Many mainlanders (but only about 2 per cent of the
Taiwanese) are Christian, and almost no mainlanders take part in the
major festivals of Taiwanese popular religion. Ahern (1981a) has
suggested that the current abundance of popular religious activity,
and especially the huge pig sacrifices (as at Co Su Kong's birthday)
express Taiwanese ethnicity in the face of mainlander opposition.
Gates (1982) suggests further that the current resurgence of popular
religion is part of a strategy by the traditional Taiwanese petty
bourgeoisie to claim support from Taiwanese local communities
against the larger economy. Pragmatic interpretations of the tie
between temple and community may thus be changing again, in ways
do not mesh simply with the ideology of gods as bureaucrats.

Region and Nation

The use of gods to support various ethnic or geographic groups
against one another fits one part of the ideologized bureaucratic
analogy: gods are the supernatural representatives of social communities. Yet community solidarity in China existed often only at the
expense of national solidarity. There has been a constant conflict in
Chinese history between the central government and the divisive
forces of regional independence. The central government made many
attempts to control these forces: officials were not allowed to serve in
their home areas and were frequently rotated (Ch'u, 1962, pp. 21–2),
political boundaries were sometimes drawn to cross-cut natural regions (Skinner, 1976, pp. 341–4), and so on. The rise of warlordism in
the early twentieth century occurred because the government was no
longer able to prevent regions from becoming autonomous. The
process that led up to this began in the Taiping Rebellion, which the
government defeated only by allowing high-level members of the
elite to set up military units in their own native areas (Kuhn, 1970).

Religion often became a tool for these divisive forces. The Qing
government was aware of this and outlawed large pilgrimages. In the

eighteenth century, even large rituals like birthday celebrations for gods were banned because they often resulted in disturbances (Hsiao, 1960, p. 231). Similar fears partially motivate the Nationalist government's discouragement of large-scale religious activities in Taiwan.

Gods and temples reflect local social communities, but the specific content of that reflection changes as social relations change. Earth God temples appear and disappear as neighborhoods come and go. Large temples emphasize ethnicity or geography as the bases of community organization change. Community solidarity opposes or supports national solidarity as the national political situation improves or worsens. Temples and their gods react to such contextual changes in the role of community, but those reactions tend to be less ideologized than the relation between god and community, which is less context-bound and more acceptable to the state.

Co Su Kong illustrates many of these themes. The temple management puts out an ideologized version of Co Su Kong's life that fits nicely with the nationalist concerns of the govenment, and confirms Co Su Kong as a loyal member of the administration. The official story relates how Co Su Kong was a military official who fought for the Song Dynasty in its losing battle against non-Chinese invaders (QSZS). He fled south with the defeated dynasty, and settled in Anxi County to perfect himself spiritually. His followers in Anxi resisted the foreign Yuan Dynasty, and supported the Chinese Ming who finally retook the throne. Co Su Kong was first officially deified by a Ming Emperor. The entire story can be read as a thinly disguised analogy for Sun Yat-sen's resistance and final victory over the Manchurian Qing Dynasty, or for the Chinese victory over the Japanese after a long occupation. Either reading fits well with the goals and public image of the government.

Yet this story is not very important to anyone beyond the temple management and the tourists who read the literature printed up by the temple. The people of Sanxia speak instead of the help Co Su Kong has given them as members of the community, but not as heroic nationalists. He used to appear in the ethnic battles of the nineteenth century, which the government was powerless to prevent in Taiwan. This was the period when the temple was tied to local ethnicity. He also helped Sanxia's soldiers in the Japanese army during the Second World War. He did not aid the cause of the Japanese or any other national government. His only concern was to save the lives of Sanxia's soldiers. People tell stories of how he helped them avoid attack, but not how he helped them win victory for (or against) the Japanese. Co Su Kong was protecting the local community, with no loyalties to any higher political unit. He apparently has the same goals under the Nationalists; a young draftee explained that Co Su Kong helped get easy assignments for draftees from Sanxia. He is protecting his citizens, but possibly at the expense of the national government. Co Su Kong is closely tied to the community; his larger loyalties change as social alliances and political conditions change. These pragmatic interpretations show local gods to be potentially much more troublesome to the state than the more general ideology of god-bureaucrats.

Gods and Elites

Temples help create local community unity, and Co Su Kong is equally the patron of everyone in Sanxia. Yet some of the actual uses of religion belie this superficial equality within the community. Sanxia's religious center, the Co Su Kong temple, ties closely with the old political elite. The man in charge of the temple's reconstruction, for example, served both as head of the township and on the township council in the early postwar years. The chairman of the temple committee is a physician, and by far the most educated man of his generation in that area. Both men are part of a political faction that began to redevelop the temple after losing political office during the murky political period in Sanxia after the Japanese departed. While the temple may serve such people in part as a retreat from politics, their very presence nevertheless makes it an informal locus of power. Tan Kim-thian, the village head and Nationalist Party member who took over the Ma Co temple, is trying to use that temple to create a similar power base for himself. Such relations between temples and politics are common in many parts of Taiwan (Baity, 1975; Seaman, 1978), where major community temples often serve as unofficial bases for local powerholders; they are the symbolic centers of the community, they are usually also major centers of informal social activity, and they tend to control relatively large budgets.

Another source of the Co Su Kong temple's power is its current reconstruction, which has made it an important economic hub. In an area with few large factories (but many small ones), the craftsmen and staff hired by the temple make it a significant employer. The scale of the temple reconstruction in Sanxia has made the temple an even larger employer and solicitor of funds than most community temples. More important, as construction progresses, the temple is becoming a well-known tourist attraction on the island, and the income from the tourist trade is potentially very important to Sanxia.

Ritual feasting also has political uses. All of the major temple festivals are accompanied by domestic feasting on a large scale. The most important occasions for this in Sanxia are the birthday of Co Su Kong, the birthday of Ang Kong (another deity), and the Universal Salvation festival. Large feasts also accompany engagements, weddings and funerals. In addition, for people in appropriate occupations, the first and last of the semi-monthly rituals for the Earth God (*thau ge* and *be ge*) also have feasts given by employers for their workers.

Food is inevitably provided for these feasts, including many ornate courses with unlimited wine and beer. The largest may feed 500–600 guests, and their great expense makes them an object of constant criticism from the government. The government campaign has had some effect: instead of rotating from one neighborhood to the next over a period of several weeks, many festivals are now celebrated on only a single day. In Sanxia, although the gigantic birthday celebration for Co Su Kong continues unabated, both the Ang Kong birthday and the Universal Salvation festival now involve only a few days. Nevertheless, hosting one of these feasts is an important opportunity for the families involved to display themselves in public. In all, the average person may attend five to ten of these feasts each year, and host one himself only once in several years.

This pattern of conspicuous consumption in feasts has several important uses, and this helps to explain the limited success of government programs against large religious expenditures. These feasts express, first of all, wealth and power. A family that serves an expensive meal for 500 guests has established itself as an important social force. Feasts also give everyone, but especially elites, the chance to create bonds of reciprocity. Such occasions are therefore particularly crucial for businessmen and politicians. During particularly busy times of the year, businessmen and politicians (and the occasional anthropologist), all anxious to maintain their contacts, can be seen going from feast to feast, stopping at each only long enough to consume the glasses of wine that courtesy requires before staggering off to the next.

At the same time, however, feasts provide no overt recognition of class distinctions – the system looks as if everyone were capable of the same thing. Yang (1961, p. 79) writes that 'while Chinese religion took a hand in trying to mitigate the oppressiveness of the rich by giving supernatural sanction to moral qualities like righteousness and generosity, it did not condemn the acquisition of wealth as such'. In fact, it did more than simply 'not condemn' wealth; it tacitly supported the wealthy through the unequal benefits of the pattern of feasts and festivals.

The choice of a *lo cu*, the 'incense pot master' who takes charge of a temple's rituals for a year, also reveals inequality beneath a surface of equality. Choice of a *lo cu* for a local Earth God temple is egalitarian; each household is registered on a list, and a randomizing divination device (*puaq pue*, throwing 'moonblocks') allows 'divine' selection of a *lo cu*. Ideally, major community temples choose *lo cu* for their major festivals in the same way. There are, however, too many households in Sanxia to give each one a chance each year. The temple instead registers a list of people who volunteer to compete for *lo cu* each year. Like throwing a feast for five hundred people, anyone can in principle volunteer, but in fact only the rich can afford this expression of religious devotion. Being *lo cu* for the Earth God is a minor responsibility, but the *lo cu* for a major community ritual has both an important social position and major expenses. The theoretical equality of families before Co Su Kong cannot override basic distinctions of wealth.

People's interpretations of gods come not simply from the ideologized analogy with bureaucrats governing a unified area, but also from pragmatic dealings with gods and temples. Gods defined ethnic communities in the nineteenth century and geographic communities in the twentieth, as the important social divisions in Taiwan changed. The ideological incorporation of local areas within a nationwide political system was questioned by an emphasis on local independence. The ideologized rule of male bureaucrats was questioned by an emphasis on a mothering goddess. The ideologized equality within local areas was questioned by a reflection of real differences in wealth, and so on.

The Temple in Action

A meeting that took place at the Co Su Kong temple on August 3, 1978, illustrates many of these cleavages. The meeting takes place annually about two weeks before the Universal Salvation festival. The temple leadership calls together all the village heads and all of the people in charge of the next birthday celebration to discuss plans for the upcoming ritual. The temple's authority to summon government officials illustrates its genuine political power.

The meeting began when Professor Li Meishu, who is in charge of the reconstruction and the most powerful man in the temple, gave a brief history of the temple and its reconstruction. After some applause a temple employee was directed to read a tentative schedule of events for the ritual. As he announced where the Four Great Pillars would place their altars, Li interrupted. He suggested that it would be simpler to put all the altars in the plaza in front of the temple, rather than scattered throughout the town. Furthermore, he felt that each pillar should supply only a single meat offering, with everyone else bringing only fruit. He was clearly echoing the government's constant efforts to persuade people to stop wasting so much money on rituals. The Taibei government had in fact been pressuring Li to cut down on ritual expenses on pain having his application for certain aspects of the reconstruction turned down. The government frowned on the expense of the project, and on the ritual expenses in which the people of Sanxia indulge. Li reacted by stressing national rather than local loyalties. He respected the government campaign for quieter rituals, and he emphasized the artistic merit of the reconstruction over its religious value.

Tan Kim-thian, the man who controls the Ma Co temple, and who is a Nationalist Party member, stood up to support Li's opinion. As village heads, he said, they were responsible to represent the government's point of view. An old man disagreed vehemently. He said it would be wrong to change because: first, the ghosts only eat meat, not fruit; secondly, the people have been preparing meat to sacrifice (especially pigs) all year, and cannot be asked not to at the last minute; and thirdly, the traditions of their ancestors should not be tampered with. Tan then softened his original position, saying that they should urge people to bring fruit instead of the more standard meat offering, although they could not force anyone. The topic was dropped and, in fact, everyone brought meat as usual. Li and Tan's attempt to use religion to support the central government failed.

At this point another man stood up and said that he was old and wanted to see a *ciou* before he died. A *ciou* is the largest ceremony a community can put on, and serves to renew its cosmic mandate (see Liu, 1967; Saso, 1972). None will be performed until the temple is completed, and none has been performed in Sanxia within living memory.[29] The slowness of the reconstruction and the lack of a *ciou* have fueled increasing hostility between Li and the community in recent years. Li became very angry at this point, and made a long speech, denying that he had misused funds, and emphasizing the temple's position as an artistic treasury and as a tourist attraction. Tan, after several unsuccessful attempts to interrupt, again supported him, and tried to cut off discussion of this topic. Feelings apparently ran too strong, however, as several more people urged a quick end to the reconstruction. The main argument is over the funds controlled by the temple. Li wanted to maintain control, and to continue his constant elicitation of donations for his project, but others wanted an end to the economic demands of the temple.

In the interstices of the argument, several of the village heads suggested revisions in the organization of the Four Great Pillars, claiming that they had a disproportionate amount of responsibility relative to their population. These revisions would have relieved their constituencies of some of the work and costs of the festival, and thus probably would have helped the village heads in future elections.

When lunch arrived, all these discussions were dropped, and the meeting was soon adjourned. Although no major decisions were made, a number of features of the meeting illustrate the political importance of religion, and the difficulty of promoting an ideology. First of all, no other organization outside the township government had the power to summon the village heads. Secondly, the argument about the reconstruction of the temple stemmed primarily from the huge sums of money that pass through the temple and the constant donations that it requests. Thirdly, the requests for readjustments in the Four Great Pillars showed that the temple's community organization is important enough to warrant the concern of the village heads. Fourthly, the political importance of the temple leadership appeared in Tan Kim-thian's constant support of Li Meishu. Tan, ever since his retirement, had been trying to become a major community leader. His first step was to get elected village head. The constant currying of favor with Li Meishu was part of the same process, which recently led him to take over the Ma Co temple as well. Finally the support for simpler rituals from both Li and Tan, and the arguments about having a *ciou*, illustrated the tension between local and national loyalties, and the failure of the temple and political leaders to impose their own interpretations. The extent and complexity of the real ties between temple and community make it very difficult to maintain a unified ideology.

Both the ancestral cult and god worship include relatively explicit, ideologized interpretations that match our usual anthropological understanding of the popular tradition (filial piety, the bureaucratic hierarchy, and so forth). Yet both also have a wide range of flexible, pragmatic ties to more complex tensions and contradictions within the society, which appear primarily where the experience of kinship and community is complex and changeable over time and place, and where local leaders cannot impose an interpretation. Such conditions encourage people to remake their pragmatic religious interpretations.

3 Pragmatic Ghosts

Ghosts contrast with ancestors and gods. The preceding chapter showed how ancestors and gods are complex, pragmatic categories, only partially ideologized. This chapter discusses how interpretations of ghosts in the popular tradition occur only partially within the structural contrast with ancestors and gods. The contrasts with ancestors and gods lead to two inconsistent readings of ghosts: ghosts as marginal ancestors are pitiful, and ghosts as marginal gods are dangerous. Pragmatic interpretations of ghosts in the Universal Salvation rites have resolved this inconsistency in different ways as social relations have changed over time in Taiwan. The ideologized, structural contrasts of gods/ghosts/ancestors set the parameters for popular treatment of ghosts, but those contrasts do not determine this treatment. The pragmatic ghosts help clarify the limits to ideology in Chinese popular religion.

Ghosts are the souls of people who died in the wrong way or at the wrong time. Only old people with many sons and grandsons, who support them while alive and worship them after they die, are able to have a proper death. Unfortunately, many people die violently – through accident, suicide, or war – and many people die before they have had children or, perhaps worse, with unfilial children who will not worship them. Ghosts are thus souls who do not occupy the correct position of the dead in the social structure. They are socially marginal beings who lack both the political standing of the gods and the kinship standing of the ancestors.

According to many informants, the dead must pass through an underworld that consists of ten bureaucratic courts. A spirit bureaucrat runs each court; he controls a staff of demonic scribes and runners who mete out the various tortures (see Figure 3.1). There is a punishment to fit each crime. In a printed tour of the underworld available in many temples, for example, an underworld official explains the suffering of one ghost:

> This criminal spirit had no proper occupation when she was alive; she specialized in striptease acts and lascivious songs and dances, customarily ruining good men. In life she did not like to wear clothes; in death, she has thus been sentenced to the Frozen Hell,

Figure 3.1   The Disintegrator Carriage Hell, Ninth Level of the
Underworld

Source: DYYJ: 11

forced to search for clothes to hide from the cold, but unable to
find them. Crime has its punishment. (DYYJ, p. 53)

Most souls avoid the worst horrors of the underworld. The living
save them by hiring priests who know how to bribe the appropriate
underworld officials. The socially marginal ghosts, however, have no
one to perform these rituals, and thus never make it through the
complexities of the underworld. Often buried without ceremony,
they must undergo lengthy punishment from which funeral ritual has
released more fortunate souls. Unworshipped, they have neither

food to eat nor money to spend in the underworld. Many thus remain in the world of the living to take what they can. The ghosts of people who died by drowning are especially dangerous: they remain in the water, hoping to regain their freedom by drowning another victim to replace them. Coal mines, military bases, old battle sites and other areas of frequent violent death also have a high concentration of ghosts. In the seventh lunar month, all ghosts are released from the underworld to enjoy a month of feasting offered by the living.

Wolf (1974b) argues that ghosts must be propitiated (*ce*) in contrast to gods and ancestors who are honored (*pai*). His argument is essentially that ghosts are metaphors for people who do not occupy proper positions in the social structure. Thus, like the beggars, thieves and strangers they represent, ghosts are dangerous and must be paid protection money. 'Although people in Sanhsia [Sanxia] differ on how one should deal with these malevolent creatures, they agree that dealing with a ghost is like dealing with *lo-mua:*, the gangs of young toughs who use threats of violence as a means of extortion.' (Wolf, 1974b, p. 170) Later, discussing the pre-Japanese period, Wolf (1974b, p. 175) writes:

The world beyond the bamboo walls that encircled each community was dangerous because it was inhabited by strangers, and strangers were feared because they were represented in experience by bandits and beggars. The ghosts are the product of this experience. They are dangerous because they are strangers, and strangers are dangerous because experience has proved them dangerous.

Ghosts are thus dangerous because they are the souls of people who fall into the interstices of the system of social categories. Asking informants to explain the ritual, however, led to some unexpected answers. I asked a broad range of questionnaire respondents two open-ended questions about the ghost-feeding ritual: 'Why do you worship the good brothers [ghosts] in the seventh month?' and 'If you did not worship them, what would happen?' For purposes of tabulation, I classed each set of answers into three groups, following the natural groupings of answers. The totals from the two questions did not match exactly because a few people gave more than one answer (see Table 3.1).

The first type of answer to why people worship ghosts was to ask for a peaceful life (*kiu pieng an*). *Pieng an* is a frequently-stated goal of religious worship. Literally 'smooth and peaceful', it means free-

Table 3.1   Questions about the Universal Salvation Festival

1. 'Why do you worship the good brothers in the seventh month?'

	Number responding	Percentage
Request a peaceful life	12	10.9%
Sympathy	49	44.5
Follow tradition	49	44.5

2. 'If you did not worship them, what would happen?'

	Number responding	Percentage
Misfortune	9	9.5%
Feel Uncomfortable	10	10.5
Nothing	76	80.0

dom from all types of misfortune. The second category covered a wider ranger of answers, but all carried some implication that the worshipper was doing an act of kindness for the ghosts. Especially common was to say that they worship in order to *chia: lang kheq* for the ghosts (have them as company) because no one else will feed them. Others said that it was to worship them, or to help them; all implied that they were acting generously toward the pitiful ghosts. A large number of people said they worship because it is the Chinese tradition, and some were unable to give any answer at all.

The categories for the second question are similar, but not entirely identical. Some people felt that misfortune would result from not worshipping: accidents, illness and loss of money were mentioned specifically. Another set thought they would feel uncomfortable (*sim bue an*; literally 'with an unpeaceful heart') if they failed to perform this ritual. This answer may include two separate types of feelings: one is discomfort at having broken with tradition, the other is discomfort at failing to be generous to the unfortunate. A few people said they would lose face if they did not worship, not for religious reasons, but because their neighbors would think they were too poor to make the offerings. The largest group thought nothing at all would happen if they did not worship, or they simply could not imagine such a situation; they told me that everyone always worships, and refused to speculate about impossible situations.

Many of these answers provide no explanation at all. For the first question, those who do not worship, do not know why they worship,

or worship only because it is 'traditional' form a category of people
who articulate no explanation for the ghost-feeding ritual. These
people add up to 44.5 per cent of the total. Even more remarkably,
80 per cent of the replies to the second question involve no interpretation of the ritual.

These results provide little support for the usual contention that
ghosts are malevolent, at least in the context of the Universal Salvation festival. Why did only 9.9 per cent of the respondents say that
misfortune would result from failure to worship? Why did only 10.9
per cent say they worship in order to maintain a peaceful life without
mishap? If the association between the malevolence and the marginality of ghosts were complete, the percentages should have been
much higher. People may not have wanted to give 'superstitious'
answers, or to antagonize the ghosts. Yet these questions were asked
much later in the year, when ghosts were not considered such a
threat, and people seemed to take the questions in a very relaxed
way. Furthermore, answering that misfortune would follow from not
worshipping is not the sort of thing that would normally antagonize
ghosts. People were also generally honest about their religious beliefs, and very few seemed to think it necessary to play down their
religious involvement. Nearly everyone, for example, insists that
they perform the ritual.

In looking for exegesis of rituals, it is easy to gravitate toward a few
especially articulate informants. Often, in Taiwan, this is the only
way to get coherent explanations of religion. However, this procedure can lead us to ignore the great mass of people who have no
ready explanations. It is unsafe to assume that the few people who
have given more thought to their rituals are expressing ideas common
to everyone. The very fact that many people have no easily verbal-
ized explanations is in itself significant.

One unspoken reason to take part in the ritual is simply aesthetic.
The seventh month is one of the big events of the year. It is second
only to Co Su Kong's birthday in the first month. There are many
feasts, a constant progression of operas and puppet shows, a night-
time parade complete with lanterns and torches, and a particularly
colorful ritual.

The entire month, and especially the events of the fifteenth, are
very *lau ziat*. *Lau ziat*, literally 'noisy and hot', is a popular aesthetic
ideal in Taiwan. In art it refers, for example, to the colorful, daz-
zlingly complex and crowded carvings that cover more admired
temples. Similarly, in festivals it refers to those with great crowds,

lots of operas, and a constant coming and going of people and rituals. The ghost-feeding ritual is very *lau ziat*, giving people yet another reason to participate.

It is also possible, however, to go beyond aesthetics to explain the lack of an established exegesis for the ghost-feeding ritual. People have no ready explanation of ghosts because ghosts are even less ideologized than ancestors or gods; the meaning lies instead in pragmatic interpretations of ghosts. The absence of an ideology of ghosts (beyond the very general structural contrast with gods and ancestors) stems from the variable experience of marginality across time and society. The following sections expand on Wolf's association of ghosts with socially marginal bandits and beggars by separating two types of marginality: ghosts as bandits are malevolent and opposed to the orthodox political order; ghosts as beggars are pitiful and should be treated with sympathy and guaranteed subsistence. Separation of these two attitudes will help clarify the different social and historical conditions that have shaped the changing pragmatic intepretations of ghosts. Ghosts do not exist simply in contrast with ancestors and gods. Sometimes they are understood in relation to ancestors alone (the more pitiful reading), and sometimes in relation to gods alone (the more malevolent reading).

Marginal Ancestors and Marginal Gods

Ghosts' similarity to ancestors is clear in some informant statements. People will not ordinarily say it, but if the right questions are asked, they will define ghosts as everyone else's ancestors. The souls of all dead are essentially alike, and the key to the division between ghosts and ancestors is the presence or absence of a kinship tie. Ghosts are strangers; ancestors are relatives. Other people's ancestors, however, like most strangers, are harmless. The problematic ghosts are really no one's ancestors. Abandoned, and therefore pitiful, these marginal ancestors form one core of the category 'ghosts'.

Other ghosts are more like marginal gods than marginal ancestors. Small temples are sometimes built for ghosts; some contain the bones of people who died in battle, and others house unidentified bones found by accident. Some of the larger ones allow people to add the bones of unworshipped relatives – usually children or childless adults. These temples have a number of names: many carry the slogan *iu kiu pit ieng* (all requests will be answered), and are thus known as *iu ieng kong* temples (Temples of the Lord Who Answers All Requests). Because *iu ieng kong* temples meet all pleas for help without regard for their morality, they are especially popular among prostitutes, gamblers and other people whose needs are not the sort for which gods, the guardians of traditional morality, would show much sympathy. Most people, if they go to these temples at all, will go only once a year during the seventh lunar month (see Table 2.3). The actual day varies from one temple to another. A few such temples are very active during the seventh month, and many people may sponsor operas or puppet shows to take place there. Over time, some of these temples may gradually develop into temples to gods, their ghostly origins forgotten (Harrell, 1974a; Baity, 1975; Jordan 1972, pp. 170–1).

The following sections expand on these two possible interpretations of ghosts. The two interpretations are not equally important for all participants, nor do they necessarily form a single clearly organized system. The structure of gods, ancestors and ghosts forms the backdrop for Taiwanese religion, but the interpretative values people put on that structure cannot be isolated from the pragmatic complexity and flexibility of everyday life.

Beggars and Marginal Ancestors

In one sense, ghosts provide a negative definition of kinship. As marginal kin – primarily deceased children and unmarried adults – ghosts clarify proper kin. Spirits of marginal kinsmen can lose their ghostly status only by becoming proper kin through spirit marriage or spirit adoption. For example, in 1978 a young man killed a young woman in a traffic accident in Sanxia. The informal settlement he reached with the woman's family included a requirement that he marry the dead woman. He would go through a marriage ceremony, substituting a picture for the living bride; in the future he would take responsibility for worshipping her spirit. The young man would remain free to marry a living wife; the young woman would be saved from being a ghost by being brought into an orthodox kinship position (see Jordan, 1972, pp. 140–55 for further examples). The ghost/ancestor boundary is permeable.

Ghosts are thus marginal kinsmen who lead a pitiful life. In this context, people worship ghosts out of sympathy, not out of fear, just as they feel pity, not terror, toward the living who occupy marginal

kinship positions. Orphans and maiden aunts need not be propitiated, but they should be supported and helped. Borrowing Wolf's
terms, they are more like beggars than bandits. Frequent and empha-
tic informant statements support this reading of ghosts. When asked
why they worship in the seventh month, a plurality of informants
replied that they worship ghosts out of sympathy and a desire to
make the ghosts more comfortable (see Table 3.1). They say they
worship ghosts because everyone ignores them throughout the rest of
the year, or because the ghosts are starving. A few said that they
worship without believing in the existence of ghosts; the ritual expresses good moral sentiments, especially respect for the dead.
People who replied that they would be uncomfortable if they failed to
worship also seemed to be implying that they would feel guilty about
not expressing these moral values. Apparently, a number of informants who said nothing would happen if they failed to worship felt
similarly. One such informant answered my questions saying: 'It's
tradition. We express our respect for the dead whom no one else
worships . . . It doesn't matter if you don't – there aren't really any
ghosts.' And another said: 'We invite the ghosts to a meal once each
year, because they are wild ghosts, living a bitter life in the underworld. It doesn't matter if you don't worship. Asking people to
dinner is just a courtesy; without this feeling of courtesy, there's no
point having company.'

Some of the offerings to ghosts also show them as pitiful beggars,
not fearsome bandits. Ghosts normally receive fully prepared food,
including, most likely, some favorite dishes of the worshipping family. This is the same kind of food offering that ancestors receive, and
emphasizes their similarity to living humans, especially kinsmen. This
theme is carried into the seventh month rituals by offering the ghosts
cigarettes, canned delicacies, and a wash basin – their basic humanity
is remembered. Gods, in contrast, usually get a standardized offering
of three or five kinds of cooked but uncut and unseasoned meat
(*sieng le*). Offerings to the gods are more standardized than those to
ancestors or ghosts because gods do not have the special human
preferences of ghosts and ancestors. Indeed, the higher ranking the
god, the less like human food are the offerings. The highest god in the
popular pantheon (Thi: Kong) receives whole, raw pigs, partially
plucked chickens, and live (unless the ritual goes on too long) fish.
Rawer, less processed food goes with more distant and powerful
beings (Ahern, 1973, pp. 167–70).

In the seventh month, however, none of the food offerings for the ghosts are fully prepared; they are given *sieng le*, which is normally reserved for the gods. People do this in part to stress the impersonal nature of ghosts in the seventh month; ghosts in other contexts appear more as individual personalities, and thus receive food more suitable for humans. People also do this in part to express special respect for the ghosts on this occasion. Like the use of a higher grade of spirit money to honor the gods at the New Year (Ahern, 1981a, p. 402), or the use of higher generation kin terms to honor certain relatives (Weller, 1981), people show special courtesy to the ghosts in the seventh month by offering them only partly prepared food. The use of two types of offerings shows the interstitial nature of ghosts: they are somewhat like gods, and somewhat like ancestors. The offerings bring out the humanity of ghosts and can be seen as generous alms as easily as the propitiatory bribes described by Wolf.

The use of paper spirit money, the currency of the underworld, clearly associates ghosts with beggars. Gods, in general, receive gold money, and ancestors receive a large and a small size of silver money. Ghosts, at the seventh month ghost-feeding ritual as on all other occasions, receive only the smaller size of silver money and a type of paper with articles of clothing and some common utensils printed on it (*kieng i*). Here, they are clearly associated with the souls of the dead in general, but in a lower position than the ancestors (larger sizes of spirit money are more respectful). The gift of clothing, like the offering of a wash basin and towel, clearly associates the ghosts with beggars: ancestors, having households of their own in the underworld, have no need for such objects. In contrast to Wolf's suggestion, generosity may well be a stronger motivation than fear in offering such gifts to ghosts.

Some people may identify directly with ghosts, rather than seeing them as either beggars or bandits. This is especially true for the old; abandonment is a great source of anxiety for the old in Taiwan, and the Universal Salvation festival is a guarantee of support for the abandoned. A metaphoric identification with the 'lonely souls' reassures the anxious worshippers that they can never be truly abandoned. Thus, the power of the idea of ghosts is not only related to fear of those outside normal structures, but also exists because the childless, abandoned ghost represents a source of anxiety, especially for older people who are increasingly dependent on others for their support. The ritual expression of the identity between ghosts and worshipper is clearest at the point in the ceremony where people try to catch the food thrown by the priest. An old woman said that when she was young, the *yang* aspect of the world was not so strong, and it was easier to see ghosts. Anyone, if bold enough, could see them by looking under the sleeves of a priest performing the ghost-feeding ritual. Some were gory and held their heads, cut off in long forgotten battles with aborigines, in their arms. No matter what their physical condition, all alike were crowding around the priest, each trying to reach the food in front of him and catch it as he threw it. Her description sounded exactly like the behavior of the living at several of the ceremonies I witnessed.

There is also some linguistic evidence for the identity of ghosts and people. None of it is decisive, but all of it is relevant. First, a number of informants described the offerings for ghosts as being determined by what the family wants for dinner. This, added to the offering of a wash basin and paper clothing, shows that ghosts have the same tastes and needs as living people. Secondly, the phrase 'to be a lonely ghost' (*cue ko*) describes a man eating voraciously. Finally, many informants told me that the purpose of the Universal Salvation festival is to *chia: lang kheq* for the ghosts. This phrase means to have company, and is used also for human guests. In fact, the food offered the ghosts serves human company later on.

People who make offerings to ghosts on the fifteenth personalize them by marking their dishes of food with individual sticks of incense and with red flags bearing their names. This practice contrasts with all other rituals, in which people place incense into a common incense pot. They are, in a sense, making a public show of generosity to the ghosts, and by the same token, staking an implicit claim to such generosity if they themselves are ever in need.

Some aspects of the ritual reinforce social categories and accepted moral values – for example, thieves *are* dangerous because they are outside the social structure, and generosity *is* highly valued – and people generally find these aspects of the ritual easy to express. Other aspects, however, like the ones discussed here, may express the darker side of people's views of the world. No informants, except with the intention to insult, would ever purposely imply that the living are like ghosts. Yet children are not always filial, and parents are sometimes dishonored and abandoned. The ritual may be important precisely because it says these things that could never be said directly; such pragmatic interpretations remain possible even when people would find an explicit, ideologized version unacceptable.

This view of the Universal Salvation festival is thus partially similar to Geertz's analysis of the Balinese cockfight:

In the normal course of things, the Balinese are shy to the point of obsessiveness of open conflict. Oblique, cautious, subdued, controlled, masters of indirection and dissimulation – what they call *alus*, 'polished,' 'smooth' – they rarely face what they can turn away from, rarely resist what they can evade. But here they portray themselves as wild and murderous, with manic explosions of instinctual cruelty. A powerful rendering of life as the Balinese most deeply do not want it (to adapt a phrase Frye has used of Gloucester's blinding) is set in the context of a sample of it as they do in fact have it. And, because the context suggests that the rendering if less than a straightforward description, is nonetheless more than an idle fancy; it is here that the disquietfulness – the disquietfulness of the *fight*, not (or anyway not necessarily) its patrons, who seem in fact rather thoroughly to enjoy it – emerges. The slaughter in the cock ring is not a depiction of how things literally are among men, but, what is almost worse, of how, from a particular angle, they imaginatively are. (Geertz, 1972, p. 446)

The Universal Salvation rites, however, do more than display disquietfulness. For the moment, at least, the ritual relieves people's anxiety. The Universal Salvation rites not only let people know how it feels to be alone, abandoned and hungry, but they promise relief.

This evidence suggests that some Taiwanese have now carried the 'beggar' metaphor to an extreme, seeing themselves, at least potentially, as abandoned beggars. This interpretation rests on a contrast between comfortable, cared-for ancestors, and miserable, abandoned ghosts. In other contexts, however, the contrast between gods and ghosts leads to a very different pragmatic interpretation of the ghost-feeding ritual.

Bandits and Marginal Gods

Considerable evidence also supports the more standard position that ghosts are like bandits – violent and dangerous outsiders who are marginal to the social and political system. People observe a number of precautions against ghostly malevolence in the seventh month. First, they put off felicitous ceremonies like weddings until a safer date. Second, *po un* (Repair of Fate) ceremonies are cancelled. Taoists normally offer this ceremony every morning at the Co Su Kong temple for people with minor problems. Finally, although some people hesitate to use the word at any time, everyone (even Kiu

Kiong Kiou's only college graduate) tries to avoid saying the word *kui* ('ghosts') during the seventh month. The word has insulting connotations: troublesome children are 'little ghosts', drunks are 'alcohol ghosts', and foreigners in some parts of China are 'foreign ghosts (devils)'. Ghosts hearing themselves called *kui* might take offense, so people usually substitute the euphemism *hou hia: ti* ('good brothers'). Ghosts can be dangerous creatures: malicious ghosts will make people sick, drowned ghosts will pull new victims into the water to take their place, and disfigured ghosts are simply terrifying. Sanxia seems to have a lot of headless ghosts – men whose arms cradle their own bleeding heads, lopped off by the non-Chinese aboriginal population of Taiwan in nineteenth-century raids.

A performance at the end of the Universal Salvation rite – an exorcism by the legendary demon-killer Zhong Kui – also indicates the ghosts' malevolent aspect (see Plate 3.1). Zhong Kui is portrayed by an opera actor in dramatic black and white make-up. He begins by setting out a row of bowls, each containing a little pork, by the side of the temple. Then, accompanied by two musicians and carrying a sword, he begins the ritual by reading a document announcing his purposes. He then takes up a big stack of lit incense sticks and hurls them over the bowls of meat. This is followed by emptying a bottle of rice wine over them, all done in a flamboyant and operatic style. He then uses a duck to write magical charms in the air (*thiek aq*); the word for duck is a pun on a word meaning to control demons. An assistant mean-while lights two large stacks of paper money on either side of Zhong Kui. Zhong Kui takes up a rolled-up bamboo mat and, lighting both ends, waves it around like a cudgel. The document that was read at the beginning of the ceremony is then burnt in the flames and the ceremony is over. The ritual is typical of Chinese exorcisms (see Chiu, 1978; Keupers, 1977). In spite of its dramatic appeal, very few people watch this ceremony. They fear attacks by the malignant ghosts that the ceremony aims to exorcise.

Ghosts are also malevolent outside the seventh month. Offended ghosts, for example, may make people sick. Priests exorcise them by expelling them from the community and preventing them from re-entering. They use techniques similar to the methods for dispelling inhuman demons, like the fire spirit, from the community. Ghosts are social outsiders in these rituals, marginal to the world of gods and politics, but irrelevant to kinship (Jordan, 1972, p. 128–33).

The place of worship and the use of incense also show ghosts to be outside the orthodox political structure. Gods and ancestors are usually worshipped inside a house or temple; ghosts are fed outside the door. On Co Su Kong's birthday, for instance, the people of Sanxia all worship together at his temple. The organization into seven shares defined by surname unites Sanxia (the administrative unit governed by Co Su Kong as magistrate) on this day by cross-cutting internal geographic divisions. The surname groupings play down more salient social differences among geographical areas. During the ghost-feeding festival, however, organization by village instead stresses the area's more salient internal divisions. The use of several different altars, none of which are at the temple (in contrast to a unified altar at the temple for the birthday festival) splits up the geographic subdivisions of Sanxia. They may even be finer divisions within each of the four great pillars, as when the people of Tiong Pho all put their offerings at the front of Zhongpu's altar table, and those from Kiu Kiong Kiou all used the back. Gods, like governments, unite communities, just as ancestors unite families. Ghosts, however, are outside this structure – they unify nothing, and this is shown by the way they are worshipped.

The use of incense at the Universal Salvation festival splits the offerings up even more finely. Instead of being united in a single incense pot, like the offerings for gods or ancestors, each stick of incense marks each individual offering (see Plate 3.2). Again, this custom stresses the divisive properties of ghosts as opposed to gods and ancestors. It serves, along with the use of red flags identifying the donor of each dish of food, to break the community down beyond the level of the neighborhood to the level of individuals. Ghosts, like bandits, can thus be seen as threats to orthodox political and kinship structures.

The lowest levels of the supernatural bureaucracy are often very ghostly. They are often evil doers who now faithfully serve the god that vanquished them. Others, like many of the ghosts of the seventh month, are the souls of good people who died by violence. These spirits are the equivalent of the yamen runners – corrupt and unreliable employees who were the most direct link between a magistrate and the people of his district. They are at the margins of respectable politics, and at the margins of the supernatural hierarchy; ghostly spirits are thus fitting players for the part. Gods who parade through their territories on a festival day (following the model of a magistrate's tour), for example, often bring along such assistants in the guise of humans in costume. The most popular pair in Sanxia are Pueq Ia (Grandfather Eight), a squat black figure whose eyes roll as he walks, and Chit Ia (Grandfather Seven), a very tall white figure with a lolling red tongue (see Plate 3.3). During their lifetimes, the pair were yamen runners known for their loyalty to each other. One day they had an appointment to meet each other. Short Grandfather Eight arrived first, but Grandfather Seven was delayed. Just at that time, there was a huge rainstorm and a flood, drowning Grandfather Eight (and turning him black). Grandfather Seven finally arrived and found the body of his friend. He was overcome with guilt – he was so tall, he could have saved his friend if only he had arrived on time. He hung himself in remorse (and thus has a lolling tongue). As a suicide and a drowning victim, they are standard ghosts. Their loyalty got them into the godly bureaucracy, but only at the lowest, most ambiguous level.

The troops of the gods never appear as clearly as Grandfathers Seven and Eight. They are even more marginal to the bureaucracy; like traditional armies, they may protect an area, but they may also devastate it, especially if not properly propitiated. Just as the line between bandits and armies was not always easy to draw in traditional times, the line between ghosts and godly troops is not always easy to draw in the religion. People worship the troops as part of the offerings on the first and fifteenth (or second and sixteenth for businessmen) of every lunar month. They burn the gold spirit money appropriate to low gods (*kua kim* and *hok kim*), but the offerings resemble offerings to the ghosts: meat for the troops is always placed outside the front door, it is cut up, and it is served with cooked rice. In fact, a few people say that this offering is really for the ghosts. Ghosts in this context are thus marginal to the gods and to the orthodox political system.

I mentioned at the beginning of this chapter how *iu ieng kong* temples also show the permeability of the god/ghost contrast. The amoral ghosts in these temples may gradually become gods if they successfully grant all requests. Prostitutes and gamblers frequent these temples because ghostly deities will grant any request; they are not yet bound by the morality of the gods. These temples sometimes evolve into full-fledged god temples, just as bandit chiefs may traditionally sometimes have become local gentry. One of these temples in Sanxia was renovated during my stay there (see Plate 3.4). A well-known gambler initiated the work and made the largest contribution. His generosity did not simply thank the ghosts; it also represented an attempt to establish legitimacy in the community.

I have tried to stress how the pragmatics of popular religion in

Taiwan move us outside a structure of contrasts into interpretations within a social context. The rebuilding of this ghost temple is another example of how the particular situation – the social maneuvers of a gambler looking for respectability – influenced the specific realization of ghosts on that occasion. Yet the structure of contrasts remains important to such interpretations. One woman who attended the celebration for the new temple showed the importance of one of these symbolic contrasts very clearly. She was confused about whether she should offer one stick of incense or two sticks. One stick (or three sticks to be more respectful) is appropriate for the gods, two sticks are for the dead. The meaning of these ghosts for her could not come solely out of this specific social situation; it had to be supplemented by placement into a set of structural contrasts for ancestors, gods and ghosts. She asked her friends what to do, and after discussion, decided to burn a single stick of incense, appropriate for a ghost becoming a god, or a gambler becoming respectable. The structure of offerings is always relevant to the interpretation of ghosts, but it is never sufficient.

From Bandit to Beggar

Ritual offerings and people's general ideas identify two readings of ghosts: a dangerous political marginality, and a pitiful kinship marginality. Both intertwine, and both are present whenever people worship ghosts. The ritual offerings that encode these two types of marginality have not changed in the last century, and yet actual performances of the Universal Salvation rites have changed a great deal. These two types of marginality, and their associated ritual codes, thus form the backdrop for any discussion of the meaning of ghost worship, but they are not sufficient by themselves to explain the changes that have taken place. The ease with which pragmatic interpretations of ghosts have changed has helped prevent them from becoming even as ideologized an ancestors and gods.

Popular performances of the Universal Salvation festival divide roughly into two periods. The period from 1860 to about 1945 saw the rise and fall of violent performances that emphasized political marginality and the bandit metaphor. The period after the Second World War has seen a resurgence of the festival, except for a few short periods of government repression. Violent performances of the festival no longer occur in the modern period; the pitiful beggar metaphor has replaced the bandit metaphor.

Violent Ghosts, 1860–1945

Changes in the popular performance of the Universal Salvation festival occurred primarily in the most violent part of the ceremony – robbing the lonely ghosts (*chiu: ko*, sometimes also translated as 'pillaging the scaffolding'). Except for simply bringing food offerings, this was the only part of the ceremony in which people directly took part. This part of the festival reached its peak of popularity and violence in northern Taiwan in the last half of the nineteenth century. A nineteenth-century Presbyterian missionary provides one of the fullest descriptions:

> The most elaborate and hideous scene I ever witnessed was the 'Seven Moon Feast' . . . The custom prevailed in all the cities and towns in north Formosa of erecting, in an open space of several acres, great cone-like structures of bamboo poles, from five to ten feet in diameter at the base, and sometimes fifty or sixty feet high. Around these cones, from bottom to top, immense quantities of food, offered to the spirits, were tied in rows . . . Meanwhile a very unspiritual mob – thousands and thousands of hungry beggars, tramps, blacklegs, desperadoes of all sorts, from the country towns, the city slums, or venturing under cover of night from their hiding-places among the hills – surged and swelled in every part of the open space . . . At length the spirits were satisfied, and the gong was sounded once more. That was the signal for the mob; and scarcely had the first stroke fallen when that whole scene was one mass of arms and legs and tongues. Screaming, cursing, howling, like demons of the pit, they all joined in the onset . . . In one wild scramble, groaning and yelling all the while, trampling on those who had lost their footing or were smothered by the falling cones, fighting and tearing one another like mad dogs, they all made for the coveted food. It was a very bedlam, and the wildness of the scene was enhanced by the irregular explosion of firecrackers and the death-groan of someone worsted in the fray. (Mackay, 1895, pp. 129–31)

A contemporary gazetteer warns that, 'With the sound of a gong, the masses begin to battle; this is called "robbing the lonely ghosts." All civil and military officials must travel to the area to repress it' (DSTZ, p. 460). The situation was so difficult for local magistrates that Liu Ming-chuan, the first Chinese governor of Taiwan, made robbing the lonely ghosts illegal in 1889 (TWSZ, 12, p. 18). The new law had little immediate effect, however, and performances of the ritual continued well into the Japanese occupation of 1895–1945.

Robbing the lonely ghosts began to occur less often under the Japanese, but when it was performed, it retained its violent flavor. A Japanese anthropologist describes performances he saw in northern Taiwan in the 1920s:

> On the day for the *chiu: ko*, they first set up a *ko pi:* about three meters wide and twenty meters high. The poles for this must be at least five centimeters in diameter, for the top will be completely covered with offerings. A 'storehouse' platform was set about six or seven meters up the *ko pi:*. On it, the offerings were piled up like a mountain, with pork, chicken and duck hanging down, and at its very top, a red flag was inserted. Because *chiu: ko* is a dangerous affair, policemen were sent to maintain order . . . The *chiu: ko* took place at 6.30 p.m., and the start was signaled by a puff of smoke, when everyone began their enthusiastic plunder. The sounds of assault and murder pierced heaven . . . At least thirty or forty thousand watched or participated in the *chiu: ko*, all forming a chaotic mass. As soon as the time arrived and the smoke was released, hordes of people began to climb the *ko pi:*, each anxious to stay ahead of the others. In the blink of an eye, the three flags had been taken. By this time, the *ko pi:* was filled with people, each enthusiastically stealing the offerings, pushing and screaming, and robbing each other. Some people were thus pushed down the platform. They say that with the ghosts' protection they will not be hurt, but in fact large numbers are always hurt and killed. (Suzuki, 1978[1934], p. 473)

Other sources from the early twentieth century also described the violence of the ceremony (e.g., Shikagane, 1902), although there was general agreement that fewer communities performed this part of the ceremony as the twentieth century wore on (TWSZ, 12, pp. 18–19). After about 1930, robbing the lonely ghosts is rarely mentioned as a living custom, although the Universal Salvation festival continued.

Descriptions of the festival from most other areas in China do not mention the violent robbing of the lonely ghosts, nor did early descriptions from Taiwan describe a violent ceremony. The Taiwan Prefecture Gazetteer (TWFZ, p. 618) mentioned only setting minia-ture rafts out to sea in the eighteenth century; each raft contained a Mexican silver dollar, and fishermen in their boats tried to collect the rafts to gain good luck for the coming year. There was no mention of violence or of a lonely ghost platform, and the compiler of the gazetteer avoided the condemnations of the ceremony that typified late nineteenth-century descriptions.

The large scale and the violence of the ceremony appeared only in later nineteenth-century descriptions from Taiwan (primarily northern Taiwan) and from Amoy, the highly commercialized treaty port on the mainland that was a point of embarkation for many Taiwanese immigrants and a point of transfer for Taiwanese goods headed to foreign markets (DeGroot, 1885, pp. 86–91; 1886, pp. 403–35). Descriptions from other times and other places paint a much more placid picture of the ceremonies, in which people give alms to the miserable ghosts, and often also to real beggars. Hunger and alms, not violence and propitiation, form the basis of the ceremony.

Why did this period between about 1860 and 1945 in northern Taiwan see so many violent performances of the ritual, which did not characterize earlier performances, and which disappeared again in later periods? The answer does not lie within the symbolic structure of the ritual itself, which continued to use the same types of food offerings, the same kinds of spirit money, and the same number of sticks of incense. The change occurred instead because, beginning around 1860, a rapid commercialization of the economy, and the uprooting of the labor force shaped new pragmatic interpretations. These developments relied on access to new world markets for Taiwanese rice, tea and camphor.[30]

In the late nineteenth century northern Taiwan commercialized rapidly. In rice agriculture, for example, the sale prices of usufruct rights tripled between 1850 and 1900, shorter leases and more frequent changes of tenant developed as competition for land increased, and the deposits required to gain cultivation rights increased as landlords felt an increasingly pressing need for cash (Wickberg, 1981, pp. 216–21).

New foreign markets for tea and camphor were even more important than rice in northern Taiwan, however. The United States became a major buyer of Formosa Oolong tea in the last half of the nineteenth century. As the new market opened up, Chinese in the foothills of northern Taiwan began to cultivate and process tea on a large scale. The many small tea farms created new demands for labor. Experienced tea workers from areas in Fujian Province, especially from Anxi County (the place of origin for most of Sanxia's population) flowed into the area. Tea required tedious, labor-intensive harvesting, after which it underwent several stages of processing, some in the countryside, and some in the commercial centers of Taibei. Processing demanded wage labor, and picking and sorting the tea required especially large new inputs of labor. Davidson (1903, p. 385) reports that 12,000 girls were brought to Taibei from the countryside seasonally to work as tea sorters. Lin (1976, p. 3) estimates that 300,000 workers were employed in the tea industry in an average year during this period. Tea thus helped to commercialize the economy in northern Taiwan by bringing in an immigrant labor force, by creating a new class of wage laborers, and by involving much of the population in the world market for tea.

The third major commercial product in northern Taiwan was camphor. It involved fewer workers than the other commodities, but it had extensive social consequences. Camphor trees grow in the northern and central depths of the massive mountain range that dominates Taiwan. Merchants in the late nineteenth century hired workers to build camphor stills up in the mountains, where they felled trees and gradually fed them into the stills. Merchants sent expeditions up into the mountains to collect the product and transport it to the coastal markets from which it was shipped abroad. Camphor was a government monopoly for much of the late nineteenth century, but government control was too weak to prevent large-scale smuggling (Davidson, 1903, p. 402). Qing registration of camphor stills was spotty at best, and the most useful statistics come from Japanese registration of stills in 1899 (Davidson, 1903, p. 415). At that time, the Japanese were discouraging camphor production by keeping the price artificially low, in order to stimulate the camphor industry in Japan. As a result, the number of stills in 1899 was considerably lower than it had been earlier. In addition, some stills surely went unregistered. There were 2057 registered stills (241 in Sanxia) in 1899, almost all of them in the mountains of northern Taiwan.

Although the total number of camphor workers, even in earlier years, did not rival the tea industry, the camphor industry was politically important. So-called 'raw' aborigines inhabited the camphor forests of Taiwan's mountains. They had always met the Chinese with violence, and their attacks on the Chinese became more frequent and vehement as their home territory was directly invaded. The late nineteenth century saw a major escalation of violence in northern Taiwan, as the Chinese met the aborigines with armed vigilantes of their own. These miniature armies help explain the success of smugglers, and also the frequency of battles between different Chinese ethnic groups in the camphor fields (e.g., Wang, 1976). Camphor work was dangerous, and it attracted young men without strong ties to home or family. Camphor helped to commercialize the economy by creating a second wage labor force and another group of people tied to the world market through the commodities they produced. Politically, it helped to reinforce local armed forces independent of the government. Sanxia's close ties to the camphor industry may help to explain why the missionary Mackay (1895, p. 159) described it as 'the most lawless region in north Formosa', where the townspeople sometimes conspired to protect 'a large band of ruffians and highwaymen' from official interference.

The political economy of late nineteenth-century northern Taiwan was thus shaped by an influx of new workers, by increasing commercialization, land scarcity and dependence on world markets, and by weak state power with extensive reliance on unofficial power. The new political economy cut off a large, new population from traditional ties to agricultural communities, and thrust them into an uncertain labor market. The state remained weak, and these people found themselves outside orthodox political and community controls.

The Japanese occupation of Taiwan brought important political changes. The most striking change was a general pacification of the countryside; the Japanese ended feuding among the Chinese, and after a few years they also ended battles between Chinese and aborigines. At the same time, changes in world demand for northern Taiwan's commodities altered some features of the economy. The tea boom decreased after the turn of the century, and the camphor market collapsed entirely with the invention of man-made substitutes. Coal became a major commodity, and the economy continued to commercialize slowly in the first few decades of Japanese rule. Yet the upheavals in the labor force, and the existence of a marginal group largely uncontrolled by the government, ended in the twentieth century with the introduction of a strong state and a routinely commercial economy. There was a steady improvement in the standard of living, but there were few major social changes until the 1930s, when Japan began to prepare for war, and when the changes the Japanese had made in Taiwanese education and infrastructure began to have a major effect (Wickberg, 1981, pp. 231–2).

The period after about 1930 saw major social transformations in Taiwan. The transportation and education systems that the Japanese had constructed began to bear fruit as the first generation of graduates from a system of modern education emerged, and as new industries and new techniques were able to move to a pacified, accessible countryside. At the same time, the Japanese were gearing up for the war, and they began to encourage industrial production in Taiwan. There was a technological revolution in agriculture, the coal industry took off, and industrial employment became a widespread alternative to farm work. Per capita income and household consumption rose more rapidly than they had in the preceding decades (Wolf and Huang, 1980, pp. 45–59). Although the years of the Second World War were difficult in Taiwan, the social changes of the period set the stage for the increasing prosperity and industrialization of modern Taiwan.

This background in the political and economic changes between 1860 and 1945 clarifies why violent expressions of the Universal Salvation rites waxed and waned during this period. The 'blacklegs and desperadoes' who robbed the lonely ghosts in the late nineteenth century probably came primarily from the new class of wage laborers. These people saw themselves as marginal to the settled communities. Like the politically marginal ghosts, they were not under orthodox political control, they were dangerous in their own right, and they required propitiation. Community temples took responsibility for warding off these ghostly people. Local elites generally controlled large community temples, and the temples sometimes served as centers of secular political organization. Sanxia's temple to Co Su Kong, for example, organized local resistance to the Japanese occupation of Taiwan (see Wang, 1967). The Universal Salvation festival emphasized this political role of the local temple. In propitiating politically marginal ghosts at the Universal Salvation, a local temple arrogated to itself the functions of the government: it collected a tax through elected officials to raise 'protection money' that could protect the community from marginal elements beyond that community's political control.

The political and economic conditions of the late nineteenth century thus conditioned the unusually large and violent performances of the Universal Salvation festival in northern Taiwan. Temples and local elites wielded authority with some independence from the weak state, while new, and sometimes dangerous, economic opportunities created a class of politically marginal wage laborers. Violent performances of the festival allowed local elites and their communities to propitiate this new marginal class, even as the new class acted out its ghostly condition in this annual riot. The local communities made no claim to control the marginal population, but only to soothe it enough to protect themselves.

Violent performances of the festival decreased under the Japanese, and apparently ended by about 1930. Violent performances ended for two reasons: the political economy that fostered the violence changed, and the Japanese attempted to repress the festival. The more important reason was the change in political and economic conditions. The camphor industry and its associated violence died out. Other aspects of commercialization became routinized, and wage laborers no longer formed a marginal group. By 1930, Taiwan had been transformed from an agricultural frontier in the throes of commercialization, into an economy with a modern industrial footing. Violent performances of the Universal Salvation festival were pragmatic realizations of this transformation. The politically marginal population of the late nineteenth century took the role of bandit–ghosts; no longer marginal by the 1930s, they no longer added their violent near-riots at the end of the Universal Salvation festival. Structural expressions of ghosts in ritual media had not changed, but pragmatic interpretations had.

The secondary reason encouraging the demise of 'robbing the lonely ghosts' was that the Japanese government discouraged the festival more effectively than had the traditional Chinese government. Yet the Japanese repression was neither systematic nor long-term. It peaked in the 1890s, when the Japanese burnt down many temples (including Sanxia's temple to Co Su Kong) in retribution for harassment of Japanese troops. It peaked again after 1937, when the Japanese invaded the Chinese mainland. The government backed off fairly quickly in both cases, and it never succeeded in ending the Universal Salvation festival. The repression did, however, lead to an odd variation on robbing the lonely ghosts. Under the Japanese the ceremony sometimes took the form of an athletic or agricultural competition. In the early days of the Japanese occupation, for example, the people who robbed the lonely ghosts in some performances were no longer a crowd of rowdies, but had been organized into village teams that competed to seize valuable prizes among the offerings (Yao and Kaye, 1976, informant statements in Sanxia).

These village teams are symbolic nonsense: if ghosts are marginal, individual outsiders according to the ritual offerings, organized village teams should not be able to replace them in the festival. The substitution makes more sense, however, as part of a general strategy that local temples used to maintain control over their rituals in the face of government opposition. Competitions to raise the most obese pig for the gods apparently began in the Japanese period as a way to legitimize food offerings as agricultural competition (Sangren, 1979, p. 131). At least one temple used the same strategy to offer pigs to the ghosts when the newly arrived Nationalist government banned the festival in 1948 (XSB, 19 September, 1948), and another temple tried to revive the robbing of the lonely ghosts in the 1970s by calling it a greased pole climbing contest, in which village teams competed against each other. Disguising the festival as athletic or agricultural competition is one way to maintain it against official pressure. It is very similar to the Taiwanese ethnic uses of temple worship discussed in Chapter 2. In this case, it was strategy of local and ethnic Chinese defense against the Japanese government. Yet the metaphorical substitution of village teams for wild ghosts remained symbolic nonsense, at odds with the ideologized contrast of ghosts with gods and ancestors, which stresses ghosts as marginal, anomic beings, not village communities. Team competition thus remained a relatively unpopular and short-lived version of the festival. Robbing the lonely ghosts had lost its earlier content when the marginal class behind the violence became unimportant; it appeared in this altered form only occasionally as a means of protest against Japanese government interference. Its occurrence makes sense only in relation to the political economy, and its relative failure makes sense only in relation to the ritual codes that contrast ghosts with gods and ancestors.

Pitiful Ghosts, 1945–1980

Popular religion suffered during the Second World War, and during the first years of Nationalist rule, while the new government was involved with the civil war on the mainland and with creating a strong base of control in Taiwan. By 1950, however, the Universal Salvation festival was again widespread in Taiwan. There was no more robbing of the lonely ghosts, but the rest of the festival remained one of the most important annual events everywhere on the island. The last three decades have brought an increasing interest and increasing investment in popular religion of all kinds. Many new temples have been built, and many old ones have been refurbished at great expense. Festivals like the Universal Salvation rites or a god's birthday are opportunities for the wealthy to invest in the local community.

The investment is public, as most temples post the names and contributions of their patrons at the ritual for their god's birthday.

The ritual texts and ritual offerings for the Universal Salvation rites are unchanged. The old robbing of the lonely ghosts, however, has been transformed. At the end of the modern ceremony, the chief priest tosses into the air a series of buns, candies and grains of rice, symbolically feeding the ghosts. A crowd of children and old people stand in front of the altar, pushing and shoving to catch the thrown food. The crowd may be large and enthusiastic on some occasions, but it never matches the violence of earlier times. One ceremony I witnessed at a small Buddhist temple, for example, drew a crowd of well-dressed, prim, middle-class old ladies who were regular devotees of the temple. As the priest prepared to throw the buns to the ghosts, this very proper crowd suddenly got unruly. They clambered over each other to catch the buns, and finally mobbed the altar, snatching buns out from in front of the priest even before he threw them. My tape recorder was an early casualty, and it was soon followed by the drums. The entire ceremony had to stop while the drummer pulled himself and his drums back together. A final plate of offerings is supposed to be saved for distribution to special devotees of the temple after the ceremony. The rampaging ladies, however, immediately swamped the young nun who was trying to carry these buns to a back room, and the platter was empty well before she reached safety. The behavior of these women looked to me exactly like their descriptions of what the ghosts were doing at the same time: pushing and shoving, twisting and turning, trying desperately to snatch some scrap of food to ease their ravenous hunger. These middle-class old women have replaced the earlier 'bandits and desperadoes' as metaphorical ghosts (although they would never discuss it this way for reasons I outlined at the beginning of this chapter). What caused this change in the realization of the ceremony?

These informants play down the violent threat of ghosts. While late nineteenth-century statements emphasized the need to propitiate ghosts. the modern informant statements I discussed earlier emphasize instead the pitifulness of ghosts. This change in the realization of ghosts at the Universal Salvation festival did not require a change in the symbolic structure of the ceremony. The ritual offerings that code ghosts have the potential for either the political/dangerous or the kinship/pitiful reading. The pragmatic interpretation of that code has changed because there is no longer a class of politically marginal camphor workers or uprooted tea laborers, and they have been replaced by a new group that is marginal in a different way – the old.

The major social changes that occurred in Taiwan after about 1930 had an important effect on old people. Some of the most useful information on this problem comes from Margery Wolf's (1975) discussion of changing suicide rates. In 1905, according to Wolf's analysis of Japanese household records, suicide rates for women in their early twenties were extremely high (57.4 per 100,000). At that time, the rate dropped off sharply for older women until it rose again for women in their sixties (to about 20 per 100,000). By 1935, however, there had been a dramatic change. The rate for women in their sixties is nearly double the rate for women in their twenties by this time. The suicide rates for old men also increase sharply between these two dates, although there is no corresponding change in the rates for young men. Wolf, concerned primarily with female suicides, attributes the change to developments in family structure:

> In generations past an emotional tie between husband and wife came later in life, if at all, and was not expected in the young strangers who were married at their parents' convenience. A young wife who enters as her husband's choice has emotional and sexual advantages over her mother-in-law from the outset. When the apparently inevitable conflicts arise between mother-in-law and daughter-in-law and the son intervenes on his wife's behalf, the effect on the older woman is stunning. All the old anxieties about physical welfare in her now near old age return. Even worse, all the years of struggle and sacrifice seem to be negated, lost to the wiles of an ignorant young woman. In despair over her powerlessness or in a fit of revengeful fury at her fickle son, the aging mother contemplates, threatens, and in some cases commits suicide. (Wolf, 1975, p. 127)

This period also coincides with what Arthur Wolf and Chieh-shan Huang (1980, pp. 193–201) have called the 'revolt of the young' in Taiwan – when young people began to refuse child betrothals, and parents began to lose their total authority over a child's marriage. Not only have changing marriage patterns weakened the position of the old in Taiwan, but new wage-earning opportunities for both young men and women have further increased their independence from their parents.[31] As a result, the old are losing the control they once exercised, and clearly realize their vulnerability.

The only suicide I was aware of while in Sanxia occurred, appropriately, on the fifteenth of the seventh month. An old woman, who had been upset with her unfilial son and daughter-in-law for a long time, quarrelled with her daughter-in-law on the morning of the fifteenth. The immediate cause was the girl's refusal to bother worshipping the ghosts. After an argument, the old woman drowned herself in the Sanxia River.

Kinship marginality has thus replaced political marginality in the Universal Salvation rites, because an increasingly insecure elderly population has replaced the commercialized population, which is no longer insecure, as the main metaphorical reference for ghosts. The structure of the ritual codes for ghosts has not changed over this period, nor has it had to change. The ritual and its offerings, abstracted from any particular political and economic context, allow equally for either type of marginality. The ritual offerings code a very general, adaptable and easily ideologized structure of kinsmen/bureaucrats/outsiders. People have not changed these offerings because they continue to make sense of experience. Yet the meaning of ghosts is not entirely contained in the symbolic structure; it has shifted pragmatically with changing political and economic experience.

Popular Religion and Pragmatic Interpretation

This chapter and the preceding one have clarified how ghosts tie partly into an abstract symbolic structure in which they contrast with both gods and ancestors. Attempts to define ghosts in ways that conflict with that structure have proved short-lived at best. Thus the popular substitution of village teams to rob the lonely ghosts could never be more than a temporary feint directed against the Japanese; ghosts are marginal outsiders according to the ritual offerings – they cannot be village communities.

Yet the interpretation of ghosts goes far beyond a set of ritual contrasts or a symbolic code. Those contrasts have not changed over the years, but the interpretations of today differ from those of the late nineteenth century. The move from dangerous political ghosts to pitiful kinship ghosts occurred because the marginal group in the population underwent a parallel change. The uprooted workers of the last century have become the insecure old of today. A change in the political economy of Taiwan has changed the daily experiences that inspire specific interpretations of the Universal Salvation rites.

These interpretations never precipitated into an explicit ideology, and there has never been any social mechanism to separate orthodox interpretations from heterodoxy, or to propagate 'correct' beliefs. The meeting at Sanxia's community temple (discussed in the preceding chapter) illustrates that even local popular temples did not have this authority; they had no mechanism with which to require people to bring certain offerings.

There is thus no explicit, self-conscious, institutionally propagated interpretation of ghosts. The structure of ritual offerings is the closest thing to such an explicit system of meanings, but it is open to various interpretations. There is, in other words, no very developed religious ideology that includes ghosts. Buddhists and Taoists do maintain such ideologies (Chapter 4), but they make little attempt to convince outsiders of them. Local temples provide institutional sponsorship of the ceremonies, but they cannot control popular interpretations and actions. In the absence of some socially organized ideology that could impose an abstract interpretation of ghosts, people are free to interpret and reinterpret ghosts in light of political and economic experience. People *make* their interpretations out of experience within the structural framework of gods, ghosts and ancestors; they do not simply act out established systems of meaning.

The preceding chapter showed much the same relationship between symbolic structure and ties to social context and political economy. The domestic cult, for example, reflects and supports the important position of the family, and it affirms the need for filial behavior even after the death of a parent. Within this framework, however, popular religion ties to specific social relations that sometimes contradict the ideals of family solidarity and filial piety: it shows distinctions of wealth in domestic altars and ancestor tablets, fraternal competition in geomancy, affinal tensions in weddings, and so on. The god cult idealizes the importance of community solidarity, and above all, the naturalness of control by a bureaucratically organized government. Yet worship of gods can also provide a flexible indicator of economic position, of local opposition to central authority, of ethnic tensions, and of personal political ambition. The abstract structure of ancestors/gods/ghosts sets the parameters for specific realizations of the popular tradition, but it remains open to new interpretations as social relations change.

Many features of ghosts appear only in the seventh month; they are not carried over into the rest of the year. Ghosts outside the seventh month are generally social aberrations who pose a violent threat to the living. No taxes are collected outside the seventh month and there is no analogy with care for the poor; no food is thrown and there is no connection to the loneliness of old age. Ghosts outside the seventh month are propitiated, not pitied. Ghosts in these contexts are often identifiable individuals who bring attention to themselves by causing sickness or misfortune. They differ from the nameless mass of suffering dead worshipped at the Universal Salvation rites. Time of year thus provides another context for varying interpretations of ghosts.

The location of the soul after death poses a similar problem of context and structure. The popular tradition represents the soul as residing permanently in the grave in some contexts, in the ancestral tablet in other contexts, in the underworld in others, in a reincarnated form in still others, and so on. This apparent inconsistency could be resolved with a concept of multiple souls, but none of my non-specialist informants ever suggested such a concept. The soul is not precipitated out of the particular contexts in which people deal with souls. Religious experts, however, do generalize across contexts to create an ideologized interpretation. Taoists solve the problem with an explicit multiple soul concept, and Buddhists solve it by pinpointing the exact location of the soul.

Harrell concludes in his analysis of the soul concept in Taiwan that, 'the perspective of the Confucian and Taoist traditions is analytical: reality must be explained. The perspective of folk religion, in contrast, is fundamentally *active*; believers experience religious reality directly through purposely behavior, especially ritual' (1979, p. 520). The following chapter shows how the pragmatic interpretation of ghosts in the popular religion is less relevant to the analytic concerns of religious specialists.

The specific set of social relations at a given time influences how the abstract structure ancestors/gods/ghosts is realized. The symbolic structure itself is not at all irrelevant. Ritual media like incense, food offerings, spirit money, and place of worship clearly code the relation between ancestors and kin, gods and bureaucrats, and ghosts and outsiders; many informants can also articulate them clearly. In worshipping at Sanxia's temple to Co Su Kong, for example, the bureaucratic analogy is obvious in informant statements, in how people address the god, and in the iconography of the temple. I have discussed how it can also tie pragmatically into Anxi origin, or local solidarity against the central government, or Taiwanese ethnic identity. Yet these relations to context are much less explicit and ideologized that the structural features. There are no symbols in the temple that show the Anxi origins of the god's followers, or Taiwanese solidarity.

The symbolic contrasts that code ancestors/gods/ghosts are thus more ideologized than the pragmatic features of the popular religion. They are defined through a set of structural, context-free contrasts, and they are more readily explicit than the contextual features. The ancestors:kin; gods:bureaucrats; ghosts:outsiders interpretation is difficult to call an ideology proper; the Buddhist, Taoist and official beliefs that I discuss in the following chapters are much more complete ideologies – elaborately structured and thoroughly explicit.

Yet the ancestors/kin; gods/bureaucrats; ghosts/outsiders interpretation remains the most ideologized part of the popular religion. Why? For one thing, this three-way model of the social world is a very simple, general scheme that easily reflects and shapes everyday experience. The simple distinction family/government/outsider remains sensible even when social relations change as fast as they have in Taiwan. It is easy to abstract out of its particular ritual realizations into a general scheme because it is so simple, and so widely applicable. The more pragmatic aspects of popular religion are by definition more fully tied to specific social relations: they cannot easily be generalized, because they change as the situation changes. Thus only the most easily generalized relations of ancestors to kinship, gods to politics, and ghosts as the residual category become explicit and abstractly structured.[32] In addition, the three-way scheme is also widely shared in Taiwan outside the popular beliefs. Taoists, educated informants, and the traditional government all shared the system. These groups constantly interacted with popular ritual and encouraged certain aspects of it. Major local temples, for example, are normally controlled by the local elite. They influence the sorts of symbolic statements that temples could make. The most idealized views of ancestors as forebears of unified patrilineages occur primarily in large lineages, which were also controlled by the elite. Groups outside the popular beliefs encouraged symbolic expression of the ancestors/gods/ghosts code because it fit the vision of the world they wanted to emphasize. We will return to these problems of ideologization in more detail, after looking more closely at Buddhist, Taoist and elite ideologies of religion in the following chapter.

The popular beliefs are open to flexible interpretations within the basically conservative frame of ancestors, gods and ghosts. They never challenge, for example, the primacy of filial behavior, but they can indicate changing family boundaries or variant lineage organizations. They never challenge the validity of bureaucratic government in general, but they can oppose specific bureaucracies or be used for personal political manipulation. New interpretations, however, could question even this fundamental structure of gods, ancestors, and ghosts. No system of beliefs is immune from radically new interpretations and uses; Protestant reinterpretations of the Bible are an obvious example. In the Chinese case, however, these basic assumptions of the popular religion were rarely questioned within the framework of the religion. Instead, people who questioned such fundamental features of their society tended to turn to entirely alternative beliefs, especially those related to Buddhism (which I include in the following chapter).

4 Specialist Ghosts

nurturing appeasing ghosts

Both Buddhist and Taoist performances of the Universal Salvation rites feature active, concrete beings, similar to those in the popular tradition. Yet specialist performances differ from popular interpretations in important ways: they draw heavily on ideologized styles of interpretation, and they rely strongly on training people to interpret religious texts and the oral traditions that accompany them. This chapter will concentrate on how specialist organization of religious knowledge differs from the more context-bound interpretations of the popular tradition. Although it concentrates on northern Taiwan, the analysis should be broadly relevant to all of Taiwan and to late imperial China.

Buddhism first gained strong influence in China in the late Han Dynasty (second and third centuries AD). It differed from earlier Chinese beliefs in important ways: it renounced the world as a place of dust and illusion caught in cycles of reincarnation, it promoted withdrawal from ordinary social life as a way of transcending that world, it added new worlds of heavens and hells populated by very human spirits, and it fostered a celibate (and thus by definition not filially pious) clergy. Many of these ideas spread throughout China, even as they remained controversial. By the late imperial period, Buddhist monasteries – many small and poor, a few large and powerful landowners – covered China. The clergy varied widely in its skill at Buddhist philosophy, although some went through a complex education leading to ordination. Monks and nuns were the main bearers of the tradition, and they are the focus of this chapter. There were also, however, some lay Buddhists who were at least partially educated in Buddhism; in Taiwan they usually join sutra-singing groups.[33]

Taoism is indigenous to China, and has a much longer history there. The roots of modern Taiwanese Taoism, however, lie less in the early philosophers like Laozi and Zhuangzi than in the creation of a religious Taoism at the end of the Han. This later Taoism, like Buddhism, featured a huge pantheon of gods, which the Taoists modelled after the political bureaucracy of the time. Unlike the Buddhists, however, the Taoists did not deny the everyday world, and advocated living in harmony with the world, not denouncing it.

This meant coming to know the world-shaping Dao (path) through ritual and meditation. Taoism had a monastic tradition, but priests could also be 'fire-dwelling', living at home and raising families. All Taoists in Taiwan are fire-dwelling; there was no monastic tradition there, and priests wishing ordination went to the mainland. Taoists in most of Taiwan divide into 'black-headed priests' (*o thau sai kong*) and 'red-headed priests' (*ang thau sai kong*). In general, black-headed priests control more prestigious ritual texts, especially for the most important Taoist ritual – the community renewing *ciou*. They also perform funerals.

Sanxia is exceptional, however, because the only Taoists are red-headed priests, and they control prestigious *ciou* texts (but do not perform funerals). Sanxia also has so-called black-headed priests who perform funerals, but they do not describe themselves as Taoists. They use only Buddhist texts, and wear Buddhist robes. People sometimes refer to them as Buddhist monks (*he-siu:*), although they have never taken Buddhist vows. The annual Universal Salvation rites at Sanxia's temple to Co Su Kong always use Sanxia's version of black-headed priests, reading Buddhist texts.

The structures of Buddhist or Taoist performances of the Universal Salvation rites, and even of their ritual texts, are remarkably similar, so much so that most laymen consider them identical. Some of the the similarities exist because the Taoist ceremony was modelled after the Buddhist original (Pang, 1977, pp. 95–6; Yoshioka, 1959, pp. 369–411). I begin by analyzing the two versions together, although I will separate them again below to analyze the underlying differences between the two systems. The ritual I describe here is based on performances by Sanxia's version of black-headed priests, and differs only slightly from the outward performances by both Taoist or more strictly Buddhist experts.

In the Universal Salvation rites the priests supervise construction of the outer altar – the long bamboo poles that invite the ghosts to the performance (*tieng ko*), and the various paper houses and god images that stand in front of the temple (see Chapter 1). They also construct an inner alter within the temple itself. In theory, this altar should move the temple's gods from the front of the temple (the position of honor) to the back, where they become spectators. The highest deities of the specialists replace them at the front altar. In Sanxia, however, because the temple is still undergoing reconstruction, the priests set up their altar in an adjoining workshop. The inner altar forms a large square, and the rituals take place in its center. The black-headed priests set up paintings of Buddhas and Bodhisattvas. At the superior end, ideally the front altar of the temple, they place a painting of Sakyamuni (the historical Buddha). In front of this image stand five rice pecks (*tau*) filled with ritual paraphernalia. These are the same as the pecks used in the *pai to* ritual I mentioned in Chapter 2; they earn good luck and long life for their sponsors.[34] In this case one rice peck represents each of the Four Great Pillars (that is, each of the four geographical divisions of the Sanxia Valley), and the fifth represents the *lo cu* (that is, the temple catchment area as a whole).

In front of the rice pecks stands an altar table holding more images of Buddhas, offerings, and some of the paraphernalia to be used in the rituals. Scrolls of Manjusri and Samantabhadra, two Bodhisattvas associated with Sakyamuni, flank the altar table. Next to these scrolls, forming the remainder of the left and right sides of the square, stand two images of the Protectors of the Dharma; these two figures accompany nearly every Buddhist altar in Taiwan. Finally, a table for the ordinary gods (including the gods of the temple) stands opposite Sakyamuni and in front of a door leading outside. Each scroll and each table has its own incense pot and food offerings.

Taoists set up identical altars. The particular images on the scrolls differ from the images of the black-headed priests, but they are painted in the same style, and few laymen could distinguish the two types of altars. Taoists replace Sakyamuni with the Three Pure Ones (San Qing), the trinity that constitutes the peak of their cosmology. Along the two sides of the altar, they place four heavenly deities (Yu Huang [the Jade Emperor], Zi Wei, Nan Chen and Bei Di). Note that these lower deities along the sides include the Jade Emperor, the highest of the popular deities. Taoists incorporate the popular cosmology, but rank their own deities higher. Ceremonies in Buddhist temples do not require special altars. Their standard layout is nearly identical to the inner altar of the black-headed priests; it includes a Buddha at the front, two associated Bodhisattvas at his sides, and the two Protectors of the Dharma next to them. Specialists need to set up their own altars only in popular temples, where they replace the local gods with their own.

The number of ceremonies performed before the actual ghost-feeding varies according to the available time and money. At the Co Su Kong temple, the ceremonies usually last for a day and a half. They begin at about 5.30 in the afternoon of the fourteenth day of the seventh lunar month. Taoists and black-headed priests perform roughly the same rituals. They have been described in detail elsewhere

(Liu, 1967; Pang, 1977; Saso, 1972), so I will be brief here. The first ceremony is a musical performance that purifies the inner altar (*lau tua:*). The next major rituals are the *huat piou* and the *chia: sin*. These consist primarily of an invitation to the gods to attend the ritual, and an announcement of the purposes of the ritual and the names of the people involved. Representatives of the Four Great Pillars and the *lo cu* attend this ritual, holding incense in special wooden sticks carved in the shape of a dragon. At least one representative of the community attends each ritual, and representatives of all four segments plus the *lo-cu* attend the more important ones. Releasing the water lanterns (*pang cui tieng*) is the final ritual of the evening (see Chapter 1).

The ceremonies start again at about 6.30 the next morning. The priests begin at the outer altar, where they worship Kuan Im and Tai Su Ia, requesting their presence to care for and control the masses of ghosts. Tai Su Ia, according to the priests, is a fearsome transformation of Kuan Im who specializes in ghost control. With the gods safely in attendance, the priests turn to the bamboo poles to ask the ghosts to come. The ceremonies then address the inner altar, where the priests read sutras on behalf of the community and renew their food offerings to the gods.[35] Late in the morning, the priests visit other local temples (out of courtesy to their gods), and they worship at the altars set up by the Four Great Pillars and the *lo cu*, inviting the ghosts to consume the offerings that Sanxia's people have prepared.

A major ritual occurs at about noon – the worship of Thi: Kong, the Emperor of Heaven (or, more officially, the Jade Emperor). Unlike most of the rituals that have occupied the day, laymen understand the purpose of this ritual and consider it important. Thi: Kong reigns as the highest deity in the popular pantheon, and only the feeding of the ghosts will outrank his worship, at least in the popular view. The ritual takes place at the inner altar, facing the open door, the courtyard outside, and a sacrificed whole pig (*ti kong*) that constitutes the major offering to the Emperor of Heaven. Several representatives of the community attend, as the priest pays their respects to Heaven.

The festivities do not really begin to attract a crowd until after lunch. By this time, an opera entertains people in front of the temple, representatives of the Four Great Pillars have brought their food offerings to the appropriate altar, and the priests have arranged a raised altar in front of the main entrance to the temple. The ceremony begins in the late afternoon, when the chief priest (in a saffron robe), leads his four assistants (in blue or black robes) and several musicians (in street clothes) around to each of the altars, to lead the ghosts back to the temple for the ceremony. Accompanied by gongs, drums and double-reeded shawms, the priests read sutras and perform mudras (esoteric hand signs) that purify the altar area in front of the temple. The priests and musicians then climb up to the altar table, which is raised about a meter off the ground. The assisting priests sit at either side of the table, the musicians sit behind them, and after a few more minutes of chanting, the chief priest sits in a cross-legged, meditative posture on a platform just behind the altar table. He has his back to the temple, and faces the small crowd that has begun to gather. He installs five powerful deities (Vairocana and four associated Buddhas for the Buddhists, and the Wu Lao, Sovereigns of the Five Directions, for the Taoists) in a crown that he then mounts on top of his ordinary hat. He thus becomes the personification of the deities. The priest again purifies the altar area with a set of chants and mudras. He invites a series of Buddhas and Bodhisattvas (or gods for the Taoists) to the ceremony, and then invites the ghosts in a long passage that describes their sufferings in flowery detail. The priest now becomes a merciful deity associated with aid for ghosts; this is Guanyin (Kuan Im) for the Buddhists, and the Great Unity Heavenly Worthy Who Relieves Suffering (Taiyi Jiuku Tianzun) for the Taoists (although the Taoist text says Guanyin, the Buddhist goddess of mercy, may be invoked instead). In this form, the priest transforms the plates of buns and candy on the altar table into quantities enormous enough to feed the starving crowd of ghosts; the offerings brought by the community could never be enough to sate the mob of ghosts. Meanwhile the priest and his assistants describe the miserable conditions of the ghosts' lives and preach to them. This is the point at which the food is thrown out to the hungry ghosts and snatched up by the waiting people. At the end of the two or three hour ceremony, the. priest sends newly reformed ghosts to the heavenly Buddhist Pure Land, where they are released from their ghostly status; he returns the unreformed ghosts back to their sufferings in the underworld.

Even this quick summary shows a systematically developed structure of contrast between ghosts and gods or Buddhas.[36] Gods dominate the beginning of the ceremony, where the priest becomes their representative; ghosts dominate the end, where they eat and, if they follow the priests' advice, repent. The gods occupy the back of the altar, in the chief priest and the temple itself; ghosts occupy the front of the altar, in their paper houses and metaphorically in the crowd that stands watching. Food offerings to the gods remain on the altar and are in token amounts; food offerings to the ghosts are thrown in front of the altar and include big sacks of raw rice, and the tables of offerings from the community. Gods are glorious, happy beings, whom the priest supplicates; ghosts are pitiful, suffering beings, to whom the priest preaches.

This structure is an important part of the specialist interpretation of ghosts in all contexts. Both the Buddhist (or black-headed priest) and Taoist performances share the structure, but a fuller analysis will show that the two specialist versions differ substantially from each other. The following sections examine Taoist and Buddhist ritual texts and the social relations in which they are embedded. They show how the style of interpretation in both specialist versions of ghosts differs from popular versions, and how Taoists and Buddhist differ from each other.

Taoism

Sanxia's red-headed (and only) Taoists earn their livings by providing religious services for their clientele. Curings are the most common service. Using a combination of divination techniques and a smattering of traditional Chinese medical knowledge, they diagnose minor ailments. The simplest, cheapest, and most common cures require the Taoist to write a charm (*hu-a*), which the patient places in his or her house, or burns to drink the ashes as tea or to wash with. More complex diseases or other problems require larger ritual solutions. Large rituals conducted for temples and their communities are rarer, but more profitable for the Taoists. These rituals range from celebrating a god's birthday, to performing the Universal Salvation rites, to the highest of all Taoist rituals, renewing the cosmic mandate of a community by holding a five-day *ciou* in its main temple.

Taoism, at least for these priests, is a profession. The meditative, mystical aspects of Taoism are important to many of them, but the need to retain a faithful clientele overrides religious interests as a determinant of the particular knowledge of a Taoist. The great majority of the curings and exorcisms that most Taoists perform involve little of the more meditative, philosophical tradition of Taoism. In fact, only one Taoist in Sanxia has much knowledge of the meditative tradition; he is also the only one who can perform a full *ciou* ritual. Two others can perform a much less prestigious one-day *ciou*, but none of them meditate regularly. One key to understanding the difference between Taoism and the popular tradition is the professionalization of Taoism.

The other key to Taoism is its textual tradition. Taoist ritual consists above all in chanting texts. The lay audience can rarely understand what it hears (the priests use an unusual pronunciation, their chanting distorts the words further, and the music usually drowns it all out), but the meaning of the ritual for the priests rests on the text and on the oral traditions that accompany them. Neither the texts nor the accompanying oral explanations are circulated publicly. Taoists learn to interpret their rituals only through a lengthy education where they apprentice themselves to more accomplished masters. While the popular tradition undergoes constant reinterpretation as the political and economic context changes, Taoist interpretations are buffered against such change by their unchanging texts, and by an indoctrination system that tries to channel their readings of those texts.

The Taoists of the northern end of Taiwan share most of their traditions, and they frequently assist each other in conducting large-scale rituals like a *ciou*. If pressed, they will explain that they follow the Zhengyi Tianshi sect of Taoism. Yet they rarely seem concerned with these large categories within Taoism, perhaps because no one in the area claims membership in any other sect. Instead, they identify themselves primarily as members of either the Lim family sect (Lim Chu Phai) or the Lau family sect (Lau Chu Phai), representing two traditions that developed from two early Taoists in the area (Liu, 1967, pp. 48–9). Many of them had studied under the same masters. Acceptance by these groups means invitations to work at the largest, most profitable ceremonies. Since these are the only Taoists in the northern tip of Taiwan likely to perform the Universal Salvation rites, they are the primary concern of this section. Only one priest from Sanxia was a member of this group; my analysis centers on him, but also draws on Taoists from other areas.

Politics, Community and Taoist Ritual

The gods/ancestors/ghosts division from the popular tradition is less useful for Taoism. Taoist ritual instead divides most easily into two categories: *tou* (Dao; 'the way') and *huat* (techniques). Taoists doing *tou* ritual are petioning the highest gods, putting themselves in the inferior position of supplicant. The *ciou* is the pinnacle of *tou* rituals, and of Taoism as a whole. The *ciou* purifies and renews a community through lengthy rituals conducted by a group of Taoists at a major community temple (see Saso, 1972; Liu, 1967). It is held for new temples, and then at regular intervals (often every twelve years) thereafter. In *huat* ritual the Taoist acts as representative of the highest gods to control various lower beings. The techniques used are coercion, threat and command, rather than the respectful petitioning of *tou* ritual. The differences between the two types of ritual are consistently marked. Taoists specializing in different types receive different titles (*tou su* and *huat su*). They wear different robes for each type of ritual: simple red robes for *huat*, and ornate embroidered robes for audiences with the highest gods in *tou*. The rituals and their texts differ, the style and instrumentation of the music differs, the official seals to be placed on all documents differ, and so on.[37]

Taoism, especially in *tou* ritual, carries the bureaucratic metaphor to extremes. The forms and titles of the documents Taoists use, for example, closely resemble traditional imperial documents (Schipper, 1974; Liu, 1967, pp. 70–1). Their ceremonial robes also recall official court dress, and in *tou* ritual they carry *hu*, narrow wooden boards that were traditionally required for audiences with the Emperor. The black cloth used to cover important documents in a *ciou* harks back to the black cloth used to cover secret memorials to the Emperor during the Han Dynasty (Bodde, 1975, p. 185n). The names and ranks of the gods also develop the bureaucracy in even more explicit detail than the popular tradition. The only real departure from the bureaucratic metaphor comes at the top of the hierarchy. The top of the Taoist cosmology is a trinity called the Three Pure Ones (San Qing). This apparent departure from the secular principle of a single Emperor at the top is resolved by the mystical unity of the trinity that is achieved through Taoist ritual and meditation (discussed further below).

Extensive use of bureaucratic trappings involves a claim of legitimacy for the Taoist: he is an official in the Heavenly government. In modern times, my Taoist informants sometimes compared themselves to lawyers in their knowledge of the proper techniques for 'talking to the gods'. This ability to deal effectively with a bureaucracy is the key to the financial success of a Taoist; it gives him a monopoly on access to the gods for any complex ritual purpose.

Taiwanese Taoism differs from elite religion (see Chapter 5), but resembles popular religion in emphasizing malevolent beings. Yet these beings differ from the Universal Salvation ghosts of popular religion – their relation to kinship is not important. Instead they generally represent malignant stellar forces or fierce armies of Heaven or Earth. The priest, as the representative of the highest gods, can control these beings through a variety of techniques (*huat*). A Taoist may also control demonic armies of his own, as described by Saso (1978, ch. 4).

These controllable demons resemble bandits – they are dangerous, but potentially allies in local political conflicts. Saso, describing Mao Shan magic, stresses the dangers of enlisting such allies:

> The Six Chia [Jia] spirits are truly terrifying demons and their control is not a matter for the weak-hearted or the pretender among Taoists . . . If the spirit comes in a terrifying shape, eighty feet in height or in the form of a monstrous demon, so hideous that the Taoist is tempted to run in terror (or 'hide himself in the earth' as the text puts it), it is absolutely necessary to show no sign of alarm, but to open the eyes wide so that they bulge and look straight at the misshapen being . . . (1978, p. 188; he goes on to describe the rest of the technique)

Only a powerful man could control either bandits or demons. Both *tou* and *huat* ritual allow the Taoist to claim power in relation to his clients; only he can petition the gods and command the demons.

The Great Year Star (Taisui Xing) provides another good illustration of such demons. In the official state cult the Great Year was an orthodox power: 'T'ai-sui [Taisui] was the powerful protector of the armies, to whom sacrifices were offered before every military enterprise' (Hou, 1979, p. 200). In popular belief and Taoism, however, he is an evil demon who must be placated. He appears on one type of paper spirit money 'as a brigand, brandishing a sabre in one hand and in the other a human head that he just cut off' (Hou, 1979, p. 201). Thus the symbol that represents official military power in the state cult is a dangerous demon in Taoism and the popular tradition, a bandit with whom people make their peace.

The political message of Taoism resembles the popular tradition; Chapter 5 shows how both differ from the elite tradition, which denies any independent power to malevolent ghost-bandits. All affirm the outlines of the secular government by recreating its bureau-racy in the heavens, but only Taoism and the popular tradition also recognize the alternative political power of ghosts and demons (or metaphorically, of bandits or rebels). They recognize some of the real political problems that the elite tradition ignores. The Taoist emphasis on powers outside bureaucratic orthodoxy also helps guarantee popular support, and thus financial success, by recognizing the complex political realities of the Taoist's clientele.

The political position of Taoism relates to the concerns of the community it serves. Taoists in Taiwan are active members of local communities, and often have ties to large community temples. In some rituals they accent their local orientation when they invoke gods from important temples elsewhere in Taiwan. Taoist ritual recitals list temples roughly in order from the farthest to the closest, and the lists concentrate on local temples. Taoists in different areas thus read lists that differ in their ordering and in some of the gods mentioned.

They perform certain rituals for entire communities, rather than for individuals. After a fire, for example, a Taoist will perform an exorcism (*siu sua:*) to expel the influence of the element fire, and to control it with the element water. The *ciou* is the most important of these community rituals; it unites communities as large as a township. Taoists, therefore, are tied to their local areas first through their financial dependence on a local clientele, and second through their position as intermediaries for the community in rituals. As a result, they share with the popular tradition an easily ideologized concern for both official and unofficial sources of power.

Kinship

Taoists, in their capacity as priests, have little to do with kinship, and ancestors are not an important part of the Taoist cosmology. The few rituals Taoists do perform that relate to kinship take bureaucratic, political forms. Taoists may assist, for example, in a spirit adoption, but their primary purpose is to draw up the appropriate documents to submit to the heavenly authorities. Taoists outside of Sanxia sometimes conduct funerals. Kinship itself is not emphasized in Taoism, which concentrates instead on the more powerful beings of the political realm.

Taoists do, however, take an active part in kinship relations independent of their role as priests. First, Taoists in Taiwan are invariably fire-dwelling, living in ordinary communities, marrying and raising families. Like their neighbors, therefore, they are members of a network of kinsmen and they take part in the cult of ancestor worship. Their priestly profession does not alter this part of their lives.

Taoist priests also take part in a system of fictive kinship. Students of the same teacher call each other 'brother', call their teachers 'father', call their teacher's co-students 'uncle', and so on. They also take on new names when they become priests. These names are used only for ritual purposes and express the same fictive kin relations. Taoists retain their secular surnames in their religious names. The first character of their personal name is taken from a poem used by all 'descendants' of a single master; each 'generation' of students is given the same character from the poem, the next 'generation' gets the next character, and so on. The second character of the religious name is individual. Outside of ritual contexts, however, Taoists use their secular names.

None of these features is unique to Taoism. Nearly everyone shares in the ancestral cult, the same kind of fictive kinship typifies all master–pupil relations in China, and the same system of naming is used in many families. While Taoists as individuals take part in real and fictive kinship relations, Taoist cosmology and ritual show little concern with kinship.

In summary, Taoism resembles the popular tradition in recognizing both official and unofficial sources of power. Like the official cult, however, Taoists have developed the bureaucratic analogy in a more detailed, thorough and systematic way — they have created a full ideology. Bureaucratic details pervade every aspect of the system. The relation of Taoism to kinship is similar to the state cult (see Chapter 5): kinship is not important within the religious tradition, but practitioners take part in the popular ancestral cult. Taoists also express their relations to the community by their connection with community temples, and by their dependence on a local clientele to stay in business. With this background, we can begin to analyze the Taoist version of the Universal Salvation festival, expanding on its relation to popular interpretations of the festival, and examining the systematic differences that Taoist reliance on texts and a particular kind of training creates, and explaining how those differences encourage a more ideologized version of the popular concern with power and hierarchy.

Taoist Ghosts

The Taoist Universal Salvation rites depict ghosts who resemble the more pitiful reading of ghosts from the popular tradition. The ceremony defines ghosts through two levels of contrast: (1) pitiful, suffering ghosts contrast with glorious, generous gods; and (2) the violent, improper deaths of ghosts contrast with the more respectable deaths of ordinary souls.

The layout of the altar and the general structure of the ritual text (the *Taishang Lingbao Zhenji Xuanke*, for Sanxia's Taoists) emphasize the contrast between ghosts and gods.[38] The priests begin by dedicating themselves to the Three Treasures of Taoism (the Dao, the ritual texts, and the Taoist masters). Then they invite various gods to attend the ceremony, including especially Taiyi Jiuku Tianzun (Great Unity Heavenly Worthy Who Relieves Suffering; he helps ghosts transcend their current state), and Tai Su Ia (the fierce transformation of Kuan Im, who will keep the ghosts under control). Only then do the Taoists lead the ghosts into the altar area in front of the temple. The priests urge the ghosts to repent, promise them salvation, and sprinkle Sweet Dew (*gan lu*) over them to quench their thirst and cleanse their sins. At this stage the Taoists are ready to climb the ritual altar to perform the longer, meditative part of the ceremony. The structure of this first segment (inviting gods – inviting ghosts – preaching repentance – providing relief) foreshadows the more elaborate performance of the meditative segment that follows.

After the Taoists climb the ritual altar, they again dedicate themselves to the Three Treasures. The chief priest puts on the five-peaked hat that identifies him with the gods, and he purifies the altar with a series of chants, mudras and visualizations. He invites a wide range of different types of gods, and worships them with incense. With these gods in attendance, he assumes a cross-legged, meditational posture, and begins to invite ghosts of all sorts, promising them relief from their suffering. Now the priest transforms the food offerings into quantities huge enough to feed the starving horde of ghosts. This step requires a complex set of mystical chants, mudras, mantras, visualizations and meditational breathing (to which I will return shortly). The longest section of the text follows, in which the chief priest and his assistants invite all kinds of ghosts to eat the offerings, describing the sins, the tragedies, and the anguish of each type of ghost in turn. The gore in these descriptions emphasizes the contrast with gods. One bloody passage, for example, compares drowning victims to Qu Yuan, a loyal Warring States period scholar and poet whose emperor suspected him of treachery, and who thus drowned himself. The emperor later repented and ordered food thrown into the river to feed Qu Yuan's ghost. Annual dragon-boat races still commemorate this event today.

> Sailing on river and sea, you suddenly meet wind and waves. Drowned in the deep swells, you float onto a sandy beach. Scattered by dogs and dragged by pigs, your corpse lies unburied. Ducks nibble and hawks tear, fresh blood flows drop by drop. Boats race on the Xiang River, and Qu Yuan is your companion. Drowned lonely ghosts, come receive the Sweet Dew! (*Taishang Lingbao Zhenji Xuanke*, n. d.)

With each description, the priest throws a small food offering to the ghosts (and to the living who watch) in front of the altar. Then he douses then with Sweet Dew again, changes the food again, and preaches to them. Finally, he sends them all back to the world of the dead, ending the ceremony. Each stage of the ritual clarifies the contrast between gods and ghosts: gods come first, ghosts come second; gods sit with the priests, ghosts stand in front of the altar; gods' food remains on the altar; ghosts' food is thrown; gods are pure, ghosts are sinners; gods are happy; ghosts are miserable, and so on.

The contrast between ghosts and the proper dead occurs primarily in the long descriptions of the various types of ghosts. Almost every description begins with the joys of a certain type of life, including everything from the glory of military victories to the pleasures of seduction. Yet every case ends with disaster – violent death like the drowning I quoted above; death caused by leading a sinful life, like the case of a shrewish woman who dies in childbirth; or death far from home, where no one will care for the remains, like some brilliant scholars:

> I bow to talented men of the colleges, students going to take the examinations. By day they write poetry and compositions, by night they read the Four Books and Five Classics. One day the examination hall opens, and all will receive an imperial audience. They enter the examination site, they leave for the examination site. Blue sky [i.e., high position] marks their road. They ascend the Dragon Gate [to glory] and enter the Phoenix Pavilion. Fame on

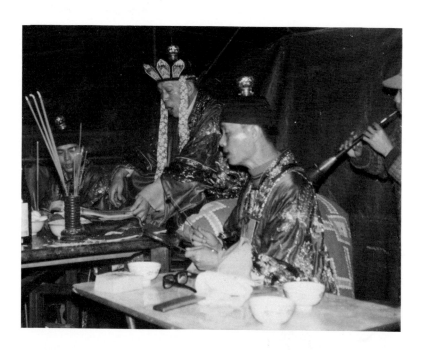

1.1 Feeding the ghosts in Taoist (above) and black-headed priest (below) versions

1.2 Tai Su la protects a temple from ghosts

2.1 Sanxia's temple to Co Su Kong

3.1 Zhong Kui exorcizes demons

3.2 Domestic offerings to ghosts using isolated sticks of incense

3.3 Grandfathers Seven and Eight on a tour of inspection

3.4 Newly renovated Iu Ieng Kong altar with offerings for ghosts becoming gods

佛陀彌阿

4.1 The Jade Emperor
(left) and Amidha Buddha
(right), showing typical
iconographic differences

the first selection of candidates! But a day is not eternal. Dead in a far-off land, they are never seen again. Thirty degree-holders are on the road. Who was to know they would die in another land? Your brave spirits cannot return home; you are lonely souls. Come to the ritual convocation! (*Taishang Lingbao Zhenji Xuanke*, n. d.)

These descriptions do not belittle worldly achievements; earthly success is a genuine possibility. Instead, they play up the contrast between worldly success and the disaster that has befallen the ghosts.

Although the Taoist text does not discuss ancestors (because kinship and ancestors are largely irrelevant to Taoism), its description of ghosts resembles one aspect of the popular tradition in emphasizing the pitiful nature of ghosts. The popular tradition's ghosts, less explicit and less ideologized, are also open to a violent interpretation. The Taoists' texts are less amenable to a violent interpretation, however, because they are so explicit about the pitifulness of ghosts, and because they contrast ghosts with happiness and success (in gods and the non-ghostly living), but not necessarily with peaceful beings. This portion of the Taoist text offers a more ideologized, explicit view of ghosts than the popular tradition, but the two views are nevertheless compatible. This compatibility is consistent with the close social and professional ties between Taoists and their communities.

Certain parts of the text refer to broader themes of Taoism that do not resemble anything in the popular tradition. Pang's (1977) outline of the Pho To text used by Honolulu Taoists includes a representation of hell, which the Taoist systematically breaks open to release the lonely ghosts. (The Sanxia text does not include this section.) Hell is divided into nine levels according to the arrangement of the Luo Shu magic square. This magic square is very old in China, and plays an important role both in Taoism and in five-phase theory (I discuss it further in Appendix A, see Figure A.4). The numerological structure of the Luo Shu is associated with the gradual decline of world order in Taoism, and Taoist priests use it in a number of ceremonies (Saso, 1978, pp. 136–40). This part of the ritual takes its meaning in part from an abstract Taoist numerological and cosmological system, and in part from the fit between a ghostly underworld and the Luo Shu as a symbol of decline. The specific social and political concomitants of a particular ritual performance are less important to Taoist interpretations than this abstract system into which they are socialized.

Figure 4.1   Correlations of the Five Phases

Element	Direction	Organ	Season	Color
wood	east	liver	spring	green
fire	south	heart	summer	red
earth	center	spleen	—	yellow
metal	west	lungs	fall	white
water	north	kidneys	winter	black

At the height of the section where the ghosts are fed, the Taoist text includes an esoteric invocation of the Sovereigns of the Five Directions, who have already been seated in the chief priest's five-peaked hat. These deities form part of an extensive system of correlations, in which each deity is associated with a direction, a color, an internal organ, a taste, a season, one of the five phases, and so on. Figure 4.1 shows some of the more important correlations. Each row of the figure interacts with all of the other rows through the orders of mutual creation and mutual destruction of the five phases (Figure 4.2). This very structured, systematized code, minus the deities, belongs to the realm of five-phase theory; I discuss it further in Chapter 6 and in Appendix A.

For the Taoist, the five phases, personified as the Sovereigns of the Five Directions, have many uses. Saso (1978, pp. 214–18) describes one of the most important, in which the priest refines the five deities into the Three Pure Ones. Taking the phases in the order of mutual creation, the priest refines east and south (wood and fire) into the Primordial Heavenly Worthy (Yuanshi Tianzun), then the center (earth) into the Lingbao Heavenly Worthy (Lingbao Tianzun), and finally west and north (metal and water) into the Daode Heavenly Worthy (Daode Tianzun, Laozi). He can then further refine the Three Pure Ones to achieve unity with the Dao. In the Universal Salvation rites, the Taoist calls up each of the five deities from the internal organ where it dwells by pressing a joint on the left hand (tied into the general system of correlations) and by performing the proper meditational acts.

This most systematically structured level of Taoist ideology is very different from the popular tradition. It stresses the creation of a personal unity with the Dao through a ritual meditation turning the gods into spiritual forces tied to the correlational system of the five phases. The Three Pure Ones, the highest figures in Taoism, stand

Figure 4.2 Creation and Destruction of the Five Phases

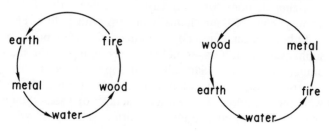

MUTUAL CREATION   MUTUAL DESTRUCTION

above all secular distinctions, especially when seen as abstract forces of meditation. This kind of meditational Taoism transcends the community and political divisions that tie in so closely with the popular tradition and to more everyday Taoist ritual.

This level of interpretation, however, was available to very few people in Sanxia. Only one person had any real knowledge of it, and his knowledge did not compare to the sophistication that Saso (1978) describes for Master Chuang. A mastery of the highly structured systems of meditational Taoism requires extensive training in texts, memorization of oral instructions, and practice in ritual performance. It thrived in the monasteries of the Chinese mainland, which allowed this extensive socialization. The monastic tradition also allowed adepts to live in relative isolation from secular social conditions. This combination of isolation within a self-defined system of social relations, and a reliance on unchanging texts, helped shield Taoism from constant reinterpretation. The monastery could not hope to forestall all reinterpretation, but it could attempt to channel and control interpretations by deciding on 'correct' readings, by imposing these readings on adepts, and by claiming an eternal truth for them. The popular tradition, in contrast, underwent constant pragmatic reinterpretation because it was more closely tied to secular political and economic events, and it had no institutional authority (like the monastery or the Heavenly Master) who could impose an 'orthodox' interpretation on unchanging texts.

Taoists living outside of strict institutional control were freer to develop individual reinterpretations. Taiwan never had a monastic tradition of Taoism, and the absence of a strongly institutionalized ideology left many Taiwanese Taoists caught between the 'orthodox' structures of meditational Taoism and the less ideologized beliefs of their clients. Some largely ignored Taoist ideology, worshipping gods and exorcizing demons for their customers, using the Taoist pantheon in ways that fit their clients' concerns with politics and community. Others became religious intellectuals, who pursued ever more sophisticated masters, sometimes even going to the mainland for training. Peq Hok-ci, Sanxia's most sophisticated Taoist, illustrates several possible ways of thinking about Taoism. He wavers about whether to explore the abstract structures of Taoist thought, or whether to fit Taoism instead into Western psychological systems.

A 'Modernized' Taoist

Mastery of an ideology requires education in its system of interpretation, and an institutionalized set of social relations to foster orthodox interpretation and channel reinterpretation. Peq partially meets these conditions for two separate systems: Taoism and modern Western education.

Peq's knowledge of Taoism comes primarily from his father, who was a leader of the Lim family sect. His father died while Peq was still serving in the army (there is a universal male draft in Taiwan), however, when Peq had not yet received all of his father's teachings. He can perform all the major rituals, but he knows he has not achieved his father's level of mastery. The other Taoists of northern Taiwan form a reinforcing group with which he interacts, but the group is tied together only loosely, and individuals guard their professional secrets from one another. There is no encompassing institution, like the mainland monasteries, to prevent Peq from interpreting Taoism in his own way or to prod him into further exploration of Taoist ideology. His partial mastery of Taoist ideology formed one context in which Peq functioned as a religious intellectual.

The other context in which Peq thinks about his work rests on a modern, Western-style education. He is a high-school graduate, which makes him more educated than many people in Sanxia, and more educated than any other Taoist I interviewed. His secular education gives him a separate abstract system for understanding Taoism. He often mentions the psychological effects of his work, speaking about the efficacy of his cures in language that would not seem unusual from a Western social scientist, and scoffing at any religious explanation. He is 'modernized', as he explains in these contexts. His psychological discourse about religion is not structured

Figure 4.3   An Antidelerium Charm (Left) and Purification Charm
(Right)

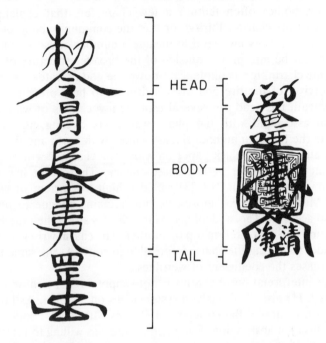

HEAD

BODY

TAIL

Source: Doré 1915:189 (left); black-headed priest's charm from Sanxia
funeral (right)

as complexly as his Taoist discourse (probably because the educational system does not address Taoist ritual), but both are equally
abstracted from everyday social experience.

I had several discussions with Peq about the charms (*hu-a*) he
writes, in which he used both types of discourse to explain them.
Sometimes he would systematize them into abstract Taoist categories.
Most charms, he explained, have a head, a body and a tail (see Figure
4.3 for two examples). There is a limited repertory of heads and tails,
but the bodies vary with the message of the charm. The heads usually
invoke the power of the Three Pure Ones, although rarely by name.
Three checkmarks at the top are a common sysmbol for the Three
Pure Ones. A stylized version of the characters 'to give an imperial
order' (*chi ling*) is also common in charm heads. Charm heads are
usually opaque to the uninitiated; to Peq, they indicate the authority

of the highest gods. Peq could not, however, explain charm tails. Each school, he said, draws the tail in its own way.

Charm bodies often feature a few characters that explain the purpose of the charm ('Purify!' or 'Let the community be at peace,' for example). They also tend to include a number of esoteric marks that cannot be interpreted outside of the broader structure of Taoism. One charm, for example, calls down the god of water, as part of an exorcism of the fire god after a fire, or to help prevent a fire. Underneath the head are several esoteric invocations of water: the trigram associated with the phase water; six circling curves that indicate the Luo Shu number six, associated with north and thus also with water, and the black paper on which the charm is written, also associated with water in five-phase theory. The charm has what Malinowski (1935, pp. 218–33) called a high 'coefficient of weirdness'. Much of it looks impressive, but remains opaque to people with no access to Taoist ideology. Many charms strengthen the effect by writing one character on top of another. The charm writer protects his trade by making the charm impossible to copy. At the same time, he increases the coefficient of weirdness.

Peq's interpretation of charms is not simply a repetition of Taoist ideology. He also abstracts and systematizes on his own. As far as I know, for example, the structure of charms with heads, bodies and tails is his own abstraction. Furthermore, he was willing to revise his charms as he understood their properties better. He once asked me to let him know if I could discover whether any of his charms really worked. He complained that he never found out, because satisfied customers did not need to see him again, and dissatisfied customers did not want to. If I would pass on what I found out when I talked to people, he would learn to write better charms.

Other Taoists showed the same empiricism within Taoist ideology. One man, for example, had just learned a technique that supposedly allowed him to control a divination system. The system, called *puaq pue* (I discuss it further in Chapter 6), consists in dropping a pair of wooden blocks. The way they fall indicates a 'yes', 'no' or 'maybe' answer from the gods. This Taoist asked me to help him test the technique. I would throw the blocks, and he would try to make them come up 'no'. The first throw indeed came up 'no', and then so did the second, the third and the fourth. By this time my own faith in the law of probability was wavering (the odds apparently favor a 'yes' answer, although they probably vary with the individual set of blocks), but his was not. When the fifth throw came up 'yes', he immediately announced that the technique was bogus, and he would not test it further. Both he and Peq functioned as religious intellectuals, working within the Taoist ideology, but continuing to abstract and to structure concepts on their own. This other Taoist had chosen to study Taoism in more depth; he was apprenticing himself to higher masters, and his interpretations would take place increasingly within the context defined by the Taoist texts, oral traditions and social relations.

Peq, in contrast, also held a competing ideology. Sometimes when he discussed his curing charms, he dismissed Taoist interpretation as irrelevant to their real psychological functions. You could write anything you wanted on the charm; it would work as long as the coefficient of weirdness was high enough to mystify the patient. He told of one woman who was so convinced he was hexing her, that she made herself sick. Another patient watched an exorcism, and felt fine until he noticed a sign that said people born in his year would get sick if they attended. He got sick, and Peq cured him with a charm. All this, for Peq, showed the fundamentally psychological nature of his business. This secular attitude toward Taoism, reinforced by the educational system and the media, sometimes made him cynical. He had a whip for use on demons in *huat* ritual. When it broke, he just used the handle instead of repairing it. The demons were invisible (at least Peq has never seen one), so he might as well use an invisible whip, he said.

At times, Peq thinks of abandoning Taoism for secular business. At other times, however, he sees events for which he has no secular explanation. He sometimes cures diseases that he feels only a Western doctor should be able to cure; he says he can keep himself healthy by manipulating the five phases through diet and meditation; he likes to tell of the spiritual powers of his father. He seems a little like Quesalid, the skeptical curer Lévi-Strauss (1963) discusses, who begins to study curing to debunk it, but ends up puzzled and at least partly convinced by the cures he effects.

Peq entered Taoism through his father, an accomplished master. He learned the rituals and a system of interpretation based on an ideology of explicit concepts. Yet Taoism, like any established ideology, survives only where it is embedded in a social structure that can maintain it. In Peq's case, the early death of his father interrupted his further indoctrination in Taoist ideology, and the lack of any strong institution allowed him to reinterpret many of his activities in individual terms that led him away from the orthodoxy of monastic Taoism.

Taoist texts, oral traditions and rituals do not determine meaning, but instead require interpretation. Reinterpretations of the Bible from Martin Luther on show the flexibility with which a set text can be read, and also show how institutions attempt to impose particular interpretations (for example, through confession or catechism). Taoism similarly allows many possible interpretations (as Peq showed), even while its institutions attempted to channel interpretation into a few ideologized forms. The most meditational Taoists were largely cut off from the contexts of the popular tradition. These Taoists looked to isolated monasteries, which could rule on orthodoxy and which were isolated from much day-to-day life of the empire. Yoshioka (1979, pp. 244–5), for example, describes the system of lectures that attempted to shape adepts' interpretations at one monastery. Saso emphasizes the importance of monastic training for the founders of a group of Taoists in Xinzhu, Taiwan (1978, ch. 2), and how one of the most meditative of these Taoists remained at the monastery as a hermit, and performed no public ritual after his return to Taiwan (1978, p. 74).

Other Taoists worked more within the social, political and economic contexts of the everyday lives of their clientele. As a result, their ordinary ritual deals more directly with gods and demons, with community interests and political power. At the lowest levels, they are simply specialists in the popular tradition – they have a more systematized knowledge of how to deal with gods and demons, but they do not draw on the spiritual abstractions of meditational Taoism. Their religion remains more ideologized than the popular beliefs, but it does not compare with the Taoist ideology of someone like Saso's Master Chuang.

Buddhism

The Buddhist version of the Universal Salvation rites, like the Taoist version, relies on a set of texts, and on a social organization that helps control how people interpret those texts. Both religions rely on more explicit and more systematized interpretations than the popular tradition, but both also differ importantly from each other. A striking superficial similarity between the two Universal Salvation texts hides underlying differences of interpretation, which stem from how the two religions socialize their priests into orthodoxy, how they relate to local communities and to national politics, and how their ideologies help create a particular view of the world.

Education, Priesthood and Community

The Buddhist clergy in Taiwan is much more centralized and organized than Taoism. This situation does not typify all of China, either spatially or historically. Rather, it results from two particular processes in Taiwan. First, the Japanese promoted Buddhism during their occupation of Taiwan from 1895–1945. Japanese versions of Buddhism served originally as a way of Japanizing the Taiwanese, and later as a tool to unite Japan's new empire, the Greater East Asia Co-Prosperity Sphere. The Japanese sponsored the construction of Buddhist temples in Taiwan, and they instituted controls over the clergy. The second influence on Buddhism was a major influx of important clergy from the mainland when the Nationalist government fled to Taiwan in 1949.[39] This new group of clergy has become a major intellectual force in Taiwan, and has helped to create an extensive system of Buddhist education.

More than any other group I spoke to in Taiwan (outside of the academics), Buddhist monks and nuns are intellectuals. Kiu Kiong Kiou's little Buddhist temple houses three nuns. The older one typifies an older generation of Taiwanese Buddhists. She is less educated in Buddhism than the younger generation, she is more willing to perform non-Buddhist ritual for her clients, and more willing to allow worshippers to use non-Buddhist offerings (like gold and silver spirit money). Yet even she has an extensive knowledge of sutras, and she promoted an orthodox education at various Buddhist centers for the two young nuns who assist her. These two young nuns were the first Buddhists I interviewed, and they stressed my own need to explore the Buddhist doctrine through its educational system. If I was not going to be a simple tourist, they admonished, I would have to read extensively, to attend public lectures in Taibei (where famous monks fill the largest auditoriums), and to visit important centers of Buddhist education, like Foguang Shan in southern Taiwan. They loaded me up with books, and sent me home to study.

Unlike the Taoists, Buddhist priests in modern Taiwan often come through an institutionalized education system that helps to insure their knowledge of important texts, and to control their interpretations of those texts.[40] The Buddhist clergy in Taiwan forms a more united, homogeneous group than the Taoists. The more institutionalized social relations of Buddhist clergy help to ensure a more uniformly ideologized concept of their religion than exists among Taoists as a group.

Buddhist monks and nuns often do not have close ties to the communities that house their temples. In many cases, the clergy do not come from the local area. Even in rural Sanxia, a mainlander runs one of the Buddhist *chai tng*. Buddhist temples also do not organize local residents in the same ways that a major community temple would, and they do not perform rituals for the benefit of the community as a whole. Unlike most Taoists, Buddhist priests do not depend on the local community for financial support. They perform their rituals instead for individual followers of the temple. Some of these adherents may come from the neighborhood of the temple, but many others will live in widely scattered areas. The monks and nuns themselves tend not to be interested in close ties with a local community. In contrast to many Taoists, they have joined the clergy to avoid the complications of secular life and thus to cultivate themselves. Although they are economically dependent on their temples, earning a living rarely seems to be the reason for their faith. Buddhists have less need for community ties than Taoists. A lack of close local ties helps solidify the institutional organization of Buddhism. Monks and nuns are less likely than Taoists to feel pulled away from the religion by ties to the secular community. They are safer, for example, from the competing ideologies that trouble the Taoist Peq.

Even the *chai tng* in Kiu Kiong Kiou, which has extraordinarily close community ties because of the local origin of its chief nun, depends primarily on outside support. Its closest and most generous followers tend to be wealthy women from Taibei and its environs. They have become involved in the temple through personal ties with the nun in charge. Another of Sanxia's Buddhist temples, found in the hills near Qibei, serves primarily an educated clientele. The head is a Pure Land monk from the mainland who does not speak Hokkien. Although he makes some effort to serve the local community, he attends especially to college students, for whom he conducts vacation retreats. A third monk lives at the mountainous edge of Sanxia. His temple is too far up in the mountains for any regular contact with a local community. His ties are instead primarily to colleges in Taibei.

The Buddhist clergy's relations to local communities thus differ from the closer ties of Taoists. The Taoist cosmology ideologizes the bureaucratic political system, Taoist demons link them to local concerns with illegitimate power, and Taoist practice ties priests to community. Buddhism, however, links neither to the national system of an interlocking hierarchy of communities, nor to local community concerns. The combination of a relatively institutionalized set of social relations that controls Buddhist interpretation, the relative absence of close ties to local communities, and the relative independence from the secular political system, allows Buddhism to maintain a systematized ideology that reflects its independence both from the local community and from the government.[41]

Equality, Buddhas and Politics

In contrast to the division into gods, ghosts and ancestors in the popular tradition, or into gods and malevolent spirits in Taoism, my informants from the Buddhist clergy conceive of ten types of beings that fall into two main categories: those who have transcended the wheel of reincarnation, and those who are still subject to the agonies of rebirth.[42] The transcended beings, called the Four Saintly Planes, include *fo* (*buddhas*, who have achieved the highest level of enlightenment), *pusa* (*bodhisattvas*, who are capable of becoming Buddhas, but choose to remain in this world in order to help others), *yuanjue* (*pratyeka-buddhas*, who have individual enlightenment but do not try to help others), and finally *shengwen* (*sravakas*, the lowest level of enlightenment, associated in China with Hinayana Buddhism). The unenlightened beings are called the Six Ordinary Planes, and consist of gods (including the entire popular and Taoist pantheons), humans, demons, ghosts, denizens of hell and animals.

The most important implication of this is that every being in the popular or Taoist world view is in exactly the same position: none has transcended the most basic feature of life, the bitter cycle of birth, sickness, old age and death. Not only have the monks and nuns ignored the precise appreciation of hierarchy found within the other traditions, but they have made the more radical assertion that everyone, whether god or man, magistrate or peasant, is fundamentally equal.

More detailed analysis shows the thoroughness of the differences between the Buddhist cosmology and the other traditions. First, although Buddhas constitute the top of the spiritual hierarchy, they are totally unlike earthly rulers or their heavenly counterpart, the Jade Emperor. There are many Buddhas, they do not take an active part in the affairs of the world, and they have no bureaucratic authority. Thus, while the Buddhist deities form a hierarchy, it is in no way bureaucratic. Position in the Buddhist hierarchy depends not on political ability to deal with the world, nor on authority to wield power, but rather on faith and a personal commitment to transcend the affairs of the secular world.

Secondly, rank is determined only by the personal merit and personal choice of the Buddhist deities; the bureaucratic principle of appointment to official position is never invoked. Bodhisattvas are not at the highest level (Buddhahood) only because they have made a personal choice to remain in this world. This contrasts with the deities of the other traditions, whose only orthodox path to power is enfeoffment (*hong*) by the emperor.

Thirdly, the beings of the Four Saintly Planes differ fundamentally from the gods of the other traditions and from men in having transcended the physical and emotional limits of humanity. Buddhist deities have unlimited vision, knowledge and abilities to transform their outward appearance; they have also given up all secular passions. Gods, on the other hand, do most things better than men, but there is no real qualitative difference. The Emperor, like the gods, is far more powerful than most people, but even he is not omnipotent. Thus, people's relationships with gods are based on their relationships with other humans; but Buddhism requires its clergy to abandon these secular principles. Faith is not an important concept in the popular religion, just as it is not an important feature of political bargaining. In Buddhism, however, faith becomes one of the keystones. The most impressive acts of worship done without faith accomplish nothing, but a simple prayer said with true faith can accomplish anything.

Fourthly, the iconography of the two religious systems also reflects their basic differences. Iconography in Taoism or the popular tradition, as I discussed above, shows the gods as traditional bureaucrats. Buddhist temples, however, are easily distinguished from popular temples by their more ordinary architecture, which makes no claims to official status. Buddhist temples in Taiwan normally avoid the curved roofs and carved pillars of community temples or magistrates' yamens. The extra-worldly vision of Buddhas and Bodhisattvas is enhanced by their images, which are painted gold, dressed in robes of a sort never worn in Chinese secular life, and seated serenely on lotus blossoms (see Plate 4.1).

Finally, the ritual offerings distinguish Buddhism from the other traditions. Both Taoism and the popular beliefs share a code of spirit money, in which silver is appropriate to ancestors and ghosts, several levels of gold are appropriate to several levels of gods, and paper with various images printed on it is appropriate to ghosts and demons. It is one of the structural correlates of the gods/ancestors/ghosts distinction in the popular tradition, and of the gods/malevolent spirits distinction in Taoism. Meat offerings reinforce the same distinctions, where the preparation of the meat (whether it is raw or cooked, cut up or left whole) encodes the type of being who will consume it (see Chapter 2; Ahern, 1981a, p. 402). Buddhism rejects both ritual codes. Buddhist temples forbid meat offerings of any form, and most also forbid, or at least discourage, the use of paper spirit money. Many Buddhist temples substitute a new form of paper offering that is more appropriate to their own cosmology. Buddhist monks and nuns urge worshippers to burn paper with sutras printed on it; there is a smaller form (*wangsheng qian*; 'rebirth money') for the unenlightened beings, and a larger form (*yanshou qian*, 'longevity money') for the enlightened beings. These Buddhist ritual offerings reject the distinctions made in Taoism and the popular tradition, substituting instead their own core distinction between enlightened and unenlightened beings.

Buddhism thus offers people an alternative interpretation of the political world. Bureaucratic hierarchy gives way to spiritual equality, political manipulation gives way to personal freedom, and secular desire gives way to faith. Buddhist cosmology levels the social distinctions that Taoism and the popular tradition emphasize, and it replaces them with an ideology that both transcends and denies the affairs of secular life. The alternative political vision of the Buddhist clergy both reinforces and relies upon their lack of close ties to secular communities. The relatively institutionalized system of Buddhist education, and the relatively closed set of social relations in which most of the Buddhists live (discussed in the next section), help maintain an ideology at odds with most secular political experience. At the same time, that ideology encourages most monks and nuns to avoid the close community ties that typify the bureaucratic cosmologies of Taoism or the popular tradition. The Buddhist critique of secular politics made it appropriate to a priesthood that cut itself off from the secular world. The same ideology, however, could take on politically active implications if it was removed from the institutionalized Buddhist control of interpretation, and placed into the secular political field. I will discuss reinterpretations of Buddhism by 'heterodox' rebels in Chapter 6. Buddhist ideology itself does not determine the beliefs of monks and nuns; their beliefs come from interpretations of that ideology, which are embedded in the social relations of modern Buddhism in Taiwan.

Celibacy and Filial Piety

Buddhism differs fundamentally from the other traditions in its relations to local communities and to secular politics. Many Taiwanese, however, ignorant of Buddhist cosmology, identify the most crucial difference between Buddhism and their own beliefs as kinship. The Taoist cosmology, like the Buddhist one, largely ignores kinship. Yet Taiwanese Taoists themselves take part in the same daily kinship relations as anyone else; Taoism may ignore kinship, but it does not reject kinship. In contrast, Buddhist monks and nuns leave their families (*chut ke*) to enter the faith, and then remain celibate. They are open to accusations of abandoning their parents by not caring for them in their old age, and even worse, by committing the most unfilial of acts – not providing their parents with descendants. This led to vehement denunciations of Buddhism for espousing unfilial acts, and to equally adamant denials by the Buddhist clergy. The clergy is quick to point out that its members, too, worship their ancestors. This is a Chinese innovation in Buddhism, and shows the truly fundamental concern of Chinese with the ancestral cult.[43] Furthermore, many of the people who become Buddhist clergy have already raised families. The head nun at Kiu Kiong Kiou's *chai tng* is a good example. Her father was a devout lay Buddhist, and she had always intended to become a nun. She was an only child, however, and therefore married uxorilocally in order to provide her parents with descendants. She became a nun only shortly after she bore a son.

Buddhist monks and nuns, like Taoists, take new names when they enter the religion. Unlike Taoists, however, they drop their original names altogether when they become monks or nuns. If surnames are needed (for official documents, for instance), they all use the character Shi, the beginning of the Chinese pronunciation of 'Sakyamuni' (Shijiamoni). The process of 'leaving the family' to join a new social group is thus marked not only by shaving the head and wearing robes, but also by changing names, even the surname. Buddhist names reinforce the end of secular kinship ties for the clergy.

Buddhist monks and nuns not only cut off most of their original kinship ties, but also take on new kinship responsibilities by worshipping dead people to whom they have no kinship ties at all. These include the remains of cremated clergy and lay Buddhists. For a price, Buddhist clergy also worship the dead relatives of other families. These are almost invariably marginal relatives – children, childless adults, and so on – whose right to a position on the ancestral altar is tenuous. By performing this service, Buddhists again place themselves outside the normal system of kin relations.

People thus have some good grounds for seeing Buddhism as opposed to normal Chinese kinship values: Buddhist monks and nuns leave their families, change their surnames, and worship other people's marginal relatives. Nevertheless, Buddhists accede at least to the most obvious outward expression of Chinese kinship ideals – ancestor worship.[44]

Buddhist Ghosts

With the crucial differences between Buddhism and the other traditions in mind, we can turn to Buddhist interpretations of ghosts in the Universal Salvation rites. The most common Buddhist text, and the only one I saw used in Sanxia, is the *Outline of the Yogacara Feeding of the Flaming Mouths* (*Yuqie Yankou*, YQYK).[45] Buddhist informants also referred me to a Ming Dynasty commentary on the text, on which I rely for some of my analysis (Zhuhong, 1976). Unlike the tightly guarded Taoist texts, both the Buddhist sutra and the commentary are easily bought in Buddhist bookstores.

Most temples precede the ghost-feeding with several days of sutra reading. Most important are sutras that relate to saving ghosts, like the story of Kshitigarba, who vows not to become a Buddha until all the ghosts are saved. Black-headed priests, and some Buddhist temples, follow the Taoists in worshipping Heaven at noon on the final day of the ceremonies, although Buddhists omit the pig sacrifice.

The actual ghost-feeding begins, as for the Taoists, in the late afternoon. The basic structures of the Buddhist and Taoist texts are almost identical, largely because the Taoists modelled their text after the Buddhists' (Pang, 1977, p. 95). Taken out of context, the two texts suggest a much greater similarity between Buddhism and Taoism than really exists. When each text is seen in relation to the full structure of Buddhist or Taoist ideology, the underlying differences appear clearly. I have argued (Chapters 2 and 3) that people understand much of the popular tradition piecemeal, as they relate their rituals to the particular situation in which they occur. Piecemeal interpretations are much less likely for the more ideologized beliefs of Buddhism or Taoism, where the priests are trained in an explicit system of interpretation. The differences between the Buddhist and the Taoist texts become clear only when they are understood in relation to the entire religious ideology.

The Buddhist text, like the Taoist, begins with a short prelude that summarizes the ceremony to come. It invites Buddhas and ghosts to attend, and explains how the ghosts will be saved. At this point the priests climb the altar, and the chief priest assumes a five-pointed crown. This crown looks nearly identical to the Taoist crown, although it has different characters written on it. Wearing the crown associates the chief priest with five Buddhas, the most important of whom is Vairocana, associated with resolute activity and wisdom (*zhi*). The chief priest purifies the altar and the offerings with a series of mantras and mudras that again resemble the Taoist purification. The priests then dedicate themselves to the Three Treasures of Buddhism (Buddha, dharma and sangha), which served as a model for the Taoist Three Treasures (Pang, 1977, p. 106). The chief priest, now sitting in a meditative posture, creates a mandala of the Diamond World (Jingang Jie, Vajradhatu) through a series of mantras, mudras and visualizations. The Diamond World is one of many universes, each associated with a particular Buddha, and each having special characteristics that allow it to help speed enlightenment. The Diamond World is associated with Vairocana, the Buddha in the five-pointed crown. This part of the text has no parallel in the Taoist text used in Sanxia, but Honolulu Taoists have a similar section in which they create a mandala of the underworld (Pang, 1977, pp. 111–13).

Now the chief priest visualizes Guanyin (Kuan Im), the Bodhisattva of mercy, sitting on a lotus blossom. The image expands until it merges with the chief priest and he becomes Guanyin. As Guanyin, the priest smashes open the gates of the underworld, and invites each kind of ghost to the ceremony. The lists of ghosts, and the descriptions of the ghosts, are very similar to the Taoist text. Each type of ghost is fed (by tossing rice and buns in front of the altar), urged to repent, fed again, and given Sweet Dew to drink, just as in the Taoist text. The ceremony ends by returning the ghosts to the underworld. A closer analysis of the text, and a comparison to the broader ideology of Buddhism, will penetrate the superficial similarities between the Buddhist and Taoist texts.

The Buddhist and Taoist interpretations of ghosts differ fundamentally from each other. The discussion of Buddhist cosmology above showed how the most important distinction is between enlightened and unenlightened beings. Hungry ghosts are a separate order of being, but their essential similarity to humans, demons, gods and the rest of the unenlightened is primary. The Universal Salvation text reinforces this view. Although it emphasizes ghosts, the ritual is really for all beings of the Six Ordinary Planes, and the priest visualizes all of them in front of his altar. This is especially explicit at one point during the actual feeding of the ghosts: the chief priest reiterates his invitation to a range of hungry ghosts, and then also invites animals, demons, living humans (with the greedy and the nobility mentioned specifically), and even the gods (i.e., of Taoism or the popular tradition) to join the ghosts in eating the offerings and listening to the sermons.

Some of my Buddhist informants explicitly analyzed the ghostly plane as a metaphor for human greed. The text includes a description of the ghost who inspired this ceremony by appearing to Ananda, a disciple of the Buddha (illustrated in Figure 4.4). 'Once the Arhat Ananda was meditating in a forest. During the night a Ghost King appeared to him. His mouth spat fire and his hair spewed smoke; his body was hideous and his joints sounded like a broken cart. His throat, entwined with flames of hunger, was as fine as a needle.' (YQYK, p. 14) Hungry ghosts have insatiable appetites and appropriately huge bellies, but their throats are so tiny that they can eat almost nothing. To make matters worse, fire consumes every bit of food they put to their mouths. There is a dual message: first, human desires can never be fulfilled and so should be transcended, and second, indulgence now must lead to suffering later. Hungry ghosts are a metaphor for human lust after worldly things.

The sections of the text that describe and preach to the ghosts stress over and over the fruitlessness of worldly endeavors. I translate a single example:

I sincerely invite you talented men of the schools. A student living in a thatched hut finds the apricot blossom [i.e., finishes third in the imperial examination] and enters the world of the literati. He travels to the thorned academy [i.e., examination hall] to take the examination. But now the glow-worm lamps [that provided light for a scholar too poor to afford oil] are scattered. Three years of work in vain! He rubbed through an iron inkslab [by writing so much and so diligently], and spent a decade overflowing with suffering. Alas! His name appears on a funeral banner in seven-foot characters [indicating high rank], and a mound of yellow earth covers his compositions. Scholars and officials of this type, all

Figure 4.4   Guanyin appears to Ananda as a hungry ghost

Source: YQYK

ghosts of this rank, take advantage of the strength of the Three Treasures [Buddha, dharma, sangha]. Rely on the esoteric mudras. Come now to the Dharma Meeting! (YQYK, p. 44–5)

The emphasis on the ultimate failure of all endeavors and the inevitability of death typifies the entire text, and it contrasts with the Taoist affirmation of the genuine worth of wordly success.

Ghosts illustrate the suffering created by being caught in the world of illusion. They are part of the consistent dichotomy in the ritual, and in Buddhism as a whole, between mortals and Buddhas, greed and selflessness, sickness and health, pity and devotion. Buddhist ghosts are a metaphor for the greed that typifies all unenlightened beings; they are not simply the improper death that Taoism and the popular tradition emphasize.

A look at the Esoteric Sect (Mi Jiao), from which the text originated, will further clarify the structure of the Buddhist Universal Salvation rites. The Esoteric Sect flourished in China in the Tang Dynasty, the period when the *Yuqie Yankou* was written.[46] The text follows the general structure of Esoteric meditation: it begins with a purification, followed by visualization of a mandala of gods and a merging of the self and the gods (during which the ghosts are fed and preached to), and concludes with a return to the ordinary world. This occurs most importantly in the Universal Salvation text where the priest merges with Guanyin. Just as part of the interpretation of the Taoist Universal Salvation rites rests on a particularly Taoist meditational tradition, the interpretation of the Buddhist ceremony rests in part on a structured meditational sequence that the ritual shares with other parts of Buddhism.

The mandalas of the ritual also typify the Esoteric Sect. These are generally circular arrangements of Buddhas (or Bodhisattvas) and their avatars, each associated with the appropriate direction, color, power and so on. Mandalas are very appropriate for a structuralist analysis: each term is meaningful only in its contrast to a set of similar terms, and each set reproduces the structure of the other sets. Freemantle and Trungpa (1975) give an elaborate example of such a mandala, as it is worked out in the Tibetan Book of the Dead. The mandala of the Universal Salvation rites is simpler, but just as tightly structured. The Diamond World is one of an infinite number of worlds, each existing at once, each ruled by a Buddha, and each with an identical structure (see Figure 4.5). The Diamond World represents the adamant, active nature of Vairocana and wisdom (*zhi*). It is opposed to the Womb World (Taizang Jie, Garbhadhatu), which is passive, represents cause and reason (*li*), and gives rise to the Diamond World. Like all of these worlds, the Diamond World rests on wheels of wind, water and land. Holy Mount Sumeru rises from its center, surrounded by seven smaller peaks. Four major continents surround the mountains. Each continent is associated with a direction, a color, a shape and a mantra; they make natural material for structural analysis. Two subcontinents flank each continent, and each

Figure 4.5   Mandala of the Diamond World

Source: Zhuhong, 1976, p. 183

of them also has a direction, color, and so on. Without going into further detail, it should be clear that each mandala makes up a structurally defined set of correlations and interrelations. The particular system differs from Taoist correlations based on the five phases, but both rely on similar coded contrasts. Both codified systems form part of the explicit ideologies that priests must learn, and differ from the more piecemeal popular worship.

Buddhism, Taoism and Ideology

The Buddhist and Taoist rituals mold a view of ghosts relatively independent from the broader political and economic contexts in which they occur. Both concepts of ghosts rely on their relationship to a broader ideology, based on a set of texts interpreted within the relatively institutionalized contexts of Buddhism or Taoism. The two Universal Salvation texts, the religious ideologies that encompass them, and the social institutions that channel their interpretation, combine to create a system of meaning relatively independent from the secular political economy in Taiwan. Reference to these broad systems of meaning differentiates Buddhist or Taoist religious interpretation from the popular tradition. In the popular beliefs, for example, ghosts may be conceived of differently when they are appeased at a curing than when they are fed in the seventh month; the vicious ghosts that cause illness receive different kinds of rituals from the pitiful Universal Salvation ghosts. The Buddhist and Taoist clergy, in contrast, always treat ghosts consistently; Taoists perform the Universal Salvation on the last day of a *ciou*, and Buddhists may perform it on any occasion. The social organization of interpretation in Buddhism and Taoism creates a more consistent, ideologized religious discourse than the popular tradition.

I do not, however, intend to imply that there is an unbridgeable void between ideologized and pragmatic interpretations. Some experts surely interpret their beliefs in light of particular circumstances, and non-experts systematize their beliefs to greater or lesser extents (see Chapter 6). As a relative distinction, however, the conclusion here is useful – expert religion is more systematized, while popular religion is more pragmatic.

This is consistent with the findings of some studies of Western political ideologies. Converse (1964) concludes that elite political beliefs are organize into a few wide-ranging systems whose objects are remote, generic and abstract. The political beliefs of non-elites are instead organized as clusters of ideas with few internal relationships, whose objects are simple, concrete and close to home. Mann (1970, p. 435) argues similarly that 'only those sharing in societal power need develop consistent societal values'.

In attempting to explain the world according to universal or eternal principles, intellectuals are striving quite deliberately to transcend context. They will make versions of a symbol that conflict in different contexts into what they view as an explicit, systematized ideology. This analysis is consistent with the views of Geertz (1964b) and Weber (1951, 1968) on the need of intellectuals to create all-encompassing systems of meaning:

> It is the intellectual who conceives of the 'world' as a problem of meaning. As intellectualism suppresses belief in magic, the world's processes become disenchanted, lose their magical significance, and henceforth simply 'are' and 'happen' but no longer signify anything. As a consequence, there is a growing demand that the world and the total pattern of life be subject to an order that is significant and meaningful. (Weber, 1968, p. 506)

Intellectuals extract meaning from the arena of everyday action and place it in a broader, more self-consciously systematized framework.

Taoists in particular range widely from pragmatic to ideologized interpretations. Some consistently interpret their rituals in reference to Taoist meditation systems, the Three Pure Ones as abstract spiritual forces, and five-phase theory. Less 'orthodox' Taoists, however, may not know much of these abstract systems, and may interact more closely with the interpretations of their clients. This range in styles of interpretation rests on a range of social relations. The most pragmatic Taoists interact extensively with a paying clientele and function as active members of the local political economy. More ideologized Taoists tie instead to a broader network of master–pupil ties and ritual schools that transcend local boundaries. The most ideologized in late imperial Taiwan often interacted only marginally with a clientele, depending instead on elite patronage for their livelihood (Saso, 1978, pp. 82–3). The ideologization of Taoism culminated traditionally in the great monasteries of mainland China, where Taoists could maintain their system of interpretation relatively free from the secular world.

The range of variation within Buddhism is smaller in Taiwan than the range within Taoism. The majority of the modern Taiwanese Buddhist clergy maintains a very ideologized style of interpretation by demanding a high level of education that is controlled by a few major centers, and enforced by a relative isolation from the secular world. Both Buddhism and Taoism share their ideologized styles of interpretation with the traditional Chinese elite, and to a lesser extent, with the modern elite.

5 Elites, Ideologies and Ghosts

Local elites join everyone else in the community in popular religious performances. Elite styles of intepretation, however, differ systematically from non-elite styles. I have so far distinguished only two main styles of interpretation – the more piecemeal, contextualized, pragmatic interpretations of the popular tradition, and the more explicit, universalized ideologies of Buddhism or Taoism. Analysis of the elite calls for further refinement: the modern elite often reinterprets the active spirits of the popular tradition as passive models that inspire good behavior. This style of interpretation grows out of the traditional state cult, an ideologized religious system that the elite generally interpreted passively, and that they used as a form of ideological control. This chapter discusses the modern elite pantheon and traditional elite uses of the state cult, especially as the elite sometimes used the cult to promote religious unities that would serve its political interests. The chapter concludes with a return to the Universal Salvation festival. It examines state attempts to repress and to manipulate the ceremony over the last century, singling out especially the effects of varying styles of interpretation (pragmatic/systematized, active/passive) on the successes and failures of the state's attempt to control a unified religion that would serve its own interests.

Elite Styles of Interpretation

I define the local elite primarily by economic position and by education, and I use a broad definition in order to capture the real range of variation in a rural township like Sanxia, which hosts very few members of the top national elite.[47] For my purposes the local elite are people with a high school (or higher) education, and whose work ties them to the modern, national economy (big businessmen, and white-collar workers in government and business), rather than to local, more traditional sectors (farmers, laborers, small shopowners).[48] I treat education and economic position together, because they correlate very strongly in Taiwan; the correlation in my questionnaire sample is so high that the two factors are largely impossible to separate. Education and economic position were even more strongly connected for the traditional elite: the elite defined itself through educational achievement, education was a prerequisite to official political power, and families that achieved wealth through land or business consolidated their position by educating their children.[49] The educational system and economic position together comprise the social relations with which religious interpretations interact.

Both the modern and traditional local elites participate actively in the popular religious tradition. They take part in daily worship at the household altar with the same frequency as everyone else, and they are visible participants in major community rituals like the Universal Salvation festival or Co Su Kong's birthday. I had originally expected that people would see a secular education (one of the elements of elite status) as leading people away from traditional religion, but I was wrong. When I asked people to agree or disagree with the claim that 'people with a high educational level are less likely to worship gods', only 22 per cent of the people interviewed agreed (16 per cent of the educated). Even more clearly, when I substituted 'ancestors' for 'gods' in the statement, only 8 per cent agreed (also 8 per cent of the educated). People perceive the educated as religious, because they feel that education develops morality.

Nearly all Chinese felt that religion serves, in part, what we would call psychological or moral functions. I was told that worshipping, drinking tea made from incense ash, and other religious acts make people feel more at ease. My next door neighbor, for example, was fond of urging me to worship at the local community temple because my 'heart would be more peaceful' (*sim khaq pieng an*), rather than because this would make the god more favorable toward me. The popular tradition, however, also sees religion as more than a psychological crutch. Gods, ancestors and ghosts are real actors who can be dealt with just like visible beings. When people go to temples they want more than just to ease their minds: they want sons, wealth, success and help with a whole range of very real problems. The objects of popular worship, as of Buddhism or Taoism, are active beings who can have a visible effect on the world.

Many of my elite informants, however, both young and old, saw the pantheon merely as a passive model, not as active beings. They scoffed at the idea of asking gods, ancestors and ghosts to grant favors. These people worshipped without expecting the objects of their worship to take any action. Instead they saw gods, ancestors and ghosts as personified representatives of moral ideals. Worship, according to these informants, should serve only to commemorate the achievements of gods or ancestors while they lived, and to encourage the living to be equally virtuous. Religion inspires people to be filial children, hard workers, and loyal subjects of the state.

Tan Kim-thian (discussed in Chapter 2), for example, says he burns incense only for his ancestors. Although he controls Sanxia's Ma Co temple, he says he only nods to gods, because so many of them do not express the proper virtues. Gods are a metaphor for a pure heart (*liong sim*).[50] Another educated old member of the elite, whose father and maternal uncle had both held imperial degrees, explained: 'Worship of gods is a matter of respect for people with worthy accomplishments. There is no need to talk about divine protection (*pou pi*). Only your heart is important. I am not afraid of any gods.' These members of the modern local elite have not worked the pantheon into an explicit ideology like Buddhism, Taoism, geomancy, or the state cult, but have instead transferred it, in varying degrees, from an active force to a passive model.

One of the items on the questionnaire asked respondents to agree or disagree with the statement 'worship of gods is only to respect their accomplishments while alive, not to request their help'. Table 5.1 shows that elite respondents are more likely to agree than non-elite respondents.[51] These answers also support the contention that educated elites tend to see as passive models the same beings who are more active in the popular tradition. Other questionnaire results lead to the same conclusion. The elite are significantly more likely than others to disagree that 'fate determines poverty or wealth' (Table 5.1). They tend to agree with non-elite informants in asserting that religion is important to people, but to disagree with claims that spirits have real powers.

Elites are also less likely than non-elites to agree that 'sooner or later science will be able to solve all problems; the power of religion will not be necessary' (Table 5.1). I found this result puzzling at first, because I would expect the opposite pattern in the United States. It suggests that the educated elite is more likely to see religion and science as serving separate functions – one is a moral model, the other is an explanation. Non-elites instead see science and religion as having overlapping functions, and can thus foresee a day when science would replace religion.

Local elites generally take part in the Universal Salvation ritual,

Table 5.1   Attitudes Toward Religion

1. Worship only for respect.

	Agree	*Don't know*	*Disagree*
Non-elite	49	11	28
Elite[a]	15	10	10

[a]$\chi^2 = 4.67$, $p < 0.1$

2. Fate determines wealth.

	Agree	*Don't know*	*Disagree*
Non-elite	49	14	25
Elite[b]	6	8	21

[b]$\chi^2 = 15.7$, $p < 0.01$

3. Science will replace religion.

	Agree	*Don't know*	*Disagree*
Non-elite	14	27	47
Elite[c]	2	7	26

[c]$\chi^2 = 4.87$, $p < 0.1$

but generally within a passive framework. Lombard-Salmon (1975, pp. 471–8) provides a good instance of elite attitudes toward the Universal Salvation festival as performed by mostly Hokkien Chinese in Java around the turn of the century. Confucian reformists were attempting to do away with the ceremony, while equally educated traditionalists felt it should be reformed. The argument centered on whether or not the ceremony encouraged filial piety – no one mentioned concern over the condition of the ghosts or fear of ghostly reprisals. In this case, the active ghosts of the popular tradition again appear as passive models for the elite.

An active principle (like the gods of the popular religion) can explain real events, and can be manipulated to achieve results in the world. Passive principles instead provide a model for ethical behavior; they can be cited to support or condemn behavior, but they cannot be used directly to achieve empirical results. Western science is an active system in this sense; moral philosophy is passive. Weber's 'magic garden of Taoism' is active.

Empirical evidence can support the existence of active forces, while it is less relevant to passive models. Thus, for example, Harrell's (1974b) conclusion that people believe more strongly in Taiwanese rituals for whose efficacy they have empirical evidence reflects these people's active cosmology: only active beings could provide such evidence. The passive elite pantheon, in contrast, explains nothing. It is only a model to illustrate traditional moral values, and many of the elite regard it explicitly as a tool for inculcating those values in people.

My characterization of elite interpretations as passive is not absolute. Active and passive interpretations are a relative distinction, and the same individual may use both in different contexts. The highly educated head of the temple to Co Su Kong, for example, always used passive interpretations in public and in interviews with me: he explained his service to the temple as a contribution to the community. Yet he was widely rumored to have become so involved in the temple because he felt that Co Su Kong had saved his son's life during the Second World War – a very active interpretation. Elites in late imperial China also occasionally wrote of active gods. Nevertheless, passive interpretation is a style that both the late imperial and modern Taiwanese elites use in abundance; in formal contexts like interviews, the modern elite (at least) uses this style almost exclusively.

State Cult, Ghosts and Political Control

The modern Taiwanese elite cosmology is more passive than popular interpretations, but it is not more ideologized. The modern local elite, on the whole, speaks no more explicitly, and no more systematically about religion than other non-specialists. The modern elite differs in this from the late imperial elite who had a strongly ideologized religious platform in the state cult.

Both traditional and modern elites, however, share their relatively passive style of interpretation of the personified cosmology. For example, Xunzi expressed similar ideas in the third century BC:

> When people try to save the sun or moon from being eclipsed, or when they pray for rain in a drought, or when they decide an important affair only after divination, they do so not because they believe they will get what they are after, but to use them as ornament to government measures. Hence the ruler intends them to be an ornament, but the common people think they are supernatural. It is

good fortune to regard them as ornamental, but it is evil fortune to regard them as supernatural. (Chan, 1963, p. 121)

Modern passive styles of interpretation have their roots in earlier times. Whether modern or traditional, passive styles lend themselves to political ends. If people see gods as active forces, they follow the gods' instructions, but if gods are a passive metaphor, they become available as tools for political rhetoric. The elite (both late imperial and modern, national and local) has a political opportunity in the passive pantheon that most of its subjects interpret actively. The late imperial national elite took particular advantage of this opportunity leading it to ideologize religion more than the modern elite. Their generally passive, personified pantheon was a metaphor for orthodoxy; their control over deification and official ritual aimed to encourage popular obedience. The late imperial state ideology used this strategy for each of the major social topics of the popular tradition – kinship, community and politics – helping to create diverse styles of interpretation within a unified set of social concerns. The following sections examine the political uses of the passive cosmology in the state cult and in the Universal Salvation festival.

State Cult and Official Morality

Although kinship did not play an important role within the state cult proper (except for worship of the Emperor's ancestors), it was always an important part of officially propagated morality. Both late imperial and modern elites (except for some Christians) take part in the ancestral cult, and both put extensive emphasis on non-religious expressions of kinship. Officials took extended leaves after the death of a parent, the *Classic of Filial Piety* was a required text, the Twenty-Four Filial Acts (a set of moral tales) were frequently cited, and so on. Even now, there is much official emphasis on the secular expression of filial piety. During my fieldwork, for example, the media carried the story of a Taibei girl who had copied one of the Twenty-Four Filial Acts – she cut off a piece of her own flesh to use as medicine for her sick mother. In spite of some initial chastisement about superstition, the government presented her with a large monetary reward to commend publicly her filial piety.

The late imperial government made similar attempts to promote proper kin morality among its subjects, by building memorial arches, for example, to chaste widows. This elite version of kinship is passive; it has no place for the active ancestral spirits of the popular tradition. It was, in part, a political tool that promoted filial obedience in a state that drew explicit parallels between itself and the family. The Emperor was a father; he would be benevolent, and his subjects would be obedient. Yet the elite treatment of kinship was not simply a cynical political tool. Lineage ties and marital alliances were very important to the elite at all levels, and their emphasis on kinship, just like the non-elite emphasis on kinship, results in part from their ties to social relations in which kinship plays a large role. The shared concern with kinship thus results both from the widely shared social importance of kinsmen, and from elite attempts to universalize a certain view of kinship.

The state cult and the popular tradition also share a general concern with community, but the styles of interpretation and their particular messages differ. The popular tradition defines communities primarily in horizontal opposition to each other. It recognizes secular administrative hierarchy only at the most local level: villages (under Earth Gods) are subsumed by the larger community (Sanxia, under Co Su Kong), but there are no further intervening units short of the central government (under the Jade Emperor). The state cult, on the other hand, explicitly and accurately followed the secular administrative hierarchy.

The state cult required that four kinds of open altars be built in all administrative cities down to the *xian* (county) level. These included: (1) altars to the land and grain (*sheji*), (2) altars to wind–rain–thunder–clouds, (3) altars to mountains and rivers, and (4) altars to the unworshipped dead (*li*) (Feuchtwang, 1976). Official rank and the place of the altar in the administrative hierarchy determined who could take part in rituals at these altars. All administrative cities also housed official City God temples and some official versions of temples to a few popular deities like Kuan Kong, who had been incorporated into the state cult. These temples were the main points of contact between the state and popular cults. When this system was actively functioning, it must have shown local communities simply as equivalent units in a nation-wide hierarchy rather than the independent, closely knit entities that the popular religion stresses.

This implies that at the local level, late imperial elites could use one or the other religious tradition to emphasize alternative messages. A magistrate, for example, would have been required to emphasize national solidarity by performing state rituals. Significantly, worship at the open altars apparently fell into disuse in the nineteenth century (Hsiao, 1960, p. 223), in a period of increasing local autonomy at the expense of the central government in China (Wakeman, 1975). A magistrate may also have chosen to bow to the local community, however, by worshipping at local unofficial temples, or by recommending a local hero for deification. After retirement, many scholars and ex-officials became involved in local temples.

The same alternatives exist for the modern elite in Taiwan, although they no longer take the same form. Local temples still express local solidarity, while national solidarity is now shown by following the government policy of opposition to large religious displays, rather than through the defunct state cult. Thus, a man like Tan Kim-thian (see Chapter 2), who is trying to establish himself both as a local leader and a representative of the government and the Nationalist Party, must play a very complex game. He publicly affirmed his local commitment by taking over management of Sanxia's Ma Co temple, but emphasized his national commitment to a group of political leaders by recommending a thriftier and simpler performance of Sanxia's most important annual festival.

Just as for kinship, the elite and popular traditions share a social concern for community, but differ in their emphases. The shared social concern, and national elite attempts to universalize their own version of community through the state cult, helped unite the elite and popular traditions; at the same time, different goals and social experiences of community helped to divide them. The local elite is in a position to take advantage of both versions.

The popular tradition and late imperial elite uses of the state cult both feature heavenly parallels of secular bureaucracy, which rest on a unified social experience of politics, diverse particular understandings of politics, and rhetorical use of the passive cosmology by the elite. One of the most important political uses of the state cult was to draft local heroes into national legitimacy by deifying them. This fostered what the government considered good moral values, but more importantly, prevented local heroes from being used as symbols by unofficial, and therefore unapproved, groups. While this plan may have worked well on some occasions, it could also lead to abuses. Powerful local elites often managed to get magistrates to recommend their ancestors for deification (Hsiao, 1960, p. 226–9). This would add to the prestige of already powerful families, but could also have effects opposed to the moral enlightenment the government intended. In mid-Taiwan, for example, influential descendants of the powerful strongman Lin Wencha convinced the government to deify him and build a temple to him in Taizhong. Lin Wencha, however, must have been a very unpopular figure in local minds, since he and his brother had taken advantage of a local rebellion to destroy their enemies and vastly increase the family's land and water holdings at the expense of their neighbors. Although the government intended to honor Lin's military achievements in Fujian, the temple probably harmed the imperial cause in the eyes of the victims of his more local tyranny (Meskill, 1979, p. 210).

The national government also used religion to claim legitimacy directly for itself. Officials and gods were part of an interdigitated hierarchy, so that secular officials could promote gods, but at the same time, a new magistrate had to present his credentials to the local City God. Officials, and especially the Emperor, also commanded the skills that keep the supernatural order running smoothly. Hsiao translates a good example from an eighteenth-century magistrate:

In the fourth month of the *chi-yu* year [1789], when I was leading my subordinates in rainprayer, [the images of] over twenty gods were carried [by rural inhabitants] . . . to the hall of the yamen. Clerks of the *Li-fang* [Division of Rituals] . . . requested me to perform the customary act of worship. I said 'This is not in accordance with the prescribed ritual form.' . . . Thereupon elders of the villages knelt and beseeched [me to comply with the request]. I told them that . . . 'the government has laid down definite rules prescribing the ritual forms to be followed by officials . . .' Now the land gods of rural areas [the images of which you carried here] are the counterparts of the *ti-pao* [constables appointed by local officials – RPW] . . . Local officials cannot treat *ti-pao* as their peers; how can land gods be treated as the equals of local officials? (Wang Hui-tsu, in Hsiao 1960, p. 632; brackets in original except as marked)

Participation in official rituals also reflected political rank. No commoners could worship at the open altars, and the higher the level of a ritual, the higher the rank of the officials involved. The implication was again that officials were needed to keep the world functioning properly, and that ordinary people had no place at such an important event. Even today, attendance at the annual ceremony for the birthday of Confucius in Taiwan (the only vestige of the official religion) is by invitation only.

The state cult allowed no independent authority to ghosts or other malevolent beings. A local populace might realize a symbiosis with bandits through the vicious 'ghosts' who pillaged the scaffold in the nineteenth century, and local Taoists might confirm such unofficial power through their alliances with malevolent spirits, but the state allowed only orthodox political arrangements. Religion for the elite was, in part, an aspect of government, and they emphasized its political facets, presented in the most orthodox light.

The State and Ghosts

The state in Taiwan has never been comfortable with popular performances of the Universal Salvation festival, and its policies illustrate the political potentials of the pantheon, as different styles of interpretation produce different versions of ghosts. Symbolically, the state could not legitimate the image of politically marginal ghosts – an illegitimate power that could demand protection money from the population. The state instead maintained that it could control the unruly and care for the needy. Politically, the state wanted to discourage the large, and especially the violent, crowds of the Universal Salvation festival. Economically, the state regretted the huge expenditures of wealth on what it considered frivolity at best. Especially in the twentieth century, the state wants to promote investment in the modern industrial sector, rather than in the traditional sectors that benefit more from popular religion.[52]

The various governments that have ruled Taiwan have tried various combinations of repressing the Universal Salvation festival and manipulating it. In the long term, neither strategy has been successful, and the explanation lies in popular styles of interpretation of ghosts. Attempts to repress undesirable realizations of ghosts largely failed because pragmatic interpretations of ghosts do not exist in any repressible social organization. The government could change people's interpretations only by changing their political and economic experiences. Manipulation failed because the government could do no more than suggest their own ideology of ghosts to replace the old one, and had no mechanism to propagate the new ideology. People continued to interpret ghosts in light of their experiences; if the state's religious ideology did not fit experience, it was safely ignored.

The Universal Salvation festival, or parts of it, was repressed at least four times between 1860 and 1980. The first occurred in 1889, when Liu Ming-chuan, the first Chinese governor of Taiwan, made robbing the lonely ghosts illegal. Liu had no way of enforcing this ban, and it had no long-term effect.

The second repression occurred in the first few years after the Japanese occupied the island in 1895. The Japanese state inserted itself much more effectively into local affairs than the traditional government could manage. The new government repressed religion at first; it burnt down a number of temples, including Sanxia's main temple, in retribution for attacks on the Japanese. After a few years, however, they relaxed their policy toward religion. Although they encouraged Japanese Shinto, Buddhism and Christian missionizing, they guaranteed religious freedom to the Taiwanese. They feared that systematic repression of popular religion would create unrest, and they preferred the minor problems of the religion to major political disruptions.

By the late 1930s, Japan was at war on the Chinese mainland, and thus again adopted a repressive policy toward Taiwanese religion. The repression was at its worst just after the Marco Polo Bridge Incident of 1937, when the Japanese invaded China. During this period, many areas (including Sanxia) set up Shinto societies under official urging. The government even removed the local god images from temples in a few areas, putting some in museums and burning others. They explained to the local people that their gods had been 'promoted' to Heaven as Shinto deities (TWSZ, 12, pp. 292–5). The government soon softened its position on religion again, not wanting to create an internal battlefront by pushing the Taiwanese toward 'Japanization' too fast. This period coincides with the low point in performances of the Universal Salvation festival. I have explained in Chapter 3 that changes in the economy were a crucial factor in changing the robbing of the lonely ghosts. The Japanese repression of the 1930s was also important. The government did not attack the festival itself, or people's ideas about ghosts. Instead they attacked the material core of all popular religion – temples and ritual perform- ances of all kinds. As we shall see, this was the only occasion on which state interference had much effect. It worked because it attacked the concrete base of popular religion, directly bypassing popular ideas about ghosts. People's changing treatment of ghosts is irrelevant as long as there can be no material expression of their ideas. Over the long run, however, the Japanese were not willing to risk further alienation of the population by repressing popular religion. Effective repression never lasted more than a few years.

The Nationalist government conducted the fourth and final repression of the festival. The new government continued to fight a civil war on the mainland from 1945–1949, and there was major unrest in Taiwan at the same time. For these first few years, therefore, the new government also discouraged massive religious demonstrations like the Universal Salvation festival. In 1948, for example, newspapers reported that police in Yilan County and in Guanyin Xiang of Xinzhu County would disperse any performances of the Universal Salvation festival as part of the government policy of 'suppressing insurrection and being frugal' (*kan luan jie yue*). Guanyin Xiang substituted a pig competition for the festival (XSB, 9 August, 1948, p. 6: 28 August, 1948, p. 6). At the same time, however, Miaoli County had a large performance of the festival by five monks and 5000 spectators (XSB, 19 August, 1948, p. 6). Even under the unsettled conditions in Taiwan, the repression of the festival was neither thorough nor completely effective. As the situation calmed down in Taiwan, the government relaxed its repression. I have found no later account of complete prohibition of the festival.

Manipulation was the other method the state used to try to control the Universal Salvation festival. The late imperial Chinese government made the most extended attempt to manipulate the popular interpretation of ghosts. The popular treatment of ghosts was unacceptable to them. They feared the violent crowds that the Universal Salvation festival drew; they regretted the large expenditures of wealth that the festival required; and they could not condone the image of ghosts as politically marginal beings who had to be propitiated because they could not be controlled. The state cult provided an entire religious ideology that was intended to supersede the popular conceptions. An altar for neglected spirits (*li tan*) stood in the suburbs of every administrative city, and it brought ghosts into the state cult.

The state cult required magistrates to perform rituals at these altars three times each year. The spirits received offerings appropriate to a 'common sacrifice' (*qunsi*) for deities at the lowest level of the cult, including Kuan Kong, the City God and others (Feuchtwang, 1976, pp. 585–7). In contrast to the popular offerings to ghosts, the official offerings thus did not mark ghosts as a marginal category. Instead, they treated ghosts as full, if low-ranking, members of the official hierarchy. The official text that the magistrate was supposed to read further emphasizes how the government claimed to resolve the marginal status of ghosts, and to make them into orthodox citizens. It instructs ghosts to serve the purposes of the government:

> The Son of Heaven sacrifices to the deities Heaven and Earth and the mountains and rivers of the world; [the officials in charge of] the kingdoms (i.e. provinces) and each prefecture, district, and county sacrifice to the mountains and rivers within their territory, and to the deities [of their territories]; the common people sacrifice to their ancestors and to the deities of the neighborhood and the local altars. The rites to be performed by high and low differ in degree . . . [The ghosts'] names have been blotted out of a sudden, the sacrificial rites to which they are entitled are unknown and unrecorded. These lonely souls have no one on whom to depend in death . . . Whatsoever persons there be among the people of our county who are obstinate and unfilial and do not hold in respect the six relationships (i.e. father and mother, eldest and younger brothers, wife, and child): who rob and defraud in defiance of the public laws; who subvert the honest and oppress good citizens; who run away from the police or maintain themselves by preying on poor households – such confirmed evildoers, such corrupt, lawless fellows you *shen* [spirits] must report to the [City God for punishment] . . . If there be persons who filially obey their parents, keep on friendly terms with their kinsmen, stand in awe of the magistrate, respect the *li* and the law, who do not act as they ought not to, who are good and upright persons – these you *shen* must make known to the [City God] and secretly protect . . . (from a Fengshan Xian, Taiwan, gazetteer, in Thompson, 1975, pp. 270–2).

The state thus denies any independent, marginal power to the ghosts, and asserts instead its control over them, and its ability to ease their suffering. The ghosts here appear almost like yamen runners or local constables (*dibao*, who help the magistrate in local control, but who are generally disliked and feared by people). An alternative text turns things around slightly: it instructs the City God to have good and upright spirits reborn as humans, and to punish evil spirits (Hsiao, 1960, pp. 630–1). Ghosts in this second text are less a part of the government than in the first text, but they are just as thoroughly under the control of the government. In both cases, the City God (as

godly equivalent of the magistrate) controls the ghosts. The state
claims to fulfill the ideal roles of a state: it protects the people from
harm, and provides welfare for its most unfortunate citizens.

Hsiao (1960, p. 223) writes that the ghostly part of the state cult
had died out in many parts of China by the beginning of the nineteenth century. This was apparently not entirely true of Taiwan.
Official altars were built and rebuilt throughout the eighteenth and
nineteenth centuries in Taiwan (TWSZ, 18, pp. 103–4). It is not clear
that official rituals were performed at all of these altars, but people
did use them to store coffins of bodies awaiting the proper geomantic
moment for burial, or of people too poor to afford a burial. Here
again, the government could legitimize itself through the ghost altars;
it provided a real welfare function for the bodies of just those people
who were most ghostly, those who were too poor or too socially
isolated to be given a normal burial. The continuing official emphasis
on *li tan* in nineteenth-century Taiwan may reflect government concern with the increasing popularity of the Universal Salvation festival
in Taiwan. The official ghost altars were the primary ideological
weapon with which the government could attempt to undercut the
popular vision of ghosts.

An early nineteenth-century subprefect of Gemalan (now Yilan
County) made one of the most inventive attempts to manipulate the *li
tan* to foster a new image of ghosts. Like much of Taiwan, this area
had been wracked by frequent battles between Chinese and aborigines, and among Chinese with different places of origin on the
mainland (primarily Hakka, Hokkien from Zhangzhou, and Hokkien
from Quanzhou). The subprefect forced about two thousand representatives of the feuding groups to attend a ritual at the official
ghost altar. Just as tablets for the ghosts were placed at the right and
left sides of the altar, he arranged all the Zhangzhou people at the
left, all the Quanzhou people and Hakka at the right, and sat all the
aborigines on the ground in the middle. Various officials made the
usual state cult offerings for ghosts, and the subprefect read a special
sacrificial text. The text described the violent settlement of the area.
He explained that the many deaths that resulted created an evil force
(*li qi*) of starving ghosts. 'Random gravemounds lie hither and
thither; the bones lie abandoned and rotten, unidentifiable. Liver
and brain are obliterated, without even five feet of land [for a proper
burial].' Fortunately, he explained, the Emperor has put a stop to the
bloodshed by his generous policies. Peaceful humans mean peaceful
ghosts:

If enemies who hate one another will discuss matters together, they themselves can dispel the evil forces . . . Thus, humans and ghosts will be at peace; the people and the aborigines will find permanent happiness. Coming from different directions and far away places, all will come to resemble the golden age of [the legendary Emperors] Shun and Yao. Stagnant souls and wronged spirits become peaceful wind and sweet rain. (Yao, 1957, pp. 85–7)

Ghosts are again clearly a metaphor for the humans of the district, but unlike the popular ceremony, this ritual denies their autonomous power. It stresses instead that the government has brought these marginal elements into orthodoxy. The government claims to have them in its control.

Even this systematic attempt to manipulate the ghost cult for specific government purposes had little apparent success. In general, the great majority of the population ignored the rites of the official cult. If the official ideology of ghosts had any effect at all, it must have concentrated primarily on the elite, who were the main people in attendance. The state had no mechanism beyond its official ritual to propagate its version of ghosts. Its alternative to the popular cult was primarily a systematized set of ideas, in which ghosts were the unfortunate dead who were brought into the official hierarchy by a generous government. The state failed to propagate this ideology successfully for two reasons: (1) They had no effective social organization that could impose this interpretation as the correct reading of ghosts. The official reading existed only in the writings of the elite (like Yao Ying's sacrificial text above) and in the performances of the state cult. Neither form had any significant contact with the bulk of the population. There was no institution through which the state could effectively impose its ideology. (2) The popular understanding of ghosts was pragmatically tied to changing political and economic experiences of marginality (see Chapter 3). It concentrated in the nineteenth century on a politically marginal population that the state did not control. The official version of ghosts thus simply did not mesh with people's real experience of marginality. The state could not manipulate the popular ideology of ghosts, because there was little worked-out popular ideology beyond the general contrast of ghost with gods and ancestors. The popular understanding of ghosts was flexible and bound to experience. It could not be fought simply at the level of ideas, and the government was incapable of fighting it at any other level.

The Japanese made no significant attempt to manipulate popular treatment of ghosts. They never accepted Chinese religion enough to offer alternative interpretations of ghosts. They thus influenced popular religion by repressing it entirely for short periods, or by offering wholesale alternatives like Shinto or Japanese Buddhism. Neither strategy was applied thoroughly enough to have many long-term effects.

Popular religion underwent a resurgence after the first few years of Nationalist rule. By 1950, the Universal Salvation festival again thrived. Markets were crowded and prices were high in the seventh month. Beggars frequented major temples. In Beitou, a northern suburb of Taibei noted for its nightlife, a major temple sacrificed 200 pigs, and the bar girls asked for the night off (XSB, 29 August, 1950, p. 5). The same article that reported the popularity of the festival made some attempt to suggest a new image of ghosts. Watching the people free to worship in Taiwan reminded the reporter of the suffering of those who could neither live nor die in peace on the mainland. Ghosts, he was suggesting, were the people living under Communist rule, and people should contribute their money to efforts to retake the mainland rather than wasting their wealth on popular religion.

The decades that followed continued to see official attempts to discourage the ceremony. As time went on, these attempts became more rhetorical and less repressive. The 1948 slogan about suppressing insurrection and being frugal became 'rigorously enforce frugality' (*li xing jie yue*) by 1955 (XSB, 2 september, 1955, p. 5), and had eased still further to 'encourage frugality' (*gu li jie yue*) by 1960 (XSB, 3 September, 1960, p. 3). Frugality became the overriding ideological theme; mutual feasting, ritual food offerings, and the festival itself were blamed for wasting precious resources that could have been used to help retake the mainland, to build Taiwan's economy, or to help the needy at home. There is an implicit similarity to the late imperial state cult view of ghosts. Ghosts are the needy, and the people should contribute to the government, who will help those in need, rather than to the ghosts themselves. The government also tried a secondary ideological theme, which held that the festival was really a Buddhist ceremony of filial piety for deceased ancestors, and that people should thus stop offering meat and forget all about pitiful or dangerous ghosts.[53] This ideal also harks back to the state cult's denial that ghosts really form a marginal category outside government control. Modern official attempts to manipulate the meaning of ghosts are not as systematized as the state cult had been, but both manipulations shared the vain effort to undercut the political and economic experience that shaped popular treatment of ghosts.

Newspaper accounts of the Universal Salvation festival in 1960 illustrate both many of the official attempts to manipulate the festival, and their general failure. By this time, the government had largely succeeded in what would be its only victory in this battle; it had gotten people to perform the ritual primarily on the fifteenth of the seventh lunar month, rather than on various days scattered throughout the month. On the lunar thirteenth (3 September), the government held meetings to discourage people from sacrificing whole pigs or from offering large feasts. They were supposed to contribute the money they saved to local reconstruction. Each area would report how much it had saved, and the most successful would receive prizes (XSB, 3 September, 1960, p. 3). The next day, however, the financial section reported that the price of pork was much higher, and that to meet the demand for pork offerings, 1500 pigs would be killed for the Taibei market that day, and 1800 were planned for the next day. This contrasted with a normal average of 1030–40 pigs per day (XSB, 4 September, 1960, p. 6).[54] On the lunar fifteenth in 1960, the papers again urged frugality and donations to the poor. Although the ceremony would not take place until that afternoon, the paper also claimed that people in Taibei were indeed more frugal than before. An editorial on the same page, however, gave a very different impression. It said that the government was holding its meetings again this year, but that they would probably have no more effect than they had in any other year (XSB, 5 September, 1960, p. 3). It was thus already clear by 1960 that the government was not having any effect.

When I saw the festival in 1976, 1977 and 1978, the government had already given up on its meetings, although it continued to editorialize about frugality, the evils of conspicuous consumption, and the real meaning of the ceremony being filial piety. The indirect effects of the government campaign appeared at the meeting in Sanxia's Co Su Kong temple (which I discussed in Chapter 2), where Professor Li and Tan Kim-thian suggested that Sanxia institute some of the government's frugality measures. They wanted to require people to bring only vegetable offerings. Various aspects of the temple reconstruction required government approval, and Professor Li was under pressure to cut down on the temple's rituals or face denial of his requests. As I discussed, the people of Sanxia simply ignored the suggested reforms. Government pressure through the temple had no effect. Each year the officials express their position, and each year the people ignore that position.

The Nationalist government failed to discourage lavish expenditures on the Universal Salvation festival for the same reasons that the traditional government failed. First, it created no institution that could impose its version of ghosts as the correct reading. The meetings it sponsored during the first years of its regime were a step in that direction, but they probably did not reach the public much better than the state cult rituals had. Second, popular interpretations of ghostly marginality are shaped by political and economic experience. As long as the interpretation of ghosts is tied to experience, it cannot be countered simply at the level of ideas.

The Limits to Mystification

The passive elite cosmology lent itself easily to political uses. Elite manipulation began with some of the unified concerns of Chinese religion – especially kinship, community and politics – trying to foster a particular interpretation that favored their position. The elite saw its passive pantheon, in part, as a mechanism of social control.

Some Marxists have argued the more extreme case that ideologies in general support the ruling class by mystifying the true nature of power, by disguising contradictions in the social system, and by supporting traditional authority. Godelier (1975, p. 84), for example, argues that religion among the Pawnee and Wichita served such a mystifying function: 'Religion legitimates the domination of the chiefs of the dominant lineages. But one also perceives that this domination is shared by both the dominated and the dominating. There inheres in religion, therefore, the source of a violence without violence, the ideal cement for exploitative social relations.'[55]

Mystification theories illuminate certain aspects of Chinese religion. The widely shared heavenly bureaucracy, for example, helps make secular politics seem natural and beyond questioning. Yet analysis of the Universal Salvation festival shows attempts at religious domination could fail. Even when much religious symbolism was shared (as for feeding ghosts), differing styles of interpretation created a greater religious diversity than mystification theories recognize.

After a review of the dominant ideologies of feudal and capitalist Europe, Abercrombie and Turner (1978, p. 149) conclude that:

> There is good evidence that the subordinate classes are not incorporated into the dominant ideology and that, by contrast, the dominant classes are deeply penetrated by and incorporated within the dominant belief system. In most societies the apparatus of transmission of the dominant ideology is not very efficient and, in any event, is typically directed at the dominant rather than the subordinate class.

The Universal Salvation festival and the state cult support the same conclusion. The government manipulation of ghosts consistently failed because it could not penetrate popular styles of interpretation. Mystification theories point to an important pressure on Chinese religion to conform to the structure of power, and the traditional elite increased those pressures through the state cult. Yet they never succeeded in fully controlling the interpretations of other groups. The particular styles of interpretation of non-elites, and the social relations in which they exist, always created a counter-pressure against a complete and effective hegemony. Unity and diversity in Chinese religion thus interlock. The general concern of the entire secular population with kinship, community and politics helped to unify religion around those concerns. Yet the varying social relations of different segments of the population led to diverse styles of interpretation, and allowed that diversity to persist in spite of official attempts to impose a unified religious ideology.

6 Unities, Diversities and Reinterpretation

Chinese religion is neither simply unified nor simply diverse. The varying social relations of its adherents allow interpretation and reinterpretation of religious symbols to create both unities and diversities. Approaching these interpretations as active processes in a social context has helped analyze three main points about Chinese religion in Taiwan:

(1) Different groups utilize fundamentally diverse styles of interpretation. At one extreme, the popular tradition offers no systematic explanations for most religious acts. People interpret much of their religion piecemeal, in relation to the immediate social context. The religious ideologies of the state cult and accomplished Buddhists or Taoists are more systematized or more passive. Institutionalized social relations, such as those promoted by the state or a monastery, develop religious ideologies most fully, and they control interpretation by enforcing their own version of orthodoxy.

(2) Religious interpretations may change as social conditions change. Less ideologized interpretations may change more flexibly, because they escape most institutional control. More ideologized beliefs change as their institutions change, or when those institutions lose control over their ideologies.

(3) Unities and diversities across styles of interpretation rest on the particular social relations of the people involved. Basic unities – like a religious concern for secular politics, community and kinship – persist because they fit the experience of many social groups. Groups like the state or the priestly elite push for unity by trying to universalize their own positions. Yet the flexibility of religion allows diverse social groups to offer very different reinterpretations of unified concerns.

This chapter examines each of these conclusions in more detail, and expands on them by supplementing the Universal Salvation rites with data from other aspects of Chinese religion. It concentrates especially on the political and social implications of religious unities and diversities.

Diverse Interpretations

I have analyzed the styles of interpretation in the Universal Salvation rites using two broad dimensions: pragmatic/systematized, and active/passive. Gods, ancestors and ghosts in the popular tradition usually get pragmatic, active interpretations. People talk about these spirits, and behave toward them, as if they were embodied beings who really affect the world. Many people recognize the moral or psychological functions of religion, and many also see it as a metaphor for the secular world, but the convincing qualities of the popular tradition stem above all from the active reality of its spirits.

Most people do not systematize their interpretations very thoroughly. The simple gods/ancestors/ghosts distinction, and its structural reflections in incense, paper spirit money, and other ritual media, sets the basis for interpretation, but it does not determine people's specific understandings. Instead their interpretations have a strong pragmatic element – ghosts, for example, exist in relation to the current political, social and economic contexts, as well as in relation to gods and ancestors. Thus, the structural contrast of ghosts to gods and ancestors has not changed over the last century, but pragmatic interpretations of ghosts have been transformed from dangerous bandits to pitiful beggars. The popular tradition has little systematized ideology of ghosts (beyond the contrast with gods and ancestors) that would lead people to a particular interpretation, nor does it have any institution that might preserve and promulgate a systematized interpretation.

Other religious traditions ideologize their beliefs by making them more systematized or more passive. Systematized interpretations claim to be aloof from the political and economic influences on popular interpretations, and they claim to resolve the contradictions across social contexts that characterize the popular tradition. Buddhist or Taoist interpretations of ghosts, for example, do not change from one ritual context to the next (as popular interpretations do).

In reality, systematized ideologies, like any system of meaning, can be reinterpreted in new social contexts. Institutions try to protect their ideologies from reinterpretation by controlling the context – they teach, legitimize, and enforce 'orthodox' interpretations, and they record those interpretations in texts, whose interpretations they must protect in turn. The form of the institution can range from the master–pupil ties of modern Taiwanese Taoism or geomancy to the more powerful control of monastic Buddhism or the traditional state cult. The popular tradition has the least control over context: there is no priesthood, there are no initiations into the religion, and popular temples make only weak attempts to control interpretation (as in the failed attempt to control offerings to the ghosts at the Co Su Kong temple). The popular tradition remains more pragmatic than the other traditions, and more open to immediate reinterpretation as the political economy changes.

The modern, and at least some of the traditional, elite often uses passive interpretations of religion. The active spirits of other traditions become metaphors that lead people to proper behavior. The elite stresses the moral and psychological functions of religion, but generally dismisses the possibility of using active spirits to achieve real empirical results. Passive interpretations encouraged the elite to use religion as a political tool, as when they deified patriots, raised memorial arches to chaste widows, or brought warring factions together to worship the ghosts.

The more ideologized styles of interpretation are strongest when an institution controls interpretation by limiting access to texts, and by channelling reinterpretation. Professionals monopolize these systems, thus protecting their means of livelihood. If everyone knew how to write charms, for example, the income of some specialists would be reduced sharply. Taoists are not content to rely on the complexity of their traditions to make it difficult for others to learn their trade secrets; they actively restrict access to their knowledge by not writing down some information, by accepting few students, and by restricting the information given even to those few students.

These limitations on learning religious knowledge encourage most people to reinterpret specialist rituals in terms familiar to them. Most people usually relate the visible bits and pieces of these systems to concepts of the popular religion, in contrast to specialists who draw on their more ideologized interpretations. In Taoism, for example, the reinterpretation is straightforward, because most public rituals share the public pantheon. Thus at a *ciou*, people see the worship of the Emperor of Heaven and of the ghosts as the two most important rituals, since both resemble rituals they themselves perform. The meditative rituals associated with the more uniquely Taoist Three Pure Ones are performed in private inside the temple. People do not understand the details of the performance, nor do they have access to the texts, even in public rituals to known gods.

I have already discussed at length how the styles of interpretation of people in different social conditions lead to diverse reinterpretations of the ghost festival. The remainder of this section clarifies this process of reinterpretation of shared symbolic systems for two further areas: geomancy and communication with the gods.

Geomancy Reinterpreted

Geomancy is a technique to harmonize the cosmological characteristics of the time, the landscape, and individual people. People hire geomancers to find the best sites for graves (*yin* dwellings) in order to benefit the descendants, and for houses (*yang* dwellings) in order to benefit the residents. Graves are invariably sited under the guidance of a geomancer. Even Christians sometimes rely on geomancers to site graves. Although modern houses are generally built without the help of a geomancer, his help is still considered necessary for houses built in the traditional style. In either case, people often ask geomancers to determine the proper placement of the domestic altar. Geomancers do not help plan new towns in Taiwan, but geomancy often becomes an after-the-fact explanation for a community's fortunes (for examples, see DeGroot, 1897, pp. 949–51; Aijmer, 1968).

The sophisticated workings of geomancy and its basis in five-phase theory were traditionally the province of the educated elite, although the elite were rarely professional practitioners. Of all the practitioners of five-phase theory, geomancers were the most respectable and had the highest elite pretensions. According to DeGroot, the geomancer

> assumes all the airs of the literati and the gentry, dresses, as they do, in a long gown, wears a pair of large spectacles, though not short-sighted, and awes his patrons by . . . speaking a mystifying, learned jargon, and by apocalyptic utterances of which the ordinary Chinaman understands nothing . . . About all their movements there is an air of classic decorum; and it is no wonder, therefore, that the masses regard the geomancers as fountains of wisdom, marvels of learning, capable of fathoming all the mysteries of heaven and earth. (De Groot, 1897, p. 1010)

Freedman also felt that because geomancers have access to a technical system not tied to popular religion, they 'are held in an esteem not shared by other religious practitioners. They are gentlemen and attract the curiosity of gentlemen' (Freedman, 1966, p. 124). My own primary informant on geomancy was a wealthy man, the son of one of Sanxia's few traditional degree-holders. Not all geomancers, however, were kindly old scholars. Some knew only enough to convince their customers, others manipulated their recommendations to increase profits, some were in it only because they failed the traditional examinations. DeGroot's sarcasm was not entirely unfounded. Nevertheless, people continue to associate geomancy, and five-phase theory in general, with scholarship. Highly structured ideologies like geomancy are difficult to learn, because an entire system must be mastered. In addition, specialists tend to guard their knowledge as trade secrets. Interpretations of five-phase theory are just as tied to institutionalized systems of socialization as other ideologies like Buddhism or Taoism. In fact, geomancers go through a system of apprenticeship much like the system I have already described for the Taoists.

Geomancy and five-phase theory provide an abstract explanation of the world that bypasses the personified spirits of the other traditions I discuss. Both five-phase theory and Western science, the two primary sets of impersonal explanations in Taiwan, are strongly ideologized. Like Western science, the concepts of five-phase theory are not self-evident, and only people with extensive educations can interpret the theory in detail.

Five-phase theory, like Buddhism, Taoism or the popular tradition, explains the world. They all answer questions like why people get sick, how they get wealthy, and so on. Yet five-phase theory differs from the others by answering these questions through the analysis of various impersonal, natural forces like *yin* and *yang*. Geomancy thus allows identification of another range in styles of interpretation, from the impersonal categories of five-phase theory, to the personified beings of the popular tradition. As this section will show, other traditions consistently reinterpret the geomancer's impersonal categories as personified beings.

I will give just a single example of how geomancers analyze a site, based on descriptions common to many geomancy manuals and generally used by Taiwanese geomancers. (Appendix A gives a more detailed discussion of professional geomancy, emphasizing techniques not discussed in the Western literature.) A structure of impersonal categories, called the four animals (*si shou*), describes the immediate vicinity of a site. These are the Azure Dragon (*qing long*, associated with east, spring, wood and the birth of *yang*), the Red Bird (*zhu que*, associated with south, summer, fire, maximum *yang*), the White Tiger (*bai hu*, associated with west, autumn, metal and the

Figure 6.1   Embracing the Site

Source: Ye, 1973, Juan 2, p. 17

birth of *yin*), and the Sombre Warrior (*xuan wu*, either a turtle or a turtle and a snake entwined in intercourse, associated with north, winter, water and maximum *yin*). Ideally, a site has its back to the North, from which the mountain protects it. The Azure Dragon is an embracing arm of hills to the left (ascendant, *yang*) side, and should be slightly larger than the White Tiger hills at the right (*yin*) side. The front of the site (Red Bird) should be a clearing proportional to the size and importance of the grave or dwelling. It should contain gently flowing water, and it should be blocked by another hill in the distance.[56] Figure 6.1 shows a mountain chain with potential sites marked by circles. Many sites, of course, do not face exactly South.

No matter what the direction, however, the Sombre Warrior is the back, the Red Bird is the front, and so on. In geomancy, therefore, the Four Animals effectively refer to the front, back and sides of the site, not to the cardinal points. Note that the concrete characteristics of dragons, birds, tigers and turtles are irrelevant; they are simply names for impersonal concepts.

Geomancy's use of such impersonal forces made it a less obvious social metaphor than the other traditions, and its esoteric, relatively institutionalized theoretical system helped guard it from easy reinterpretation. The specialist interpretation of geomancy is relatively insulated from the political economy; geomancers do not constantly reinterpret the general meaning of the White Tiger, the way the popular tradition reinterprets ghosts. Geomancy is not, however, apolitical for the elite; specific applications of geomancy do react to the political context. Geomancy could claim a morally neutral empirical basis (and thus avoid the official damnation that met some religious groups), but the particular uses of its findings often had political implications.[57]

On the one hand, geomancy can support traditional authority. It ties directly into the system of Neo-Confucian philosophy, which the imperial government adopted as its basis. It emphasizes a balanced interaction between man and the world, which is controlled best by people with intellectual and temporal power (especially the Emperor). It affirms the official view of society as a meritocracy where the most capable are the most educated and thus given the most power.

On the other hand, however, geomancy's reliance on morally neutral impersonal forces allows the use of geomancy without respect for authority, or even in opposition to it. For example, insurgents in imperial times sometimes destroyed imperial tombs, hoping to undermine the dynasty by ruining its geomancy (DeGroot, 1897, p. 1052). DeGroot (1897, p. 1052) even suggested that 'should European armies have for a second time to march on Peking, it will be worth while trying whether the campaign cannot be shortened and loss of life spared by a military occupation of the burial ground of the Imperial Family'.

Geomancy also helped ignite the lineage feuds that often plagued the traditional government; one group would try to steal the propitious dragon veins of another (e.g., Baker, 1979, pp. 219–25). The authorities frowned on this use of geomancy, as in a section of the Qing legal code translated by DeGroot:

If some one, coveting another's burial ground which brings good luck (to the offspring), has fraudulently dug up a grave of ancient date, and the descendants of that dead person lodge a complaint against him with the magistrates, who, on investigating the case, find incontestable proofs of the crime, the perpetrator thereof shall be condemned to strangulation. (DeGroot, 1897, p. 878)

Geomancy also allowed people to challenge the building of missions and railroads in the nineteenth century (DeGroot, 1897, pp. 1042–9). Similarly, people in the New Territories often demand government restitution for the geomantic damage done by new construction. Thus, among the elite, geomancy sometimes supported traditional authority, and sometimes opposed it. This political ambivalence was possible because the systematized, active and impersonal style of interpretation in elite geomancy allowed it to appear politically neutral.

Freedman (1966, p. 126) described geomancy as an amoral system in which 'the dead were passive agents, pawns in a kind of ritual game played by their descendants with the help of geomancers'. He contrasted the competitive uses of geomancy to ancestral tablet worship, which he saw as stressing moral goals and family harmony.

Whereas in ancestor worship men are under the dominance of their dead fathers (and of the dead of remoter generations), so that a hierarchy of forebears imposes a restraint upon the relations of living descendants, in the geomancy of burial men liberate themselves from their ancestors to give themselves up to an anarchic pursuit of narrow self-interest. (Freedman, 1966, p. 142).

Freedman's distinction supports the claim that members of the educated elite distinguish between a moral, animate, 'religious' system (including tablet worship) that affirms traditional values of harmony, filial piety, etc., and an amoral, impersonal 'theoretical' system (including geomancy) that can make more varied statements, and can even go against the grain of official moral principles like fraternal respect.

Several authors, however, have suggested that Freedman's distinction may be valid only for professionals in the theory (Ahern, 1973; Li, 1976; and, briefly, Freedman himself, 1966, p. 126). Indeed, a closer look shows that the popular tradition thoroughly reinterprets geomancy, transforming it from a systematized, impersonal theory to a pragmatic, personified set of beliefs. Geomancy may contrast with religion and morality for the elite, but it is part of religion in the popular tradition.

Few people can afford the geomantic manipulations that can create intra-family competition. The great majority of families bury their dead in public graveyards, where geomancers only align the direction of the coffin. My findings in Sanxia tally with Ahern's (1973, pp. 185–8) that geomancy is not an important weapon in fraternal competition. Thus the poor, who cannot afford to find ideal geomantic sites, are also unlikely to challenge official kinship morality by using geomancy as an amoral tool for the pursuit of narrow self-interest. Amoral geomancy remained a technique for the elite.

Freedman, however, argues that the interpretations of geomancy by different people are essentially alike:

> Just as in Neo-Confucian philosophical writings the concretizing words *shen* and *kuei* [*gui*] (which are ordinarily translatable as gods and demons, respectively) are used for positive and negative spiritual forces, beings stripped of their anthropomorphic connotations . . . so in popular religion a reverse transformation is worked by which the disembodied forces of the geomancer are turned into personal entities. (Freedman, 1969, p. 10)

Freedman concludes that this change is a surface transformation (from impersonal to personified) of a shared deep structure. Yet this transformation has more far-reaching implications than Freedman discussed. The popular version of geomancy is personified and active, as Freedman contends. It is also combined, however, with the personified and active world of gods, ghosts and ancestors. As a result, popular geomancy shares the political and social messages of the popular cosmology, and contrasts with the elite versions of both. In the popular version, ancestors in the grave become active beings who enforce kinship values. Geomancy is no longer the amoral, flexible, impersonal system of the professional.[58]

There are several types of evidence for this popular reinterpretation of geomancy. First, spirit mediums (*tang-ki*) often ascribe problems of the living to geomancy (Li, 1976). Although the reasons for these problems sometimes include the grave being in the wrong location, other reasons run counter to the professional tradition: the ancestor is uncomfortable or unsafe in the grave, the descendants neglect the spirit in the grave, an ancestor regrets being buried with a person he or she does not like, and so on. Geomancy in this view is a world of animate, moral beings.

Secondly, in ordinary conversations people often stress the physical comfort of the ancestor in a grave. Many say they do not want to be buried with people they do not like. The scenery must also be pleasant, and eyesores detract from the geomancy of a site. Only a comfortable ancestor will bring harmony to his or her descendants (see also Ahern, 1973, pp. 180–2, Anderson and Anderson, 1973, p. 132).

Finally, the way that non-professionals occasionally used technical terms clearly personifies the impersonal system of the geomancer and ties it into the popular cosmology. One woman, for example, explained that the geomancy of her house was bad, and that her daughter had lost a lot of money as a result. She hired a geomancer who told her that a hill in front of the house was a White Tiger. In geomancy, as I explained above, White Tiger is the hill to the right of the site, and is not automatically good or bad. The geomancer probably concluded that the five-phase value of the shape or position of the hill conflicted with that of the home and its residents. In Taoism and the popular tradition, however, the White Tiger is a demon who must be exorcised. In addition, the hill was a public graveyard, and, according to this informant, it resembled a tiger's head. She had reinterpreted the morally neutral, impersonal geomantic 'White Tiger' as an evil demon. Ahern cites a similar example where an informant claimed a factory chimney 'hit' (*chiong*, Mandarin *chong*, also 'clashed') the grave of his ancestor. *Chiong* is a technical term for an unlucky relation between pairs of Earthly Branches in the professional's version of geomancy (see Appendix A). This informant, however, meant not only that the smoke from the chimney might make his dead grandmother unhappy (Ahern, 1973, p. 182). The impersonal, systematized concepts of expert geomancy have become concrete and context-bound.

Taoists often reinterpret geomancy in a similar way.[59] Taoists occasionally serve as geomancers, but they do not use the expert system. Instead, they adapt their own system of a powerful, active bureaucracy to meet the requirements of geomantic siting. They rely entirely on the techniques of *huat*, ignoring the geomancer's specialized forms and principles. Taoists use their position and power in the heavenly bureaucracy to get imperial approval (*chi*) of every aspect of a site.[60] Their concrete pantheon replaces the geomancer's abstract categories.

Taoists also perform a ritual at the opening of all new temples, based on their own version of geomancy. The ritual is called Settling the Dragon and Sending Off the Tiger (*an long song hu*). The dragon can be interpreted either as the mountain chain leading to the site of the temple (*shan long*), or as the Azure Dragon which, in geomancy, represents ascending yang, spring, left and so forth. The Tiger is the geomancer's White Tiger, associated with ascending yin, autumn, right, and so forth. Both beings are embodied in paper figures in the ritual, and a second dragon is also formed from rice, coins and oil lamps. The Taoist addresses both personified spirits: he threatens the evil Tiger and bribes him to leave, while he convinces the beneficent Dragon to stay. As in the popular version of geomancy, the professional's impersonal categories become personified and tied to a cosmology filled with similar beings.

Professional geomancy and chronomancy include a technique called the Unique Gate of the Hidden Jia, and Taoists have a system of magic that uses the same name. The geomancer's technique correlates nine of the ten Heavenly Stems with the nine squares of a magic square called the Luo Shu (Liang, 1976; see also Appendix A). The remaining stem, *jia*, is replaced by one of the other nine, which explains the term 'Hidden Jia' in the title of the system. In the cycle of sixty stem-branches, *jia* (like every other Stem) appears six times, each time associated with a different branch. The Taoist technique (described by Saso, 1978, ch. 4) uses many of the same technical terms, but reinterprets them as personified spirits. The six combinations of *jia* and a branch in the cycle are called the Six Jia Spirits.

> Each of the Six Chia [Jia] Spirits is a general leading an army of spiritual soldiers. All are ready to leap forth at the summons and call of the Taoist, provided he has gained power over them by a knowledge of the talismanic charms and mantric incantations of the nine polar stars. (Saso, 1978, p. 142)

The 'nine polar stars' are the Big Dipper and two nearby stars; they are the residence of the Six Jia Spiritis. Again, the impersonal relations of five-phase theory have become personified and bureaucratized. They are part of the general Taoist pantheon.

Reinterpretations of geomancy are not simply surface transfomations of a shared deep structure, as Freedman suggested. These diverse styles of interpretation instead lead to diverse political roles for geomancy. The impersonal forces of elite geomancy allowed the elite to engage in some actions against official authority, and in fraternal competition, even though such behavior contradicted officially sanctioned Confucian morality. The impersonal style of interpretation behind geomancy makes the political ethics of the system seem safe – geomancy appears as politically neutral, empirical truth. The government could never damn it as immoral, the way it damned troublesome religions that relied on personified beings.

In contrast, popular geomancy ties into the personified bureaucracy of gods, ghosts and ancestors. If Grandmother is happy in her grave, her family will prosper; if she is miserable, her descendants will suffer. The personified spirits of the popular tradition cannot become the mere pawns that Freedman discusses in elite geomancy. Popular geomancy merges into the rest of the popular religious tradition, and both share the same political advantages and disadvantages. Both have the possibility of flexible interpretations in new contexts, and both have the limitations of being part of a cosmology that ties closely to the traditional social order. Elite geomancy, in contrast, channels reinterpretation through its institutions, and has greater possibilities to justify politically improper behavior (like fraternal competition) because it relies on impersonal forces.

Talking to the Gods

There are various ways of communicating with the gods in Taiwan; they illustrate the social grounding of different styles of interpretation, and the various political potentials of those styles. This communication takes place in two major contexts: (1) in temples, the most important of which (like Sanxia's temple to Co Su Kong) are controlled by the elite and thus associated with traditional authority; and (2) at spirit medium sessions, which are often opposed by the elite and can sometimes protest against traditional authority.

The simplest way to communicate with gods in a temple is by throwing moonblocks (*puaq pue*). Moonblocks are pairs of crescent-shaped blocks of wood which are flat on one side (*yin*) and rounded on the other (*yang*). After burning incense and offering food and paper spirit money to the gods, a patron may ask questions using the moonblocks. After giving his or her name, address and birthdate, the person asks a question and drops a pair of moonblocks on the ground. If both land with flat sides up, the answer is 'no'; if one is up and the other is down, the answer is 'yes'; and if both land with flat sides down, the god is 'laughing', usually because the person failed to provide enough information in the initial question.

A more complex system is available in a set of lots (*chiam*). The number of lots varies, although sixty is a very common number. This also begins with worship of the god, followed by throwing the moonblocks to ask permission to choose a lot. If permission is granted, one lot is chosen from the set, and the patron throws the moonblocks again to make sure it is the correct lot. Each lot has a number on it, and the patron can get a verse that goes with that particular lot. These verses are generally very condensed and metaphoric, and most people turn to the temple management for interpretation. The slip of paper on which each verse is printed usually includes a list of possible questions and very brief indications of how the poem answers them. The types of questions supplied are very limited in range; there is no way to ask, for example, about whether a rebellion will succeed or whether to join a heterodox sect (see Ahern, 1981b, pp. 88–9). Unusual questions can be asked only by turning to the temple management for help. The inherent ambiguity of the verse permits more flexible interpretations. As I showed in Chapter 2, however, the temple management are often members of the educated elite. They are unlikely to provide interpretations that challenge their own positions of authority. In general, choosing lots allows only a very narrow range of interpretations.

While this system of verse interpretation is not nearly as systematized as Buddhism, Taoism, or the state cult, it still shares some features with those traditions. It is more institutionalized than much of the popular tradition; the temple management may base its interpretations on written texts to which they limit access; and the management can partially monopolize interpretation, especially by limiting the number of questions that can be asked. The management's monopoly on interpretation is hardly complete, because new questions and new readings of the verses are always possible. Any text is open to potential reinterpretation. Yet this system in practice tends to accept (if not necessarily to serve actively) the interests of the local elite who control it. In general, drawing lots allows for harmless answers to politically safe questions.

Spirit medium (*tang-ki*) sessions provide a second context for communicating with gods. Spirit medium sessions in Sanxia do not occur in the major temples, but instead use small temples, ancestor halls, or private houses. A god possesses the medium, who will speak or write the god's answers to people's questions. For a small fee, anyone can speak directly to the god. The god's speech may be slightly stylized, but everyone understands it, and the interactions often resemble natural conversation. Bystanders sit and talk casually, and they show little special respect for the god. Unlike the system of drawing lots, no one has direct control over the questions asked, and everyone is in a position to provide his or her own interpretation. Interpretation is very pragmatic because no institution really controls it. With minor variations, spirit mediums practice in this fashion throughout Taiwan, and practiced similarly in late imperial times throughout southeastern China.

Politically safe interpretations of spirit medium sessions are the rule, at least in modern-day Taiwan. Most of the questions concern illness, and about half of the diagnoses refer to relatives of the questioner rather than to some group with wider political significance (Li, 1976, p. 330). Yet spirit medium sessions offer a potential for much more flexible interpretation than drawing lots. Because people are free to ask their own questions, and to provide their own pragmatic interpretations grounded in the political context, spirit mediums create the possibility for political dissidence. Seaman (1978, pp. 106–18), for example, describes how spirit mediums representing several political factions in central Taiwan waged a supernatural battle. In the turbulent years after the Japanese departure from Taiwan in 1945, two mediums battled for supremacy. One was tied to a group of landlords and their supporters; the other was tied to a group of freeholders. One evening, the same god possessed both mediums at once, a paradox that required immediate resolution:

> Chiu announced himself as 'The Second Brother Chen-Wu' and so did Pan: a long argument, of accusation and counteraccusation, followed. Then the two shamans [mediums] began a 'magical struggle'. The struggle became more and more intense, until at last Chiu picked up a sawfish bill sword, one of the ritual weapons of the shaman, and split Pan's forehead with it, knocking him senseless. Pan was never again possessed after this, and the authenticity of Chiu's possession was admitted by all concerned. (Seaman, 1978, p. 115)

Chiu's faction continued by discrediting and then destroying a religious plaque important to Pan's group. This turned out to be an error, because Pan's allies had Chiu arrested, and Chiu too was never again possessed. Communication with gods through spirit mediums can transcend passive approval of political orthodoxy, because the style of interpretation remains more pragmatic and flexible than communication with gods in elite-controlled community temples.

Both the traditional and modern elites actively discourage spirit mediums. The traditional Chinese government passed laws against spirit possession (see, for example, Overmyer, 1976, p. 24). The Japanese colonial government in Taiwan frowned on cults whose mediums urged a boycott of Japanese goods (Seaman, 1978, pp. 26–7). The current government often accuses mediums of fakery and extortion; it is taking gradual steps to outlaw them. These governments did not oppose mediums simply when they made dissident statements; the great majority of spirit medium sessions are politically innocuous. Instead these governments opposed them because their pragmatic flexibility immunized interpretation completely from state control, and thus created a great *potential* for dissident interpretation.[61]

Three Dimensions in Styles of Interpretation

People involved in different social relations interpret shared ritual codes in systematically diverse ways. Geomancy can be personified or impersonal, the cosmology can be active or passive, and both can be more or less systematized, depending on who interprets them (see Table 6.1). These three dimensions of interpretation – pragmatic/systematized, personified/impersonal, and active/passive – clarify one of the basic diversities in Chinese religion. Even shared religious concerns, like politics or community, are realized differently as people see them through different styles of interpretation embedded in different kinds of social relations. Thus the popular tradition I described in Chapters 2 and 3 is less explicit, less abstracted from the immediate social context, less dependent on structural systems of contrast, more active, and more personified than the other traditions.

Systematized, self-conscious ideologies typify elite and specialist traditions. The Buddhists and Taoists I have discussed so far share with geomancy and the state cult extensive education in a complex system of meanings. The Buddhist and Taoist intellectuals who developed these systems and who use them with the greatest sophistication were in fact closely tied to the elites. Officials themselves were sometimes learned contributors to Buddhism and Taoism. Furthermore, the large land-holdings of some mainland monasteries made

Table 6.1   Styles of Interpretation

	Systematized	Passive	Impersonal
Popular tradition	−	−	−
Buddhism	+	−	−
Taoism	+	−	−
Modern elite pantheon	−	+	−
State cult	+	+	−
Five-element theory	+	−	+

them structurally similar to secular power holders. Like elite ideologies, the Buddhist and Taoist traditions are the product of a leisured intelligentsia. Such uses of time are limited to those whose livelihood is guaranteed, and social institutions like the state and the monastery control access to such guarantees. They reinforce their control by reserving the right to determine orthodox interpretations, and thus channel some of the flexibility of the popular beliefs.

There is thus no mechanical dichotomy between pragmatic and ideologized interpretation. Religion becomes ideologized (that is, more systematized, passive, or impersonal) in various ways, and to varying degrees, according to the social relations of the people involved. Even the more complex sets of dichotomies I summarize in Table 6.1 should not disguise the fundamental flexibility of all styles of interpretation.

Thus, Buddhism and Taoism share some of the 'magical' character of the popular tradition: they deal with active, concrete beings. They are, however, more highly ideologized than the popular religion as a result of their long histories of intellectual systematization. The elite really makes use of two separate systems. The first is their version of the pantheon, which tends to be more passive and more systematized (in the case of the state cult), but which still consists of concrete, animate beings. The second is five-phase theory, which is abstract and highly systematized, but which deals with active forces (recall that Weber calls it 'magical'). There is no simple dichotomy between rationalized and magical thought (although some traditions have developed more elaborate structures of explanation), between literate and illiterate thought (although some traditions rely heavily on texts), or between logical and illogical thought (although some traditions show inconsistencies if social context is ignored). Instead, styles of interpretation change with social conditions.

Certain styles of interpretation help or hinder attempts at political mystification. The passive style of the state cult made it a good vehicle for official morality, while the impersonal style of elite geomancy made it difficult to bend entirely to the political ends of the state. In general, the state is always trying to use religion to legitimize itself. Diverse reinterpretations, however, guarantee that mystification never succeeds entirely. State manipulations of religion never had the desired effect on the populace, because the pragmatic, uninstitutionalized (and thus relatively uncontrolled) style of interpretation in the popular tradition produced flexible re-readings of official ritual, rooted in the everyday experience of the populace (as for the failed attempts to manipulate the ghost cult). We must look beyond shared ritual codes to style of interpretation, and to control over interpretation.[62]

Making Ideologies

My emphasis on interpretation over code, on how people actively make meaning in particular social relations, implies that any ritual act allows many interpretations. Strong institutions may try to monopolize the right to determine 'orthodox' interpretation, but they never entirely succeed in eliminating alternate styles of interpretation. I have stressed that different styles of interpretation are embedded in particular social conditions, both reflecting and changing those conditions: the alternative world-view of Buddhism rests on its isolated monastic institutions; the political uses of the passive state cult rest on the political interests of the government; the flexible reinterpretations of the popular tradition rest on its lack of strong institutions; and so on.

The constant making of new meaning allows styles of interpretation to merge into one another. This section explores some of the conditions under which interpretations change. In the following three examples, adherents of the popular tradition systematize initially pragmatic interpretations. Each example concerns a relationship to Buddhism, but each also shows one of the major processes that can create ideologized interpretations. In the first example, an individual religious philosopher gradually explores various ways of systematizing his beliefs. In the second example, the Buddhist clergy gives its lay adherents a conscious push into Buddhist ideology and institutions. In the third example, religious sects rework Buddhist ideology when the original institutions lose control over interpretation.[63]

Looking for the Way

In many communities on Taiwan individuals create idiosyncratic ideologies by combining pragmatic ritual traditions and some contact with religious specialists. These people are the Chinese equivalent of Radin's (1927) 'primitive philosophers' – contemplative individuals who develop complex theories out of a less systematized set of popular traditions. Ong A-liong, an artist employed in the reconstruction of Sanxia's Co Su Kong temple, is one such individual.

When I first met Ong in 1976, he did not appear especially concerned with religion, although his job as a religious artist gave him a more systematized understanding of iconography than most people have. By the time I returned to Taiwan in 1977, however, Ong had begun a more intensive search for religious meaning. While my assistant, a friend and I stood in the temple plaza one day, Ong beckoned us over. He was expecting us, he said; that morning, while he meditated, Co Su Kong had given him an insight that three good people would visit. Ong knew from our faces that we must be the visitors. We had a long conversation, during which Ong outlined the systematized ideology that he was creating out of his pragmatic religious experience. His discourse centered on Co Su Kong and many of the religious images he had carved. In this early stage of his search, he still concentrated on his extensive immediate experience with the temple. Yet he also expanded on some ideas that are common in the popular tradition, but rarely thought through. He talked about face-reading, a skill based on five-phase theory, which everyone knows about, but few people practice. Ong had apparently not studied the five-phase techniques of face-reading, but began to develop his own system that combined facial features and personality features. He had also expanded and systematized the common cliché that 'the five religions (Buddhism, Christianity, Confucianism, Islam and Taoism) are one'. He spoke with more facility about Western religion than anyone in Sanxia, and constantly pressed me for details about Christianity and Judaism. He still concentrated his efforts, however, on the Co Su Kong temple.

By the end of the year, Ong seemed less interested in developing his own, idiosyncratic, ideology and more interested in mastering an extant system. He began to read more Buddhist sutras, and asked me to buy him a Bible. Most importantly he had found a master in a nearby town. This master was idiosyncratic in his own right, but relied most heavily on Taoism and five-phase theory. Like a Chinese storybook holy man, he usually looked ragged and poor, and few people (except for Ong, of course) trusted him. Ong absorbed his master's ideology in the usual master–disciple pattern – he received esoteric knowledge in dribs and drabs, as the master gradually tested his faith, patience and loyalty. As Ong began to pull together this new knowledge, he passed some of his secrets on to me, swearing me to secrecy, and warning of their power. The most important was a Taoist meditation technique that symbolically placed the five phases in the order of mutual creation. This second stage of Ong's search saw him looking to his master's already established, but not very institutionalized ideology.

By the end of 1978, Ong had largely broken his ties with his master, perhaps because he began to believe the rumors about the master's iniquities, perhap because he had grown beyond what his master could teach. He began to turn toward a more thoroughly systematized, ideologized set of interpretations – Buddhism. The five religions remained valid paths, but Buddhism had become the most powerful for Ong. At the end of 1978, he joined me on an interview with a very famous nun in the northern suburbs of Taipei. By the time I left in 1979, Ong had taken lay Buddhist vows, with the nun as his new teacher. He seemed satisfied, both intellectually and emotionally, for the first time since he had begun his systematizing two years earlier.

Individuals face great difficulties systematizing their beliefs on their own. Not only is the intellectual challenge considerable, but publicly proclaiming truly idiosyncratic ideologies can lead to accusations of eccentricity and superstition. Ong never tried to be completely idiosyncratic – he always consulted religious texts, and soon turned to his semi-Taoist master. This path had its own problems. Ong's master and his other disciples formed the beginnings of a religious counter-institution, centered on a small temple with which the master was involved. As such, this network faced opposition from more established institutions, especially the state. Eccentricity at this point becomes heterodoxy, and adherents face serious social pressure. In response, Ong turned toward Buddhism, an established, institutionalized religious ideology.

Buddhists and Laymen

The most standard path to a systematized ideology is through the institution that fosters it. This section briefly examines how Buddhists interact with most of the visitors to their temples – followers of the popular tradition. The general strategy is to keep people coming to the temples by encouraging their pragmatic interpretations of Buddhism, and then gradually substituting more orthodox interpretations for new adherents, while bringing them into ever greater social contact with Buddhist institutions.

An example of popular reinterpretation of Buddhist iconography began this book. Although Buddhist temples generally look very different from temples in the popular tradition, popular reinterpretations smooth out these differences, as my neighbor showed me in the early days of my research. Buddhist altars usually contain three primary images representing three associated Buddhas or Bodhisattvas. To the ordinary worshipper, however, all are Hut Co (the Buddha Patriarch), just as many of the images in Sanxia's main temple are all Co Su Kong. Statues of the Buddhist Protectors of the Dharma become the door gods found on all large popular temples. Most people offer the Buddhas paper spirit money, which is one of the clearest ways people ritually mark the non-Buddhist distinction among gods, ancestors and ghosts (Wolf, 1974b). Some Buddhist temples even offer some rituals from the popular tradition, like the *po-un*.

Taoists and geomancers encourage popular ignorance of their traditions because it guarantees their control, but Buddhists have a different attitude. They are aware of the popular reinterpretation but do little about it for two reasons. First, like all temple managers, their income depends heavily on popular support and donations, and they are thus afraid to antagonize people by challenging their traditions. The second reason is the Buddhist concept of *upaya*, teaching at the level that best suits the student. Any kind of contact with Buddhism, the clergy feel, is a useful first step. Later, perhaps, they can lead their adherents to stop eating meat, join a sutra recitation group, and gradually come to accept a more sophisticated version of Buddhism. Some Buddhist temples take the stronger step of forbidding people to burn paper spirit money from the start.

The progressive reinterpretations of the Protectors of the Dharma provide one example of how Buddhists transform popular, pragmatic interpretations of temple iconography into more systematized Buddhist ideology. Most worshippers see the statues of the Protectors of the Dharma as door gods, who guard the entrances of temples.[64] The Buddhists do nothing to discourage such readings, but they may suggest a further interpretation to special followers – the red-faced 'door god' is actually Kuan Kong, the red-faced god of war and patron of business, one of the most important figures in the popular tradition. Kuan Kong, according to the clergy, converted to Buddhism, and now protects the faith. This reinterpretation does not bring the adherent especially far into systematized Buddhist ideology – it is a piecemeal adaptation of a critical figure from the popular tradition. This adaptation makes special claims about Buddhism; if Kuan Kong himself guards Buddhist temples, they must be special indeed. Further reinterpretation brings followers still more fully into Buddhist ideology. The Protectors of the Dharma are *really* two Bodhisattvas. At this stage, the Protectors of the Dharma no longer mesh with the popular tradition, but become part of the iconographic representation of Buddhist ideology; they are enlightened beings dedicated to saving souls by guarding the Law (dharma; one of the Three Treasures of Buddhism).

The use of paper spirit money provides an even clearer case of successive reinterpretations fostered by the clergy. The Buddhist temple in Kiu Kiong Kiou allows people to use gold (for the Buddhas and Bodhisattvas here, but normally for the gods) and silver (for the ancestors or ghosts) spirit money, although it does not approve. The chief nun, however, often encourages people to use only gold money, telling a story of how a paper manufacturer solved a crisis of overproduction by tricking people into burning silver paper for the dead. This seemingly minor ritual point in fact cuts out one of the structural underpinnings of the popular cosmology: spirit money no longer distinguishes gods from ghosts and ancestors. From this stage, it is only a short step to the crucial Buddhist assertion of equality – all unenlightened beings are really alike. The alternative paper money of the Buddhists, according to their interpretation, fully substitutes the Buddhist cosmology for the popular tradition, as one form of money goes to enlightened beings, and the other to the unenlightened. The final stage toward Buddhist ideology is not to use spirit money at all. The nuns at Kiu Kiong Kiou's temple burn no money themselves, since the only real value of the money is the sutras printed on it, and they can read the sutras out of books.

In addition to their gradual replacement of popular interpretation with Buddhist orthodoxy, Buddhists maintain control over interpretation by bringing disciples into Buddhist social institutions. They bring followers together by inviting them to special ritual occasions, and some temples offer classes in Buddhism. The most widespread institution is the sutra-singing group, a collection of (usually female) adherents who meet periodically to recite sutras. Such groups may also recite sutras for paying customers, especially at funerals. Sutra-singing groups allow the clergy to encourage and control mastery of the Buddhist system of beliefs. The controlled transformation of pragmatic interpretation into systematized ideology succeeds best when some institution, such as the sutra-singing group for lay Buddhists, master–disciple ties for Taoists or geomancers, or the traditional educational system for the state cult, fosters and organizes reinterpretations of religious acts (like burning spirit money, or worshipping the Protectors of the Dharma).

New Institutions and New Interpretations

Interpretations embedded in static social relations like the monastery may be slow to change. Yet Buddhism again illustrates how the loss of institutional control can lead to drastic reinterpretations. The Buddhist renunciation of the secular political hierarchy led to occasional official denunciations. For example, 'in 624, the powerful minister Fu I summarized the political objection to Buddhism: in teaching the renunciation of all worldly ties, it led people to become disloyal to the ruler and unfilial toward parents' (Yang, 1961, p. 200).

Fu I was probably overconcerned; Buddhist temples rarely showed disloyalty, and Chinese Buddhism made constant efforts to combat the perceived lack of filial piety (see Chapter 4). Yet rebellious groups did occasionally rework Buddhist ideology. Buddhism gave rise to a number of sectarian offshoots, which reinterpreted doctrine free from the institutional control of Buddhism itself. Most of these sects were never violent (Overmyer, 1981; see also Jordan, 1982, for a Taiwanese example), but these sects nevertheless shared the rebellious reputation of some of their relatives, like the White Lotus that inspired frequent violence against the Qing government.

Orthodox Buddhism renounced secular politics for a quiescent life in the monasteries. Outside monastic institutional control, however, rebellious sects easily reinterpreted the Buddhist alternative as a call for political action. Many sects share not only a part of the Buddhist cosmology, but also many sutras (including the Heart Sutra and the

Diamond Sutra), the hope of rebirth in a paradise, and a belief in the eventual arrival of a new Buddha, Maitreya. They had close historical relations with Pure Land Buddhism (Overmyer, 1976, p. 85–9). The sects, like monastic Buddhism, reject the popular pantheon and its concomitant approval of the secular political hierarchy. They emphasize instead faith, equality and compassion.

Yet the sects reworked some of the Buddhist concepts to fit their own needs. Sectarian use of Maitreya is the best example of re-interpretation of a Buddhist symbol. Both orthodox Buddhism and the sects speak of history as a series of kalpas – long periods of time begun by the arrival of a Buddha, after which human values steadily deteriorate, until the kalpa ends in the devastation preceding the beginning of the next kalpa. In orthodox Buddhism kalpas are extraordinarily long; one illustration says that if a soft cloth is passed over a solid rock forty *li* in size once every hundred years, a kalpa still will not have passed by the time the rock is entirely worn away (Soothill and Hodous, 1937, p. 242). In the sects, however, the period is shortened to the point at which the end of the kalpa is imminent. Sect leaders sometimes proclaimed themselves to be Maitreya, the Buddha whose arrival marks the beginning of the new kalpa and the end of the old. The orthodox Buddhist interpretation was appropriate to a pacific life of moral cultivation, while the sectarian interpretation of Maitreya could be used instead to justify violent political action.

The symbol of the future Buddha was thus made potentially useful for rebels. The scheme of successive kalpas resonated with the traditional Chinese concept of changes in the Mandate of Heaven, which justified revolt against an emperor who no longer enjoyed divine approval. At the same time, a claim to be the incarnation of Maitreya could also give supernatural sanction to the actions of a sectarian leader. The difference between monastic Buddhism and these sectarian ideologies stemmed in large part from the different social relations that support them. Sectarian reinterpretations become possible when Buddhist institutions lose control over how people interpret their texts and rituals. The sectarians then developed their own institutionalized, systematized ideologies. As in each of the cases examined in this section, transformed interpretations accompany transformed social relations.

Unities and Diversities

I have concentrated so far in this chapter on two major points about diversity: that diverse social relations foster diverse styles of interpretation, and that all beliefs become open to reinterpretation when the institutions and other social experiences behind them change. The pressures toward unity in Chinese religion, however, are just as important, and just as grounded in social relations as those pressures toward diversity. Widely shared social experiences produce one pressure toward unity. China was a politically and economically unified country, and most of the population shared certain basic experiences of kinship, politics and community, though they may often have had different points of view. The same is true of Taiwan today. Institutions' active attempts to create unified beliefs produce a second pressure toward unity. Buddhists offer classes in their doctrines; Taoists or geomancers reveal enough to keep their clients; and most importantly, the state tried to subordinate much ritual to its political goals.

The most clearly shared concern in Taiwan or late imperial China is kinship: nearly all Chinese worship their ancestors. Ties through marriage and descent affect everyone, and large lineages often helped unite rich and poor in an area. Lineage and descent receive regular ritual attention because they concern everyone, and because the elite promoted lineage ritual (by building ancestral halls and supporting lineage banquets) wherever kinship ties gave them a political and economic base of support.

Kinship is thus a unifying concern, but each of the religious traditions treats it differently. Taoism and the state cult pay little attention to kinship. Taoists and elites worship their ancestors in the same way as the popular tradition, although elites may systematize the ancestor cult more (for example, by codifying lineage rules and genealogies), and they use more passive interpretations than the popular tradition. Taoism and the state cult themselves confine kinship to other contexts, elaborating instead on the political metaphor. Buddhists are the exception – they contradict some otherwise shared basic assumptions about kinship. By asserting that everyone is really equal, and by leaving their families to join the clergy, Buddhists imply that they have no more attachment to their own relatives than to anyone else's. They strengthen this implication by worshipping tablets to other people's ancestors in their temples. Buddhism supports its ideological emphasis on equality and transcendence of the secular world by maintaining a self-supporting monastic tradition that could freę its followers from dependence on their natal families.

Geographical community provides another unified religious concern for everyone (except the Buddhists), because community concerns unite all classes of people. Taoism (to the extent that it depends on local support) and the popular tradition emphasize the primacy and unity of local communities. The state cult instead presented communities as units in a nation-wide hierarchy, and the modern government promulgates much the same message by disapproving of local religious festivals. The shared experience of community favors a unified religious concern with community. The government attempt to use religion as a claim for its own centrality also emphasized unity, but the varied interests of local communities countered official moves toward national unity. The realization of a particular ritual performance depends on how these various forces interact in real historical conditions. Buddhism is again the exception, because it is less dependent on community support; Buddhist temples typically rely on geographically dispersed communities.

Politics is the theme most elaborated in the popular, elite and Taoist cosmologies. The state cult reflected government interests by combining with and echoing orthodox political arrangements; it ignored or ritually controlled heterodox power. The popular tradition, and Taoism in even more detail, also recognize this orthodox political system. Yet they also recognize heterodox sources of power (in bandit-ghosts, for example), taking a more realistic view of power at the local level, but putting the central government in a less favorable light. Buddhism, the black sheep once again, renounces both orthodox and heterodox power, substituting instead its own egalitarian vision, and thus appealing to a wide range of the dissatisfied. These differences make sense in relation to the political positions occupied by the adherents of each tradition: the power-holders traditionally emphasized their own authority, ordinary subjects (Taoists and adherents of the popular tradition) are more willing to emphasize heterodox power, and the Buddhists (who generally managed to avoid the government) emphasize equality. These various forces of unity and diversity played and counterplayed each other in a widely shared ritual like the ghost-feeding. Changing social experience promotes diversity (as when popular interpretations of ghosts changed over the last century), while shared experience promotes unity (as for the common concerns with kinship, community and politics). Varied styles of interpretation push people toward diversity (as when the active spirits of the popular tradition receive passive interpretations from the elite), while institutions push people to unify around fixed interpretations (as in state attempts to manipulate the Universal Salvation festival).

The particular unities and diversities I have discussed are specific to the historical development of northern Taiwan in the last century. The broader conclusions, however, can clearly also be applied to the rest of China, at least for the late imperial and Republican periods. All evidence points to shared concerns with kinship, community and politics, and at least suggests the importance of distinctions between pragmatic and systematized, active and passive, and personified and impersonal styles of interpretation. Even more generally, I would suggest that this study's emphasis on interpretation over code, on the diversity of styles of interpretation across social lines (going beyond simple identification of an ideology), and on the possibilities of making and reinterpreting meaning can help clarify issues of culture and ideology in any complex society. My conclusions suggest in particular that 'ideologies' are more complex and flexible than usually granted. Thus various styles of interpretation in Taiwan combine in various ways to form different *types* of ideologies, each open to reinterpretation by people in different positions.

Summary

Mystification theories stress primarily unified ideological support for an entire social system, promoted especially by the ruling class. These theories provide an important insight into unity and diversity in Chinese religion: certain basic structures are indeed widely shared, and they may benefit one class more than another. Yet mystification theory underestimates the counter-pressure toward diversity. More than one religious tradition, and more than one style of interpretation exist in Taiwan. No integrated set of beliefs permeates the entire society. Only trained specialists, for example, use Buddhist or Taoist styles of interpretation, and different participants interpret even shared rituals like the Universal Salvation rites in diverse ways.

Other theories emphasize only the forces of diversity, losing sight of the pressures that mystification theorists stress. 'Moral economy' (Scott, 1976, 1977), for example, maintains that peasants develop their own ideologies:

Woven into the tissue of peasant behavior, then, whether in normal local routines or in the violence of an uprising, is the structure of a shared moral universe, a common notion of what is just. It is this moral heritage that, in peasant revolts, selects certain targets rather than others, and that makes possible a collective (though rarely coordinated) action born of moral outrage. (Scott, 1976, p. 167)

Scott (1977, p. 33) suggests that 'any moral order is bound to engender its own antithesis, at least ritually, within folk culture'. He writes later that peasant culture and religion 'contain almost always the seeds of an alternative symbolic universe . . . This symbolic opposition represents the closest thing to class consciousness in pre-industrial agrarian societies' (1977, p. 224) Thaxton (1982), for example, has applied this principle to rural China by arguing that Communist organizers succeeded only by accepting the demands of the traditional peasant moral economy.

Yet peasant ideologies, in so far as they exist, may be new orders rather than simple inversions of old ones. Buddhism in Taiwan, for example, offers a radically egalitarian message, which contradicts both the secular political hierarchy and the standard cosmological hierarchy that supports it (Chapter 4). Only the clergy and some heterodox sects however, generally recognized this message. In normal times, most people reinterpreted the Buddhist pantheon as favorable to the secular social order. The public recognized the egalitarian potential of Buddhism only occasionally, generally in times of rebellion. A *potential* alternative ideology exists, but it is not the particular property of the peasantry or any other class.

There is no simple case either for cultural unity and ideological mystification, or for class diversity and ideological opposition. Different social strata may share the same religious traditions, as for the general themes of kinship, community and politics shared by all non-Buddhists in Taiwan. On the other hand, a single social stratum may hold diverse or even contradictory beliefs. For example, local elites draw on both popular and elite traditions as they suit the particular purposes of the individuals involved (Chapter 5), and villagers may interpret the ghost-feeding ritual differently depending on their age. For Taiwan, at least, it is not possible to assert that any given social position is invariably associated with any unified system of religious beliefs. Religious unity or diversity depends in large part on how much intellectuals (who develop the ideologies), their backers, and their institutions succeed in influencing the conceptual systems (and the social relations that ground those systems) of other groups in the society.

Still other theorists (e.g., Gramsci, 1971; Sallach, 1974), argue that ruling classes deliberately keep the ideas of subordinate classes in fragments, that is, they prevent them from becoming ideologized. Such pragmatic, unsystematized styles of interpretation create tacit acceptance of the social order by keeping the majority of people unaware of alternative values. According to this theory, ideological confusion, not consensus, is created. Official ideologies are restricted because most people do not have access to the training needed to master them. Development of new ideologies is inhibited because the state can usually control the institutions that foster them.

This recognition of diverse styles of interpretation realizes that the popular tradition is not automatically an oppositional ideology (in contrast to the claims of moral economy), yet it also need not simply reinforce the structure of power (in contrast to mystification theory). The very fact that the popular tradition is not institutionalized, which inhibits the development of oppositional ideologies, also inhibits state control of popular culture, as the state's vain attempts to manipulate the Universal Salvation festival illustrate.

Some elements of the popular tradition may support the power structure, but others may oppose it. These latter can be the roots of an oppositional ideology, but that ideology will develop fully only in future conflicts. 'The social group in question may indeed have its own conception of the world, even if only embryonic; a conception which manifests itself in action, but occasionally and in flashes – when, that is, the group is acting as an organic totality' (Gramsci, 1971, p. 327). Gramsci's more flexible view of culture rests on the kind of argument that this book shares: people actively make their interpretations; they do not simply inherit an established code of meanings. This view makes visible the counterplay of forces that create a mosaic of unities and diversities in religion. Groups in different social positions use diverse styles of interpretation even for shared rituals like the ghost-feeding, and for shared concerns like politics. Styles of interpretation can change as social relations and institutions change. At the same time, shared experience helps unify religious concerns, and certain groups may actively promote unity, as when the government encourages a favorable reading of the hierarchical cosmology by bringing local deities into the state cult. Popular traditions and ideologies, unities and diversities, form parts of historically developing systems of social relations, tied to institutions, to everyday experience, and to structures of power. Seeing beliefs as mechanical correlates of class or society hides the flexibility of interpretation in light of ongoing historical experience. People use, manipulate and create culture (including religion) as part of everyday life within a system of social relations.

Appendix A: Geomancy

This appendix serves primarily to illustrate some of the complexities that make up highly systematized expert systems of interpretation, and will also help fill some gaps in the English literature on geomancy. There are very few discussions of the experts' system of geomancy. There are several nineteenth-century accounts (e.g., DeGroot, 1897; Eitel, 1873). Feuchtwang (1947b) is the most complete study, and Freedman (1966, 1969) remains the most important theoretically. Needham (1954–, vol. 2) and Porkert (1974) give some of the theoretical underpinnings of the system.

The most important sources, however, remain the many handbooks published for use by geomancers. These include modern discussions of geomancy (e.g., Kong, 1977; Lin, 1977; Nanhai, 1976; Wang, 1968), as well as traditional sources (which I consulted in Jiang, 1967; Wang, 1976; and Ye, 1973). In addition, I consulted several professional geomancers. This appendix summarizes some of the basic techniques of geomancy, emphasizing aspects not usually discussed outside the geomancy manuals.

Geomancy traditionally constitutes one of the Five Arts (Wu Shu), which include fate-calculation (*ming*), divination (*bu*), reading appearances (*xiang* (including face-reading, palm-reading, and geomancy), medicine (*yi*), and meditation (*shan*, literally 'mountains'). A few sources classify geomancy as *shan* rather than *xiang*, and ignore meditation entirely. A shared theory based on the five phases unites the Five Arts.

The geomancer's goal is to determine the *qi* or 'configurational energy' of a site. (I rely on Porkert (1974) for definition of terms, although I do not always adopt his ponderous translations.) *Qi* is an active force, and its movements can be seen in its effects on the mountains and streams of Earth. The geomancer examines the shapes and movements of mountains and water in order to determine the flow of *qi* through conduits (*mo*, literally 'veins'). Chinese medicine looks at the flow of *qi* in the veins, nerves and other conduits of the body. Geomancers look at the flow of *qi* in mountain ranges, watercourses and other geographical conduits. Geomancy functions because certain conduits connect lineal relatives, and the *qi* flowing through the Earth can be controlled to flow through the conduit of descent. The term 'dragon' (*long*) or 'dragon-vein' (*long mo*) is sometimes a synonym for geographical conduits, although it refers often only to mountain chains. The problem posed to the geomancer is how to identify the characteristics of the invisible, impersonal *qi*. Is the *qi* of a site propitious or dangerous? Is it strong and concentrated or weak and dispersed? How does it relate to the *qi* of the clients and of the time period?

The geomancer approaches his analysis by dividing every site into four aspects: (1) the mountain chain (*shan long*, literally 'mountain dragon'); (2) the site, sometimes called the 'den' (*xue*, more properly, any point of a conduit where *qi* can be tapped; it also refers to acupuncture points), sometimes called the 'direction' (*xiang*, when referring to the direction it faces), and sometimes called the 'mountain' (*shan*, when referring to the direction directly opposite the *xiang*); (3) water (*shui*); and (4) other mountains, hills, boulders, etc. (*sha*).

Either or both of two techniques determine the characteristics of a site. The first is the physical form (*xing*) of the hills and streams at a site. The second is the cosmological principles (*li*), like the five phases, which invisibly influence the *qi* of a site. I discuss each technique below. Ideal sites are not always available, and the geomancer must compensate by using a third technique – *fa* ('methods', Hokkien *huat*). This may involve physically reshaping the site, but more often demands non-geomantic techniques. This is, in fact, the realm of the Taoist, and is not part of the standard body of geomancy.

Forms

Analysis of the physical form of a site follows the same principles as analysis of the physical form of a person's face or hand. At the most basic, certain shapes relate to the system of five phases (*wu xing*) – the very structured system of abstract categories that characterizes nearly everything in geomancy, and that I introduced when I discussed Taoism (see Figure 4.1). Among their many associations are a set of five shapes that correlate with the shapes of physical objects: Wood is narrow and rounded, Fire is pointed, and so on (see Figure A.1).

The shapes of the five phases are not considered accurate enough to analyze all mountains, and most geomancers rely on two other systems. Feuchtwang (1974b, pp. 121–6) describes one, called the Method of the Twelve Staves (Shi'er Zhangfa, attributed to Yang Yunsong). The other, called the Nine Stars (Jiu Xing; they are associated with the stars of the Big Dipper plus two nearby stars), is a variation on the five phases. Five of the Stars are equivalent to the five-phase shapes, and the other four are combinations. Each of the Nine Stars subdivides into various numbers of subsidiary shapes (Figure A.2 show the subtypes for one of the stars). Similar schemes exist for the classification of the shapes of water courses (see 'Gui Hou Jing' in Jiang, 1967).

Geomancers sometimes also borrow non-geomantic terms to describe the shape of a site. Objects may resemble an official's cap, a writing-brush stand, the character for 'king', a carp, a fishnet, and so on (DeGroot, 1897, gives several examples, and Feuchtwang, 1974b has a more systematic discussion). Lists of these shapes occur in some geomancy manuals, but there is no established system. Choice is limited only by the whimsy of the geomancers. These terms, however, tend to be secondary descriptions of sites that already fit more standard categories.

The shape of the entire mountain range can also be analyzed. It is best if all the phases occur in the order of mutual creation; it is bad if only one phase appears and the range never changes. Mountain ranges may be lively, with many peaks and valleys, or they may be smooth and quiet. The *qi* may meander slowly along a range with many curves, or it may charge down a straight chain of mountains. As with the relationships among the five phases, balance is a crucial goal. The mountains and the water should have a lively

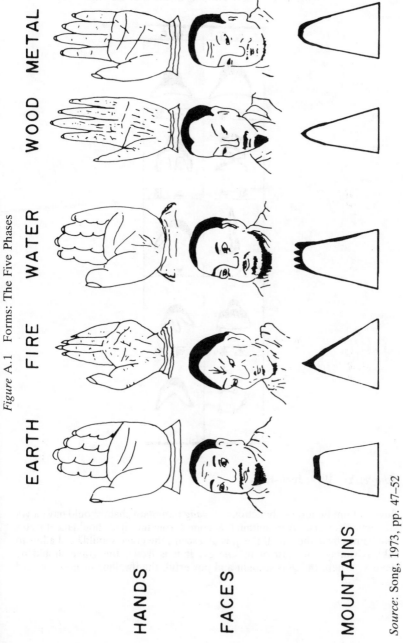

Figure A.1 Forms: The Five Phases

EARTH   FIRE   WATER   WOOD   METAL

HANDS

FACES

MOUNTAINS

Source: Song, 1973, pp. 47–52

Figure A.2   Main Variants of the Star Lu Cun

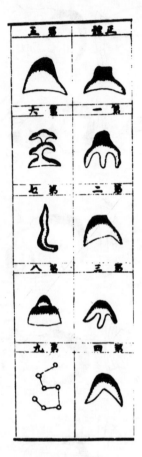

Source: Ye, 1973; Juan 1, p. 7

flow, but not be too rambunctious. A *yang* mountain chain should have a *yin* site, and vice versa. A mountain that comes from the right should meet water that comes from the left. If the *qi* is quiescent, the grave should be shallow to take advantage of most of its energy. If it is lively, the grave should be deeper. Where the *qi* is straight and powerful, the dwelling or grave should be off center to avoid its force. Where the *qi* is weak and meandering, it should be in the center of the conduit to tap all the force.

Principles

The geomancer's compass is the key to discerning the cosmological correlations (*li*) of a site. These devices consist of concentric rings around a central magnetic compass. The rings inscribe a wooden circle, which can be rotated around the compass to allow them to be aligned with the magnetic South. (Chinese take South as their focus instead of North.) Each direction then correlates with a five-phase value, and with a whole host of ther cosmological principles. Thus, for example, a geomancer can use the compass to assign a five-phase value to the direction of the gravesite, and to each of the prominent land forms and watercourses in the area. None of the five phases is good or bad by itself, although all have specific properties. The quality of a site depends on how they interact through the order of mutual creation (*xiang sheng*) and the order of mutual destruction (*xiang ke*) (see Figure 4.2). Geomancers combine these interactions to create much more complex structures than the Taoists use. Thus, for example, if a mountain has characteristics of both Metal and Fire, it is probably unlucky because Fire destroys Metal. Metal and Earth would be good, because Earth creates Metal. The amounts of the phases must always be balanced; none should overwhelm the others. In some cases, for example, where Metal is overpoweringly strong, Fire may be a lucky influence because it controls Metal's strength. This same situation may be complicated further by the presence of Water, which also helps to control Metal because (1) it creates Fire which destroys Metal, and (2) Metal is weakened because it creates Water and thus sacrifices some of its own power. Geomancy is highly structured – no phase can be understood without reference to the others.

    Yin and *yang*, the five phases, and all the rest are impersonal forces that act on the world. In medicine their balance causes health or illness, in geomancy it causes success or failure. The forces it discusses are invisible and generalized away from concrete objects, and the relations and implications of *yin* and *yang*, the five phases, and all the rest are meaningful regardless of the particular material situations in which they occur. The concepts of geomancy are also systematically interrelated with each other. The various systems of classification it includes had separate origins, but are now united into a single theoretical scheme.

    Much of the Western literature mentions a Jiangxi [Kiangsi] school of geomancy based on Forms, and a Fujian school based on Principles. The two are no longer clearly distinguished. I often heard, however, about a different distinction between two schools that differ in the types of cosmological principles they depend on. The San He school concentrates on analysis of the

Figure A.3   The Six Gods

	Both yin or both yang	One yin and one yang
B destroys A	Seven Noxious Breaths	True Official
B creates A	Biased Seal	Seal Ribbon
A destroys B	Biased Wealth	True Wealth
A creates B	God of Food	Injurer of Officials
A equals B	Matched	Destroyer of Wealth

ten Heavenly Stems and twelve Earthly Branches, and the San Yuan school concentrates on the eight trigrams and sixty-four hexagrams. Both systems compare and evaluate characteristics of the time, the clients and the landforms. These systems again show geomancy to be ideologized, based on a systematized set of contrasting categories, and impersonal.

The San Yuan and San He schools use different types of compass. Both Martel (1972) and Feuchtwang (1974b) include illustrations of a San Yuan compass, but both they and most other writers on geomancy analyze only San He geomancy. Martel, whose analysis is purely formal, points out that the San Yuan compass he illustrates does not fit the structure he derives for San He compasses, but he goes no further. I will sketch the broad outlines of both systems below.

Compasses of either school, as well as mariner's compasses, contain at a minimum a magnetic needle (Heavenly Pool) and a ring of twenty-four characters (the Twenty-four Mountains), which name the directions. The larger San He compasses contain three rings of Twenty-four Mountains, each slightly offset from the others, and each associated with some of the other rings. These three rings divide the compass into three sections, called the Heaven, Earth and Man Plates. Geomancy manuals differ on how each ring of Twenty-four Mountains and its associated Plate should be used. One common recommendation is to use the Heaven Plate (the outermost section) to judge water (*shui*), the Earth Plate (the innermost section) to judge the site itself (*xue*), and the Man Plate (the center section) to judge the other prominent land forms (*sha*).

The five phases are important in understanding forms; they are even more important in understanding principles. Nearly every cosmological principle correlates with the five phases, and the most common way to compare any two things is to take their five-phase value as a least common denominator. The various possible relations between the five phases and *yin-yang* (the latter is most important for stems and branches) are called the Six Gods (to be distinguished from the Six Jia Spirits discussed in Chapter 6), which I summarize in Figure A.3. One of the characters represents the individual (A in the table), and the others are compared to it by means of this table. In geomancy the point of reference (A) is usually the site of the grave or house (*xue*). The approximate values of each relationship are clear from their names. (The seal ribbon was a symbol of official office.) Balance, as always, is crucial. Thus, for instance, if there is too much Wealth, the Destroyer of

Figure A.4   Luo Shu Magic Square

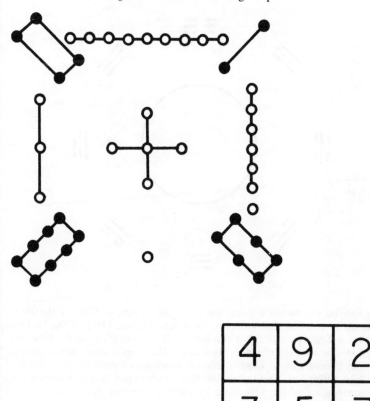

Wealth is propitious. Chao (1946) goes into more detail about the use of this system for eight-character divination of fate; geomancy adopts precisely the same system.

The trigrams, hexagrams, stems and branches can also be classified according to a numerological scheme based on the Luo Shu (see Figure A.4). Pairs of Luo Shu numbers correlate with the directions: nine and four are south, eight and three are east, one and six are north, two and seven are west, and five is the center. Anything that people conceive as a cycle (e.g.,

Figure A.5   Eight Trigrams in Former Heaven Order

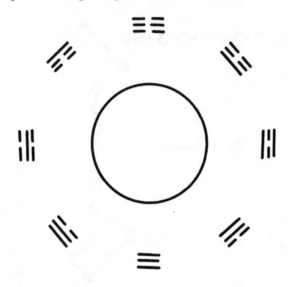

time) can be enumerated using the Luo Shu numbers. One of the most important systems of chronomancy, called the Unique Gate of the Hidden Jia (*Qimen Dunjia*), correlates the time with various lucky and dangerous influences. Because the numbers are also used to identify the compass points, the same system can be used to choose propitious directions (see Zhang, 1977; Ngo, 1976; Tai, 1965). The Luo Shu numbers can also tie together the various elements of the Five Arts by using a complex numerology (e.g., Wang, 1968).

Another major category of compass symbols are the twenty-eight asterisms, which occupy the outermost part of all larger compasses. Geomancy manuals claim that these twenty-eight star groups divide the celestial equator. The asterisms are all different sizes, and the compass also gives the number of degrees occupied by each. Many compasses do this in two rings: one using the traditional Chinese division of the circle into 365 ¼ degrees (based on the length of the solar year), and one using the division into 360 degrees introduced by the Jesuits. The asterisms, like everything else, correlate with the five phases. These readings are compared to determine the relation between the site and the surrounding landforms (*sha*). The phase of the asterism of a site should also be in a relation of creation with the phase of its Earth-Penetrating Dragon, that is, the sexagenary stem-branch of its direction.

The trigrams and hexagrams are more crucial to geomancy, and form the basis of the San Yuan school. The trigrams are combinations of three broken (*yin*) or unbroken (*yang*) lines. Traditionally, they were discovered in the Former Heaven Order (see Figure A.5) by the legendary emperor Fu Xi.

The most *yang* trigram (three unbroken lines) is at the top, a position associated with South, fire and pure *yang*. The most *yin* trigram (three broken lines) is opposite it, and the other trigrams are logically ordered between them so that the top is most *yang* and the bottom is most *yin*. This is associated with the mutual production order of the five phases. The eight trigrams can also be ordered in another sequence, called the Latter Heaven order.

The specific techniques for manipulation and comparison of the hexagrams come from Yi Xue (study of the Yi Jing). The actual interpretations in the Yi Jing are not emphasized. Yi Xue concentrates instead on the logical and cosmological associations of the hexagrams (see, for example, Kong, 1977). The hexagrams can be used to classify time, space and individuals, and geomancers compare the results using the five-phase characteristics and the Luo Shu numbers associated with each.

There is one important system based on the trigrams that is not part of San Yuan geomancy, called the Nine Stars of Shape (Xingzhuang Jiuxing). In the form used to compare the direction of a grave with the surrounding land-forms, the geomancer first determines the trigrams associated with the direction of the site and the landform in question, using the ring of trigrams on the compass. He then uses the 'root trigram' that is, the trigram for the direction of the site, and generates the other seven trigrams by changing the top line, the middle line, the bottom line, the middle line again, and so on. Each resulting trigram is respectively correlated with one of the Nine Stars in a pre-determined order. Thus, for example, the 'root trigram' Qian generates the following: Dui (star: Tan Lang, phase: Wood), Zhen (star: Ju Men, phase: Earth), Kun (star: Lu Cun, phase: Earth), Kan (star: Wen Qu, phase: Water), Sun (star: Lian Zhen, phase: Fire), Gen (star: Wu Qu, phase: Metal), Li (star: Po Jun, phase: Metal), and Qian (stars: Zuo Fu and You Bi, phase: Wood). Landforms in the directions of the trigrams associated with Tan Lang, Ju Men and Wu Qu are propitious; the others are not. With minor variations, the same system is used to compare the direction of a site with the direction of a watercourse (Fu Star Water Method).

The sixty-four hexagrams – all the possible combinations of the eight trigrams – are the basis of San Yuan geomancy. A Yuan is a time period of sixty years, and three of them (San Yuan) is the period it takes to cycle through all sixty-four hexagrams, where each hexagram dominates for two and a half years. Each Yuan is subdivided into three twenty-year periods (Yun). The nine Yun are named after the Nine Stars, and each contains eight hexagrams. Actually, sixty-four 2½-year hexagrams only last 160 years; one Yun is missing. For the sake of theoretical elegance, geomancy manuals always leave this central Yun blank, and distribute the hexagrams among the other eight (see Figure A.6).

If the eight trigrams in the Prior Heaven order are superimposed on the Luo Shu, each trigram can be assigned a number. Each hexagram in the San Yuan system is given the Luo Shu number associated with its upper trigram. Each hexagram thus has two numbers: its Yun number (numbered one through nine), and its Luo Shu number (also numbered on through nine). The geomancer proceeds by finding the correct hexagram for the current time period (by looking in an almanac) and the hexagram for the directions

Figure A.6 The Sixty-four Hexagrams for San Yuan Geomancy

Yun Number	1	2	3	4	5	6	7	8	9
Yuan	upper	upper	upper	middle	middle	middle	lower	lower	lower
Hexagram and Luo Shu Number	Qian 9	Dazhuang 8	Xu 7	Daxu 6		Jue 4	Dayou 3	Xiaoxu 2	Tai 1
	Dui 4	Kui 3	Zhongfu 2	Lin 1		Lu 9	Guimei 8	Jie 7	Sun 6
	Li 3	Ge 4	Mingyi 1	Jiaren 2		Feng 8	Tongren 9	Bi 6	Jiji 7
	Zhen 8	Wuwang 9	Yi 6	Tun 7		Shike 3	Sui 4	Fu 1	Yi 2
	Sun 2	Sheng 1	Daguo 4	Ding 3		Jing 7	Gu 6	Gou 9	Heng 8
	Kan 7	Meng 6	Song 9	Jie 8		Huan 2	Shi 1	Kun 4	Weiji 3
	Gen 6	Jian 7	Xiaoguo 8	Dun 9		Qian 1	Jian 2	Lü 3	Xian 4
	Kun 1	Guan 2	Jin 3	Cui 4		Po 6	Bi 7	Yu 8	Bi 9

of the various aspects of a geomantic site (by consulting the rings of hexagrams on his compass). Each hexagram is compared with the direction of the
site. If the Luo Shu number of the hexagram in question equals the number
of its current Yun, it is considered flourishing (*wang*). If the Luo Shu and
Yun numbers do not match, they should at least both be 'east of the river'
(*jiang dong*, i.e., both numbered 1, 2, 3, or 4) or both be 'west of the river'
(*jiang xi*, i.e., both numbered 6, 7, 8, or 9). The 'river' is the middle Yun,
which has no hexagrams associated with it. If the numbers are on opposite
sides of the 'river', the relationship is called 'weakening' (*shuai*).

The hexagram for the mountain chain should be 'flourishing', and the spot
where the water leaves the site should be 'weakening'. In other words, the
mountains and the water should be on opposite sides of the 'river'. The
direction of the grave or dwelling should be on the same side of the 'river' as
the Yun and the mountain range. Ideally, all should have the same Yun
numbers; the farther away the Yun numbers are, the slower the geomantic
benefits will be realized.

In addition, the Luo Shu numbers of any two aspects of the site should be
in one of the following relationships: (1) 'birth and completion' (*sheng cheng*,
so that the Luo Shu numbers for each direction are paired), i.e., 1 and 6, 2
and 7, 3 and 8, or 4 and 9; (2) 'harmony of ten' (*he shi*, so that opposites on
the Luo Shu diagram are paired), i.e., and 1 and 9, 2 and 8, 3 and 7, or 4 and
6; and (3) *yin-yang* (so that the lowest and highest pairs of *yin* and *yang*
numbers are together), i.e., 1 and 7, 2 and 6, 3 and 9, or 4 and 8. Any other
relationships are not propitious.

Each hexagram is also associated with one of the five phases via its Luo
Shu number (1 and 6 are Water, 2 and 7 are Metal, 3 and 8 are Wood, 4 and 9
are Fire). It is good for the *xiang* (direction of the site) to create or destroy
the five-phase value of the *shan* (back of the site). The reverse relations are
unlucky.

It is also propitious if the two hexagrams being compared are inverted (*dao
pai*, where the top and bottom trigrams are switched), or reversed (*fan*,
where the entire hexagram is turned upside-down). Thus, for example, if the
mountain chain belongs to the hexagram ☰☰ (Lo Shu number 1), a good
direction for the *shan* would be its inverse ☷☷ (Lo Shu number 8). The *xiang*
☰☰ (Lo Shu number 2) is the direct opposite of the *shan*, and water flowing
out at its inverse ☷☷ (Lo Shu number 9) would be lucky. Note also that the
long and *shan* are on one side of the 'river', and the *shui* and *xiang* are on the
other; this is the correct relationship. Furthermore, all four hexagrams are in
the eighth Yun, making it especially propitious.

The arc covered by each hexagram is too large to allow precise alignment.
The compass thus subdivides each hexagram into six units, each represented
by one line of the hexagram. Whichever line is chosen to align the site
changes from *yin* to *yang*, or vice versa, creating a new hexagram. The upper
and lower trigrams of the new hexagram are compared. Their Luo Shu
numbers will be in a relation of 'birth and completion' or 'harmony of ten' if
the site is propitious. The Yi Jing associates each trigram with a kin relation.
Geomancers can thus also compare the benefits for various relatives by
examining the production or destruction of the five-phase values of the two
trigrams. If no satisfactory alignment is available, the site can be put between

two lines, which changes two lines in the hexagram and thus creates more possibilities.

The ten Heavenly Stems and twelve Earthly Branches of San He geomancy also classify space, time, and individuals. Each has a *yin-yang* value, and each is associated with one of the five phases. Running through both sets at once results in a cycle of sixty stem-branches, which are used to classify time. The eight characters used for fate-calculation are the stem and branch associated with the hour, day, lunar month and year.

Each Stem goes through a life cycle described by the twelve Branches (see Chao, 1946). The peak of the life of each Stem occurs at the Branch belonging to its phase. Various combinations of Stems and Branches are lucky or dangerous. The most important combination is the Three Harmonies (San He) of each phase, and the San He school of geomancy takes its name from this relationship. Propitious relationships are generally called harmonies (*he*) and harmful relationships are generally called clashes (*chong*). The system works by finding a site with a propitious combination of the Stems and Branches of the current time, the clients, and the land and water. Feuchtwang (1974b) contains a more thorough discussion of San He geomancy.

Appendix B: Character List

Note: M indicates Mandarin words, H indicates Hokkien words.

an long song hu (M) 安龍送虎
an tau (H) 安斗
an thai sin (H) 安胎神
an thai sui (H) 安太歲
ang ke touq (H) 紅格桌
Ang Kong (H) 翁公
ang thau (H) 紅頭
Anxi (M) 安溪

bai hu (M) 白虎
be ge (H) 尾牙
Bei Di (M) 北帝
biou kong (H) 廟公
bu (M) 卜

Cau Kun (H) 灶君
ce (H) 祭
chai tng (H) 菜堂
Chan (M) 禪
chi (M) 勅
chi ling (M) 勅令
chia: lang kheq (H) 請人客
chia: sin (H) 請神
chiam (H) 籤
chiong (H) 沖
Chit Ia (H) 七爺
chiu: ko (H) 搶孤
chong (M) 沖
chut ke (H) 出家
ciou (H) 醮
Co Su Kong (H) 祖師公
cu ciou (H) 主醮
cu hue (H) 主會
cu pho (H) 主普
Cu Si: Nia:-nia: (H) 助生娘娘
cu tua: (H) 主壇
cue ko (H) 做孤
cui tieng pai (H) 水燈徘

dao pai (M) 倒徘
Daode Tianzun (M) 道德天尊
Daxi (M) 大溪

185

dibao (M) 地保
Dingpu (M) 頂埔
Dui (M) 兌

En Cu Kong (H) 恩祖公

fa (M) 法
fan (M) 翻
fo (M) 佛

gan lu (M) 甘露
Gen (M) 艮
gin-a pho (H) 孩仔普
gu li jie yue (M) 鼓勵節約
Guanyin (M) 觀音
gui (M) 鬼

Hai Shan (M) 海山
Hanlin (M; Frozen Forest) 寒林
Hanlin (M; Imperial academy) 翰林
he (M) 合
he shi (M) 合十
he siu: (H) 和尚
Hengxi (M) 橫溪
hok kim (H) 福金
hong (H) 封
hong sui (H) 風水
hou hia: ti (H) 好兄弟
hu (M) 笏
hu lo cu (H) 副爐主
hu-a (H) 符仔
huat (H) 法
huat piou (H) 發表
huat su (H) 法士
Hufa Shen (M) 護法神
Hut Co (H) 佛祖

iu ieng kong (H) 有應公
iu ieng kong biou (H) 有應公廟
iu kiu pit ieng (H) 有求必應

jia (M) 甲
jiang xi (M) 江西
jiang dong (M) 江東
Jingang Jie (M) 金剛界
Jiu Xing (M) 九星
Ju Men (M) 巨門

Kai Zhang Sheng Wang (M) 開漳聖王

Kan (M) 坎
kan luan jie yue (M) 戡亂節約
kham hun (H) 搚魂
kho kun (H) 搞軍
Khui Kui Mng (H) 開鬼門
kieng i (H) 經衣
Kim Bo (H) 金母
Kiu Kiong Kiou (H) 九芎橋
kiu pieng an (H) 求平安
ko pi: (H) 孤棚
kua hiu: (H) 刈香
kua kim (H) 刈金
Kuan Im (H) 觀音
Kuan Kong (H) 關公
kui (H) 鬼
Kui: Kui Mng (H) 關鬼門
Kun (M) 坤

Laozi (M) 老子
Lau Chu Phai (H) 劉厝派
lau tua: (H) 鬧壇
lau ziat (H) 鬧熱
Li (M; trigram) 離
li (M; measure of distance) 裏
li (M; village) 里
li (M; reason or principles) 理
li (M; ghost) 厲
li qi (M) 厲氣
li tan (M) 厲壇
li tiu: (H) 里長
li xing jie yue (M) 厲行節約
Lian Zhen (M) 廉貞
Lim Chu Phai (H) 林厝派
Lingbao Tianzun (M) 靈寶天尊
liong sim (H) 良心
lo cu (H) 爐主
lo mua: (H) 流氓
long (M) 龍
long mo (M) 龍脈
Lu Cun (M) 祿存
Luo Shu (M) 洛書

Ma Co (H) 媽祖
Meizhou (M) 湄州
Mi Jiao (M) 密教
ming (M) 命
mng-sin (H) 門神
mo (M) 脈
mua: po (H) 麻布

Nan Chen (M) 南辰

o thau (H) 烏頭
o thau sai kong (H) 烏頭師公
ong si: ci: (H) 往生錢

pai (H) 拜
pai to (H) 拜斗
pang cui tieng (H) 放水燈
Peq-ke (H) 白鷄
Pho To (H) 普度
pieng an (H) 平安
Po Jun (M) 破軍
po un (H) 補運
pou pi (H) 保仳
puaq pue (H) 賭筶
Pueq Ia (H) 八爺
pusa (M) 菩薩

qi (M) 氣
Qian (M) 乾
Qimen Dunjia (M) 奇門遁甲
qing long (M) 青龍
Qu Yuan (M) 屈原
Quanzhou (M) 泉洲
qunsi (M) 羣祀

San He (M) 三合
San Qing (M) 三清
San Yuan (M) 三元
Sanxia (M) 三峽
sha (M) 砂
shan (M) 山
shan long (M) 山龍
sheji (M) 社稷
shen (M) 神
sheng cheng (M) 生成
shengwen (M) 聲聞
shengyuan (M) 生員
Shijiamoni (M) 釋加牟尼
Shi'er Zhangfa (M) 十二杖法
shuai (M) 衰
shui (M) 水
Shulin (M) 樹林
si shou (M) 四獸
si tua thiau (M) 四大柱
Sian Kong (H) 仙公
sieng le (H) 牲禮
sim bue an (H) 心不安

sim khaq pieng an (H) 心較平安
sin (H) 神
Siong Te Kong (H) 上帝公
siu kia: (H) 收驚
siu sua: (H) 收煞
Sun (M) 巽

Tai Su Ia (H) 大士爺
Taisui Xing (M) 太歲星
Taiyi Jiuku Tianzun (M) 太乙救苦天尊
Taizang Jie (M) 胎藏界
Tan Lang (M) 貪狼
tang ki (H) 童乩
tau (H) 斗
te-a po (H) 袋仔布
Te Cong Ong Pho Sat (H) 地藏王菩薩
Te Ki Co (H) 地基主
te li (H) 地理
thau ge (H) 頭牙
thiek aq (H) 勅鵶
Thi: Kong (H) 天公
tho te biou (H) 土地廟
Tho Te Kong (H) 土地公
ti kong (H) 猪公
tieng ko (H) 燈篙
Tiong Pho (H) 中埔
tou (H) 道
tou su (H) 道師

wang (M) 旺
wangsheng qian (M) 往生錢
Wen Qu(M) 文曲
Wu Lao (M) 五老
Wu Qu (M) 武曲
wu xing (M) 五行
Wusheng Lao Mu (M) 無生老母

xian (M) 縣
Xian Tian (M) 先天
xiang (M; direction) 向
xiang (M; appearances) 相
xiang ke (M) 相尅
xiang sheng (M) 相生
xing (M) 形
Xingzhuang Jiuxing (M) 形狀九星
xuan wu (M) 玄武
xue (M) 穴

yang (M) 陽

yanshou qian (M) 延壽錢
yi (M) 醫
Yi Xue (M) 易學
Yi Guan Dao (M) 一貫道
yin (M) 陰
Yingge (M) 鶯歌
You Bi (M) 右弼
Yu Huang (M) 玉皇
yuanjue (M) 緣覺
Yuanshi Tianzun (M) 元始天尊
yulanpen (M) 盂蘭盆
Yun (M) 運

zhen (M; township) 鎮
Zhen (M; trigram) 震
Zhengyi Tianshi (M) 正一天師
zhi (M) 智
Zhongzhuang (M) 中庄
Zhong Kui (M) 鍾馗
Zhongpu Li (M) 中埔里
Zhong Shan Tang (M) 中山堂
zhu que (M) 朱雀
Zi Wei (M) 紫薇
Zuo Fu (M) 左輔

Notes

1.   Others have developed similar arguments for other parts of the world. Probably most important for studies of China is Louis Dumont (1970[1966]). Dumont, who is strongly influenced by French structuralism, suggests that the idea of hierarchy based on purity/impurity forms a foundation for the apparently endless diversity of Indian caste beliefs. He does not deny that there are major differences in caste ideology between modern versions and historic, textual versions, between North India and South India, or even between one caste and another, but he looks below these differences to identify a basic structure of purity and impurity.

      Moffatt (1979) makes a similar argument about Indian religious worship. Indian villagers of all castes, he argues, share a divine hierarchy that reproduces, and thus legitimates, the human caste hierarchy. He writes that religious differences across caste have been over-emphasized, and that even Untouchables share a 'deep consensus' with all other groups. See Maloney (1975), however, for a very different view that emphasizes diversity over unity.

2.   Several more general theories support the hypothesis of fundamental ideological or cultural unity. Functionalist 'strain theory', for example, holds that ideologies resolve social and psychological conflicts, and thus help to maintain social homeostasis; ideology creates a cohesive society by supplying a set of shared values (e.g., Apter, 1964). Others argue that ideologies support a mode of production, and especially the security of its ruling classes, by mystifying people about the true nature of power and exploitation in the society (see Chapters 5 and 6 for a fuller discussion).

      Clifford Geertz (1964a, p. 207) criticizes these theories for failing to address symbol formation adequately. For Geertz, ideology (including religion) is a separate system of socially negotiated meanings (i.e., a 'culture') that resolves *cultural*, rather than social or psychological strain. 'Ideologies . . . are, most distinctively, maps of problematic social reality and matrices for the creation of collective conscience' (Geertz, 1964a, p. 220). Geertz rightly shifts attention to meaning formation, but he continues to assume, like the strain theorists, that ideologies help everyone by helping the society as a whole. Ideologies can give differential benefits to different groups. Furthermore, as we shall see, the possibility of reinterpretation means that no ideology may be accepted (at least not intact) at all levels of a society.

3.   An earlier anthropological distinction between an urban, educated, elite Great Tradition, and a village, uneducated, peasant Little Tradition (e.g., Redfield, 1956, ch. 3) has recently been revived by 'moral economy' theorists, especially Scott (1977). This early affirmation of cultural diversity in complex societies is no longer common in anthropology because: (1) the elite tradition may not be as homogeneous as

191

the theory suggests; (2) the two traditions may not be as separate as the theory maintains; and (3) the theory does not allow the possibility of a shared underlying structure of the sort described by Dumont for India and suggested by Freedman for China (see Tambiah, 1970, pp. 3–4, 367–72 for a fuller discussion of these problems). I discuss moral economy in more detail in Chapter 6.

4. Sapir is urging anthropologists to consider individual variation more seriously, emphasizing studies of socialization in particular. His more flexible view of culture leads equally, however, to the examination of the group and class constraints that this study will pursue. We also need studies of individual variations in Chinese religion, on differences within households, on differences by sex, and on socialization, but they must be set in the context of the broader influences on religious practice.

5. Barnett (1977) re-examines changes in Indian caste ideas in this light. He discusses the unifying symbol of caste that Dumont also discussed: blood purity. Some South Indian castes now see blood purity simply as inherited substance, rather than as the traditional combination of substance with a code for conduct. These castes are thus beginning to resemble ethnic groups, and to function as regional power blocs. These changes occurred in conjunction with a Dravidian nationalist movement – there were political motivations behind the change in caste definition. There is thus both a basic unity that no one questions (the central symbol of blood purity), and an equally basic diversity (some groups have redefined caste hierarchy as ethnic difference).

6. He dismissed Weber's (1951) study of China in a footnote as sociologically inadequate. Its general theoretical impact as part of Weber's sociology of religion, however, was probably greater than any of the others.

7. Much of DeGroot's evidence came from personal observation, but it cannot be considered systematic ethnography.

8. I chose to work in Sanxia primarily because the research of several other anthropologists there has provided a solid base for understanding popular religion. Ahern (1973) and Harrell (1974b, 1982) have studied religion in two Sanxia villages with different social structures. Wolf (1970–1974b) has studied popular religion in the town of Sanxia. Wolf and Huang (1980) include a bibliography of works on Hai Shan, the traditional name for the area that included Sanxia, and Wang (1976) has a brief history of the area.

9. A township (*zhen*) is an administrative unit below the county (*xian*) and above the village (*li*). Taiwan has 15 countries, Taibei County has 29 townships (including Sanxia), and Sanxia Township has 22 villages. Locally recognized villages or neighborhoods may differ from official administrative villages. I will use Hokkien names for locally recognized units, and official Mandarin names for administrative units. I romanize Mandarin terms in Pinyin, and Hokkien following Bodman (1955). Appendix B gives characters and identifies dialect for all Chinese terms used. I have not disguised place names, or the names of individuals too well-known to be disguised. I use pseudonyms for all other individuals.

10. I will not examine Christianity here. Catholicism is not important in Sanxia, but there are about one hundred Protestant families.

11. I revised the questionnaire from one developed by Xu Jiaming, Li Yih-yuan and John McCreery at the Academia Sinica. I am very grateful to them for their help and generosity.

12. On the first day of the seventh month, temples most closely associated with the underworld carry out a special ritual, called Opening the Ghostly Gate (Khui Kui Mng). The temple management opens a little door at the side of the temple, and shuts it again after all the ghosts have returned to the underworld on the last day of the month, during the Closing of the Ghostly Gate (Kui: Kui Mng). The temples most likely to do this are City God temples (City Gods rule over traditional administrative capitals, and were recognized by the state cult), and Buddhist temples to the Bodhisattva most closely associated with the underworld, Kshitigarba (Te Cong Ong Pho Sat).

13. The Universal Salvation rites go back to the Six Dynasties period in China. They were originally Buddhist, but the text was soon adapted by Taoists. The ceremony was widely performed from the Tang Dynasty on. Yoshioka (1959, pp. 391–401) describes the development of the Buddhist and Taoist texts. Chen (1973, pp. 24–34) outlines the Yulanpen Jing, the sutra that describes the origins of ghost feeding in Mulian's attempt to save his mother from ghosthood with Buddha's help. Lombard-Salmon (1975, pp. 29–30) discusses possible meanings for the term *yulanpen*, which is one of the Buddhist names for the festival.

14. Other temples in Sanxia may also hold smaller ghost-feeding rituals. The first and last days of the month are especially popular for these smaller ceremonies, but any time during the month is possible. Traditionally, many occupational groups also held their own ceremonies during the seventh month. Now, to my knowledge, only the butchers, who are most closely associated with death, still hold their own ceremony in Sanxia. Some people also make an offering to the ghosts of children (*gin-a pho*), but although people had heard of it in Sanxia, I never saw it performed. Especially devout people may thus worship the ghosts half a dozen times or more during the seventh month.

15. In other parts of Taiwan, this parade may be on a much larger scale, including up to a hundred water lanterns, and also twenty-foot-tall scaffolds (*cui tieng pai*) hung all over with electric lanterns powered by generators on accompanying trucks. This still occurred in Sanxia as recently as 1972 (Stevan Harrell, personal communication).

16. Meat is never offered at Buddhist temples. Partially prepared vegetarian dishes are substituted for *sieng le*. Often, an artificial *sieng le*, entirely vegetarian but shaped to resemble meat, is offered instead.

17. Some of the smaller temples in Sanxia conduct ceremonies that are simplified from the elaborate and expensive performances at the Co Su Kong temple. No other temple in Sanxia has an organization to rival the Four Great Pillars of the main temple, none has the same influence, and thus none has ceremonies on the same scale. All these temples substitute the cheaper puppet shows for operas. Some of them

do not even conduct rituals; people simply bring offerings, burn incense and watch puppets. Buddhist temples (*chai tng*) also put on Universal Salvation ceremonies. At the Buddhist temple in Kiu Kiong Kiou, the entire ceremony takes three days. The first two are devoted to reading Buddhist sutras, and the last to feeding ghosts. A Pho To altar similar to the one at the Co Su Kong temple is set up inside the *chai tng*. The chief priest is an ordained Buddhist, but again, his performance looks to most people exactly like the performance at the Co Su Kong temple.

18. Black-headed priests are Taoists in other parts of Taiwan (Saso, 1972, ch. 5). I discuss them further in Chapter 4.

19. Buddhists change the characters to read 'Frozen Forest Academy'. The two pronunciations are identical except for tone. The Buddhist version is a metaphor for the bitter suffering of the world of reincarnation.

20. Such arguments have their roots in Saussurian structural linguistics, and have entered anthropology especially through the works of Claude Lévi-Strauss. Saussure (1959[1916]) argues that the relation in the mind between a word (signifier) and its referent (signified) is arbitrary; there is no natural connection, for example between the English phonetic string [tri] and the idea 'tree'. The meaning of a word must therefore come from its relation to other words (value). The sound [tri] means 'tree' because it contrasts with other sounds to encode the parallel contrasts of 'tree' with 'bush', 'flower', etc. Words thus form a complex structure of contrasts, which can encode the structure of thought. The social context in which a word is uttered is irrelevant; its meaning comes solely from position in an abstract structure.

21. Much of the material in this chapter will be familiar to specialists. I present it here to provide necessary background for non-specialists, and to recast it in the theoretical framework of Chapter 1.

22. Some of the material in this section is based on Weller (1984), which develops some of these ideas further for Taiwanese affinal kinship.

23. I divide old from young at age 45 primarily to distinguish those who entered their teens before and after the end of the Japanese occupation.

24. The boundaries are less clear for areas with very scattered settlement patterns and no clear neighborhoods (see Harrell, 1981).

25. Zhongzhuang is administratively part of neighboring Daxi township, although it has always had strong economic ties to Sanxia. Sangren (1979, pp. 243–7) discusses an interesting case of a Chen lineage there, whose members take part in both the ritual cycle for Co Su Kong in Sanxia, and the one for Daxi's equivalent, Kai Zhang Sheng Wang.

26. Both of these restrictions are originally Buddhist. Buddhist attitudes toward spirit money will be discussed in Chapter 4.

27. The system did permit, however, criticism of specific gods or specific magistrates for misbehavior.

28. I refer only to division among the long-time residents of Taiwan. The division between these residents and the post-1945 wave of exiles remains strong. There is no significant number of Hakkas in Sanxia,

although conflicts between Hakkas and Hokkiens have been important in other parts of Taiwan.

29. Actually, the annual birthday ceremony contains a ritual technically called a one-day *ciou*. It is performed outside the sight of most people, and few know about it. It is not, technical definitions aside, the elaborate ceremony most people have in mind when they talk about holding a *ciou*.

30. Sugar became another crucial export from Taiwan during this period. I do not consider it here because it was grown primarily in the southern part of the island.

31. The proportion of the old in Taiwan (and presumably the number of dependent old) has generally increased during the twentieth century, from about 3.7 per cent over 60 in 1905 (Ho, 1978, p. 316) to 5.8 per cent in 1974 (Economic Planning Council, 1975, p. 14). Over the same period, the proportion of employment in agriculture (where the old can retain more control) has decreased from 68 per cent in 1905 to 33 per cent in 1970 (Ho, 1978, pp. 324–6). (These figures are for males, because only male employment figures are available for the early period. Total figures would be slightly higher.)

32. Silverstein (1976, pp. 49–50, n.d.) argues that informants recognize the referential functions of language much more explicitly than the indexical features. They recognize most easily forms that exist in continuous segments, that are not bound to social contexts (i.e., they are not pragmatic), and that do not alter the social situation (i.e., they are not creative). This is similar to the Taiwanese cosmology in which the more abstracted, ideologized gods/ancestors/ghosts model is more explicitly recognized than are the elements more thoroughly tied to pragmatic interpretations.

33. For the sake of simplicity, this chapter concentrates only on the clergy. Chapter 6 briefly examines popular reinterpretations of Buddhism and some popular sects based on Buddhism. Much work remains to be done, however, on lay Buddhists.

34. See Liu (1967, pp. 118–27) for details on the specific symbolism of *tau*.

35. They read the *Cebei Sanmo Shui Chanfa*.

36. I will discuss the general irrelevance of ancestors to Buddhism and Taoism in the sections that follow.

37. See Saso (1972) and Liu (1967) for descriptions of *tou* ritual; Keupers (1977) and Liu (1974) for *huat*.

38. Pang (1977) describes another text used in Honolulu. The outlines of the two texts appear similar; I mention the major differences below.

39. Some Taoists, including the Heavenly Master (the titular head of Taoism) also arrived from the mainland, but they did not have the numbers or the influence of the Buddhists.

40. Welch (1967) has the fullest discussion of the social organization of Chinese Buddhism; it concentrates on the large monastic tradition.

41. The different relations of Buddhism and Taoism to local communities may have a historical basis in the native origin of Taoism and the foreign origin of Buddhism. The problem requires greater historical depth than is possible for this study.

42. These informants were generally more influenced by Pure Land Buddhism than any other school, but with only two exceptions, they refused to identify themselves with any one school.
43. Catholics in Taiwan now also worship their ancestors.
44. Dudbridge (1978, pp. 85–91) shows how the legend of Miaoshan, which has ties both to Guanyin and to the Universal Salvation rites, constitutes a Buddhist attempt to resolve the conflict between entering the clergy and maintaining filial piety. Miaoshan uses her Buddhist faith and purity to save her father.
45. A few Buddhist temples read sutras to Dizang Wang (Ksitigarbha; Hokkien: Te Cong Ong) in a much simpler ceremony.
46. The priests who perform the ritual in Taiwan are not followers of the Esoteric Sect. Their own interpretations of the ritual do not depend heavily on the specific features of the Esoteric Sect, but draw instead on the more general features of Taiwanese Buddhism that I have just discussed.
47. Sanxia also had very few members of the national elite in traditional times. There were only three *shengyuan* (the lowest degree) at the end of the Qing Dynasty (1895 in Taiwan).
48. This class analysis is simplified from Gates (1979). Clearly, my simple distinction between elites and non-elites is only a beginning. It clarifies some of the differences in styles of interpretation, and it illustrates some of the forces toward unity and diversity, but it will require finer division.
49. Meskill (1979) gives a good example, where the Lins of Wu-feng consolidated their local strongman position by educating a younger generation.
50. Although Tan and other members of the local elite may have been aware of the history of a term like *liong sim* in Chinese philosophy, they would rarely know the details of the philosophical arguments. Instead, such concepts have come to be a kind of general knowledge.
51. High education correlates with youth in the sample as a whole, but in this case, there is no significant difference between young and old informants. Youth is a factor, however, in the correlations of the other two parts of Table 5.1.
52. Gates (1982) has suggested that the resurgence in popular religion has been funded primarily by a traditional middle class – largely Taiwanese (as opposed to mainlander), and largely cut off from the government and big business sectors that provide most opportunities for social mobility. She argues that these people spend money on religion as a way of gaining status and investing in the local community, independent of (and possibly in opposition to) government and big business. This argument does not specifically address the ghost cult, but my data are nevertheless consistent with Gates's interpretation.
53. The state does not usually show any special support for Buddhism. In this case, however, they are making an opportunistic use of the Buddhist origins of the festival in order to promote their own political goals.
54. By 1965, this had grown to 2500 pigs, fully double the average at the time (XSB, 10 August, 1965, p. 5).

55. The final chapter of Weber's *Religion of China* suggests that Taoism and Confucianism stunted the autonomous growth of capitalism in China. Two factors prevented the development of a modern economy: the 'rational' Confucianists never opposed the popular dominance of 'magical' Taoism; and Confucianism did not create the tension with the secular world that Weber considers essential for the development of capitalism.

> Completely absent in Confucian ethic was any tension between nature and deity, between ethical demand and human shortcoming, consciousness of sin and need for salvation, conduct on earth and compensation in the beyond, religious duty and sociopolitical reality. Hence, there was no leverage for introducing conduct through inner forces freed of tradition and convention. (1951, pp. 235–6)

The specifics of Weber's argument are no longer accepted; Metzger (1977), for example, suggests that Confucianists did not simply strive for harmony with the world, but instead experienced a fundamental tension with it. Weber's broadest claim, however, that Chinese religion impeded 'rational' development because it supported traditional authority, is similar to more modern mystification theories. Weber looked less at exploitation than mystification theory does, but both emphasize religion's support for the status quo.

56. Several authors (e.g., Anderson and Anderson, 1973; Feuchtwang, 1974b) have pointed out that these structures, plus requirements about water flows, soil types, and so on, make good ecological and architectural sense.

57. Ahern (1981b, pt. I) makes a similar distinction between interpersonal ritual and non-interpersonal ritual. Interpersonal ritual involves communication with personified spirits, similar to the kinds of interpersonal communication in the ordinary world. Interpersonal ritual is strictly defined by rules and uses a restricted code, much like communication with humans who are physically removed (like signal flags on ships) or socially distant (like a petition to a high official). Non-interpersonal ritual, most of which is based on five-phase theory, uses a more elaborated code, and attempts to determine natural causes, not human (or godly) wishes. Ahern's distinction thus also clarifies the greater potential of interpersonal communication to act as a metaphor for society.

58. Responses to two questionnaire items illustrate the general acceptance of geomancy. I asked, 'will problems develop if a geomancer is not consulted when building a house or finding a grave?' Only 22 per cent of the respondents felt that no problems would arise. I also asked people to agree or disagree with the statement: 'If the rooms of a house face in the wrong direction, there will be trouble.' Only 28.5 per cent disagreed. The young and the elite, however, are much more likely to disagree. The figures for older educated people do not differ significantly from older uneducated people. The apparent correlation between education and doubts about geomancy is thus caused by specifically Western education, rather than by education in general.

59. Some Buddhists deny the usefulness of geomancy, while others hire professional geomancers; the Buddhist tradition itself says nothing about geomancy.
60. I am indebted to John McCreery for introducing me to the *huat-su* who explained his views on geomancy to me.
61. Weller (1982) discusses spirit mediums in heterodox, sometimes rebellious sects of Buddhism. I address them again below, but only very briefly to avoid further complicating the argument, and because such sects were not very powerful in Sanxia.
62. Maurice Bloch (1974, 1975, 1977) has suggested that religious language is very formalized – it has impoverished syntax, and makes extensive use of metaphor and condensation. Formalized codes are frozen; they cannot address concrete events. Bloch argues that such codes can only affirm accepted generalities, can never challenge the status quo, and thus support traditional authority. His 'formalized codes' are similar to my 'ideologies', especially to systematized styles of interpretation. My finding that institutions tend to systematize their interpretations, and to use them to support their authority (as for drawing lots in temples, or for any of the major religious traditions), fits Bloch's suggestion. Yet Bloch's emphasis on code over interpretation leads him to underestimate the possibility of reinterpretation. Thus, for example, even a highly formalized ritual like the Universal Salvation festival undergoes regular reinterpretation outside the control of priests or other authorities. Use of the code, and control over its interpretation are at least as important as the code itself.
63. A fourth process of ideologization is socially secondary, but it can be a methodological problem: some informants will construct spontaneous theories when the anthropologist asks them about an aspect of religion normally taken for granted. For example, many Taiwanese burn three sticks of incense each day: one is for the ancestors, one is for the gods, and one is placed outside. I elicited three kinds of responses to questions about who the last stick was for. Many informants simply did not know and would not speculate; they gave the frustrating answer one hears so often, 'It is just our custom'. Many other informants hesitated at first, but then answered either that it was for Thi: Kong, the Emperor of Heaven, or for the door gods (very low deities), or for the ghosts. All these beings are normally worshipped outside. Each of these explanations is plausible, and each is ethnographically interesting, but they are also mutually exclusive. These explanations are spontaneous constructions created out of pragmatic interpretation that does not ordinarily address such questions. Burning incense outside is ordinarily something one does, not something one thinks about. The explicit religious ideologies anthropologists often report may represent, in part, theories created by the very process of fieldwork.
64. Door gods come in different types, appropriate to different kinds of temples, but for most people door gods are all the same. Only people like temple artisans have such systematized knowledge of iconography.

References

ABERCROMBIE, NICHOLAS and BRYAN S. TURNER (1978) 'The Dominant Ideology Thesis', *British Journal of Sociology*, 29, pp. 149–70.

AHERN, EMILY MARTIN (1973) *The Cult of the Dead in a Chinese Village* (Stanford: Stanford University Press).

—— (1974) 'Affines and the Rituals of Kinship' in Arthur P. Wolf (ed.), *Religion and Ritual in Chinese Society* (Stanford: Stanford University Press).

—— (1981a) 'The Thai Ti Kong Festival' in Emily Martin Ahern and Hill Gates (eds), *The Anthropology of Taiwanese Society* (Stanford: Stanford University Press).

—— (1981b) *Chinese Ritual and Politics* (Cambridge: Cambridge University Press).

AIJMER, GORAN (1968) 'Being Caught by a Fishnet: On Fengshui in Southeastern China', *Journal of the Hong Kong Branch of the Royal Asiatic Society*, 8, pp. 74–81.

ANDERSON, E. N. and MARJA L. ANDERSON (1973) 'Feng-Shui: Ideology and Ecology' in E. N. Anderson and M. L. Anderson (eds), *Mountains and Water: Essays on the Cultural Ecology of South Coastal China* (Taipei: Orient Cultural Service).

APTER, DAVID E. (ed.) (1964) *Ideology and Discontent* (Glencoe, Ill.: Free Press).

BAITY, PHILIP (1975) *Religion in a Chinese Town* (Taipei: Asian Folklore and Social Monograph Series, No. 64).

BAKER, HUGH D. R. (1979) *Chinese Family and Kinship* (New York: Columbia University Press).

BARNETT, STEVE (1977) 'Identity Choice and Caste Ideology in Contemporary South India' in Janet L. Dolgin, David S. Kamnitzer and David Schneider (eds), *Symbolic Anthropology* (New York: Columbia University Press).

BERNSTEIN, BASIL (1970) 'Social Class, Language, and Socialization' in Pier Paolo Giglioli (ed.), *Language and Social Context* (Harmondsworth: Penguin).

—— (1972) 'A Sociolinguistic Approach to Socialization; with Some Reference to Educability' in John J. Gumperz and Dell Hymes (eds), *Directions in Sociolinguistics* (New York: Holt, Rinehart and Winston).

BLOCH, MAURICE (1974) 'Symbols, Song, Dance and Features of Articulation', *European Journal of Sociology*, 15, pp. 55–81.

—— (1975) 'Introduction' in Maurice Bloch (ed.), *Political Language and Oratory in Traditional Society* (London: Academic Press).

—— (1977) 'The Past and the Present in the Present', *Man* (N.S.) 12, pp. 278–92.

BODDE, DERK (1975) *Festivals in Classical China* (Princeton: Princeton University Press and the Chinese University of Hong Kong).

BODMAN, N. C. (1955) *Spoken Amoy Hokkien* (Kuala Lumpur: Grenier and Son).

199

CHAN WING-TSIT (1963) *A Source Book in Chinese Philosophy* (Princeton: Princeton University Press).

CHAO WEI-PANG (1946) 'The Chinese Science of Fate Calculation' *Folklore Studies*, 5, pp. 279–315.

CH'EN, KENNETH K. S. (1973) *The Chinese Transformation of Buddhism* (Princeton: Princeton University Press).

CHRISTIAN, WILLIAM A. (1972) *Person and God in a Spanish Valley* (New York: Seminar Press).

CHIU KUEN-LIANG (1978) 'Dance of Chung Kuei', translated by Earl Wieman, *Echo of Things Chinese*, 6(7), pp. 7–24.

CHIU, VERMIER Y. (1966) *Marriage Laws and Customs of China* (Hong Kong: Chinese University of Hong Kong).

CH'U T'UNG-TSU (1962) *Local Government in China Under the Ch'ing* (Stanford: Stanford University Press).

COHEN, MYRON (1976) *House United, House Divided: The Chinese Family in Taiwan* (New York: Columbia University Press).

CONVERSE, PHILIP E. (1964) 'The Nature of Belief Systems in Mass Publics', in David E. Apter (ed.), *Ideology and Discontent* (Glencoe, Ill.: Free Press).

DAVIDSON, JAMES W. (1903) *The Island of Formosa, Past and Present* (London: Macmillan).

DEGROOT, J. J. M. (1885) 'Buddhist Masses for the Dead at Amoy', *Actes du Sixième Congrès International des Orientalistes, tenu en 1883 à Leide*, Section 4 (Leiden: E. J. Brill).

——— (1886) *Les Fêtes Annuelement Célebrées à Emoui*, translated by C. G. Chavannes, *Annales du Musée Guimet*, 11, pp. 1–399; 12, pp. 400–830.

——— (1897) *The Religious System of China*, vol. 3 (Leiden: E. J. Brill).

DORE, HENRI (1915) *Researches into Chinese Superstitions*, vol. 2 (Shanghai: T'usewei Press).

DOUGLAS, MARY (1966) *Purity and Danger* (New York: Praeger).

DSTZ (1872) *Danshui Tingzhi* 淡水廳志 (Danshui Prefecture Gazetteer), compiled by Chen Peigui 陳培桂 in *Taiwan Quanzhi* 台灣全誌 (Taibei: Taiwan Jingshi Xinbaoshe, 1922).

DUDBRIDGE, GLEN (1978) *The Legend of Miao-shan* (London: Ithaca Press).

DUMONT, LOUIS (1970 [1966]) *Homo Hierarchicus: The Caste System and Its Implications* (Chicago: University of Chicago Press).

DYYJ (1978) *Diyu Youji* 地獄遊記 (Record of a Journey Through Hell). Edited by the Shengxian Tang 聖賢堂 (Banqiao: Sanyang).

Shengxiah Tan (Banqiao: Sanyang).

ECONOMIC PLANNING COUNCIL (1975) *Taiwan Statistical Data Book, 1975* (Taibei: Economic Planning Council, Executive Yuan).

EITEL, E. J. (1873) *Feng-Shui: or, The Rudiments of Natural Science in China* (Hong Kong: Lane, Crawford and Co.).

FEI HSIAO-T'UNG (1939) *Peasant Life in China: A Field Study of Country Life in the Yangtze Valley* (London: Routledge & Kegan Paul).

FEUCHTWANG, STEPHAN (1974a) 'Domestic and Communal Worship in Taiwan' in Arthur P. Wolf (ed.), *Religion and Ritual in Chinese Society* (Stanford: Stanford University Press).

___ (1974b) *An Anthropological Analysis of Chinese Geomancy* (Laos: Vithagna).

___ (1976) 'School-Temple and City God' in G. William Skinner (ed.), *The City in Late Imperial China* (Stanford: Stanford University Press).

FREEDMAN, MAURICE (1966) *Chinese Lineage and Society: Fukien and Kwangtung*, London School of Economics Monographs in Social Anthropology, No. 33 (London: Athlone).

___ (1967) 'Rites and Duties, or Chinese Marriage' in Maurice Freedman, *The Study of Chinese Society: Essays by Maurice Freedman*. Selected and introduced by G. William Skinner (Stanford: Stanford University Press, 1979).

___ (1969) 'Geomancy', *Proceedings of the Royal Anthropological Institute of Great Britain and Ireland*, 1968, pp. 5–16.

___ (1974) 'On the Sociological Study of Chinese Religion' in Arthur P. Wolf (ed.), *Religion and Ritual in Chinese Society* (Stanford: Stanford University Press).

FREEMANTLE, FRANCESCA and CHOGYAM TRUNGPA, trans. (1975) *The Tibetan Book of the Dead; The Great Liberation Through Hearing in the Bardo, by Guru Rinpoche According to Karma Lingpa* (Boulder, Col.: Shambala Publications).

GALLIN, BERNARD (1966) *Hsin Hsing, Taiwan* (Berkeley: University of California Press).

GALLIN, BERNARD and RITA S. GALLIN (1982) 'Socioeconomic Life in Rural Taiwan: Twenty Years of Development and Change', *Modern China*, 8, pp. 205–46.

GATES, HILL (1979) 'Dependency and the Part-time Proletariat in Taiwan', *Modern China*, 5, pp. 381–407

___ (1982) 'Are Two Bourgeoisies Better Than One?' (unpublished manuscript).

GEERTZ, CLIFFORD (1964a) 'Ideology as a Cultural System' in Clifford Geertz (1973), *The Interpretation of Cultures* (New York: Basic Books).

___ (1964b) ' "Internal Conversion" in Contemporary Bali' in Clifford Geertz (1973), *The Interpretation of Cultures* (New York: Basic Books).

___ (1972) 'Deep Play: Notes on the Balinese Cockfight' in Clifford Geertz (1973), *The Interpretation of Cultures* (New York: Basic Books).

GODELIER, MAURICE (1975) 'Toward a Marxist Anthropology of Religion', *Dialectical Anthropology*, 1, pp. 81–5.

GORDON-CUMMING, Constance Frederica (1900) *Wanderings in China* (Edinburgh: Blackwood).

GRAMSCI, ANTONIO (1971) *The Prison Notebooks* (New York: International).

GRANET, MARCEL (1975[1922]) *The Religion of the Chinese People*, Maurice Freedman (trans. and ed.), (Oxford: Blackwell).

HARRELL, STEVAN (1974a) 'When a Ghost Becomes a God' in Arthur P. Wolf (ed.), *Religion and Ritual in Chinese Society* (Stanford: Stanford University Press).

___ (1974b) *Belief and Unbelief in a Taiwan Village* (Ph.D. dissertation, Department of Anthropology, Stanford University).

___ (1976) 'The Ancestors at Home: Domestic Worship in a Land-Poor

Taiwanese Village' in William Newell (ed.), *Ancestors* (The Hague: Mouton).

_____ (1979) 'The Concept of "Soul" in Chinese Folk Religion', *Journal of Asian Studies*, 38, pp. 519–28.

_____ (1981) 'Social Organization in Hai-shan' in Emily Martin Ahern and Hill Gates (eds), *The Anthropology of Taiwanese Society* (Stanford: Stanford University Press).

_____ (1982) *Ploughshare Village: Culture and Context in Taiwan* (Seattle: University of Washington Press).

HO, SAMUEL P. S. (1978) *Economic Development of Taiwan, 1860–1970* (New Haven: Yale University Press).

HOU CHING-LANG (1979) 'The Chinese Belief in Baleful Stars' in Holmes Welch and Anna Seidel (eds), *Facets of Taoism* (New Haven: Yale University Press).

HSIAO KUNG-CHUAN (1960) *Rural China: Imperial Control in the Nineteenth Century* (Seattle: University of Washington Press).

HYMES, DELL (1974) *Foundations in Sociolinguistics, an Ethnographic Approach* (Philadelphia: University of Pennsylvania Press).

JIANG GUOZONG 蔣國宗 (1967) *Dili Zhengzong* 地理正宗 (Orthodox Geomancy)(Xinzhu: Zhulin Chuban She).

JORDAN, DAVID K. (1972)*Gods, Ghosts, and Ancestors: The Folk Religion of a Taiwanese Village*(Berkeley: University of California Press).

_____ (1982) 'The Recent History of the Celestial Way: A Chinese Pietistic Association', *Modern China*, 8, pp. 435–62.

KEUPERS, JOHN (1977) 'A Description of the *Fa-ch'ang* Ritual as Practiced by the *Lu Shan* Taoists of Northern Taiwan' in Michael Saso and David W. Chappell (eds), *Buddhist and Taoist Studies*, vol. 1 (Hawaii: University Press of Hawaii).

KONG ZHAOSU 孔昭蘇 (1977) *Kongshi Yipan Yijie* 孔氏易盤易解(Master Kong's Explanation of the Hexagram Compass)(Taipei: Jiwen Shuju).

KUHN, PHILIP A. (1970) *Rebellion and Its Enemies in Late Imperial China* (Cambridge: Harvard University Press).

LABOV, WILLIAM (1969) 'The Logic of Nonstandard English', Georgetown Monographs on Language and Linguistics, vol. 22.

LÉVI-STRAUSS, CLAUDE (1967) 'The Sorceror and His Magic' in Claude Lévi-Strauss, *Structural Anthropology*, vol. 1 (Garden City, NY: Anchor).

LI YIH-YUAN (1976) 'Chinese Geomancy and Ancestor Worship: A Further Discussion' in William Newell (ed.), *Ancestors* (The Hague: Mouton).

LIANG XIANGRUN 梁湘潤 (1976) *Qimen Dunjia Rumen* 奇門遁甲入門 (Introduction to the Unique Gate of the Hidden Jia)(Taibei: Xingmao Chuban She).

LIN MANHONG 林滿紅 (1976) 'Wan Qing Taiwan de Cha, Tang ji Zhangnao Ye' 晚清台灣的茶糖及樟腦業 (The Tea, Sugar, and Camphor Industries in Late Qing Taiwan), *Taibei Wenxian* 38, pp. 1–9.

LIN ZONG 林縱 (1977) *Yijing yu Sanyuan Dili* 易經與三元地理(The Yijing and San Yuan Geomancy)(Gaoxiong: Longshan Chuban She).

LIN YUEH-HWA (1948) *The Golden Wing: A Sociological Study of Chinese Familism* (New York: Oxford University Press).

LIU ZHIWAN 劉枝萬 (1967) *Taibeishi Songshan Qi'an Jianjiao Jidian* 台北市松山祈安建醮祭典 (Great Propitiatory Rites of Petition for Be-nifecence at Songshan, Taibei, Taiwan)(Nangang, Taiwan: Academia Sinica, Institute of Ethnology).

—— (1974) *Zhongguo Minjian Xinyang Lunji* 中國民間信仰論集 (Collected Writings on Chinese Popular Beliefs), Academia Sinica Special Monograph No. 22 (Taipei: Academia Sinica, Institute of Ethnology).

LOMBARD-SALMON, CLAUDINE (1975) 'Survivance d'un Rite Boud-dhique à Java: La Cérémonie de Pu-du (Avalambana)', *Bulletin de l'École Française d'Extreme Orient*, 62, pp. 457–93.

LÜ ZIZHEN 呂子振 (1975[1880]) *Jiali Dacheng* 家理大成 (Outline of Family Rites)(Tainan: Qibei Publishing).

LURIA, A. R. (1976 [1974]) *Cognitive Development: Its Cultural and Social Foundations* (Cambridge: Harvard University Press).

MACKAY, GEORGE LESLIE (1895) *From Far Formosa* (New York: Fleming H. Revell).

MALINOWSKI, BRONISLAW (1935) *Coral Gardens and their Magic*, vol. 2 (London: George Allen & Unwin).

MALONEY, CLARENCE (1975) 'Religious Beliefs and Social Hierarchy in Tamil Nadu, India', *American Ethnologist*, 2, pp. 169–91.

MANN, MICHAEL (1970) 'The Social Cohesion of Liberal Democracy', *American Sociological Review*, 35, pp. 423–39.

MARTEL, FRANCOIS (1972) 'Les Boussoles Divinatoires Chinoises', *Communications*, 19, pp. 115–37.

MESKILL, JOHANNA MENZEL (1979) *A Chinese Pioneer Family: The Lins of Wu-feng, Taiwan, 1729–1895* (Princeton: Princeton University Press).

METZGER, THOMAS A. (1977) *Escape from Predicament: Neo-Confucianism and China's Evolving Political Culture* (New York: Columbia University Press).

MOFFATT, MICHAEL (1979) 'Harijan Religion: Consensus at the Bottom of Caste', *American Ethnologist*, 6, pp. 244–60.

NANHAI ZHUREN 南海主人 (1976) *Kanyuxue Yuanli* 堪輿學原理 (Principles of Geomancy)(Taipei, Jiwen Shuju).

NAQUIN, SUSAN (1976) *Millenarian Rebellion in China: The Eight Trigrams Uprising of 1813* (New Haven: Yale University Press).

NEEDHAM, JOSEPH (1954–) *Science and Civilization in China*, 7 vols (Cambridge: Cambridge University Press).

NGO VAN XUYET (1976) *Divination, Magie et Politique dans la Chine Ancienne* (Paris: Presses Universitaires de France).

OVERMYER, DANIEL L. (1976) *Folk Buddhist Religion: Dissenting Sects in Late Traditional China* (Cambridge: Harvard University Press).

—— (1981) 'Alternatives: Popular Religious Sects in Chinese Society', *Modern China*, 7, pp. 153–90.

PANG, DUANE (1977) 'The *P'u-tu* Ritual' in Michael Saso and David W. Chappell (eds.), *Buddhist and Taoist Studies*, vol 1 (Hawaii: University Press of Hawaii).

PASTERNAK, BURTON (1969) 'The Role of the Frontier in Chinese Lineage Development' *Journal of Asian Studies*, 23, pp. 551–61.

PORKERT, MANFRED (1974) *The Thoretical Foundations of Chinese Medicine* (Cambridge: The MIT Press).

POTTER, JACK M. (1970) 'Land and Lineage in Traditional China' in Maurice Freedman (ed.), *Family and Kinship in Chinese Society* (Stanford: Stanford University Press).

QSZS (n.d.) 'Qingshui Zushi Liechuan' 清水祖師列傳, photocopy (Sanxia: Changfu Yan Chongjian Weiyuanhui).

RADIN, PAUL (1927) *Primitive Man as Philosopher* (New York: D. Appleton).

REDFIELD, ROBERT (1956) *Peasant Society and Culture* (Chicago: University of Chicago Press).

SALLACH, David L. (1974) 'Class Domination and Ideological Hegemony', *Sociological Quarterly*, 15, pp. 38–50.

SANGREN, PAUL STEVEN (1979) 'A Chinese Marketing Community: An Historical Ethnography of Ta-Ch'i, Taiwan' (Ph.D. dissertation, Department of Anthropology, Stanford University).

SAPIR, EDWARD (1934) 'The Emergence of the Concept of Personality in a Study of Cultures' in Edward Sapir (1949), *Culture, Language and Personality* (Berkeley: University of California Press).

SASO, MICHAEL R. (1972) *Taoism and the Rite of Cosmic Renewal* (Pullman: Washington State University Press).

_____ (1978) *The Teachings of Taoist Master Chuang* (New Haven: Yale University Press).

SAUSSURE, FERDINAND DE (1959 [1916]) *Course in General Linguistics* (New York: Philosophical Library).

SCHIPPER, KRISTOFER M. (1974) 'The Written Memorial in Taoist Ceremonies' in Arthur P. Wolf (ed.), *Religion and Ritual in Chinese Society* (Stanford: Stanford University Press).

SCOTT, JAMES (1976) *The Moral Economy of the Peasant* (New Haven: Yale University Press).

_____ (1977) 'Protest and Profanation: Agrarian Revolt and the Little Tradition', *Theory and Society*, 4, pp. 1–38, 211–46.

SEAMAN, GARY (1978) *Temple Organization in a Chinese Village*, Asian Folklore and Social Life Monographs, vol. 101 (Taipei: Orient Cultural Service).

SHIKAGANE KAKUTARO 鹿鉅赫太郎 (1902), 'Shinhen Nenju Gyoji' 新編年中行事 (New Compilation of Annual Rituals) *Taiwan Kanshu Kiji*, 7, pp. 67–9.

SILVERSTEIN, MICHAEL (1976) 'Shifters, Linguistic Categories, and Cultural Description' in Keith H. Basso and Henry A. Selby (eds.), *Meaning in Anthropology* (Albuquerque: University of New Mexico Press).

_____ (n.d.) 'The Limits of Awareness', (unpublished manuscript).

SKINNER, G. WILLIAM (1976), 'Cities and the Hierarchy of Local Systems' in G. William Skinner (ed.), *The City in Late Imperial China* (Stanford: Stanford University Press).

SMITH, ROBERT (1974) 'Afterword' in Arthur P. Wolf (ed.), *Religion and Ritual in Chinese Society* (Stanford: Stanford University Press).

SONG DEHAI 德海 (1973) *Shan Yi Ming Bu Daquan* 山醫命卜大全 (Great Collection on Mountains, Medicine, Fate and Divination)(Taizhong: Ruicheng Shuju).

SOOTHILL, WILLIAM E. and LEWIS HODOUS (1937) *A Dictionary of Chinese Buddhist Terms* (London: Kegan Paul, Trench, Trubner).

SUZUKI SEIICHIRO 鈴木法一郎 (1978[1934]) *Taiwan Jiuguan Xisu Xinyang* 台灣舊慣習俗信仰 (Old Customs and Traditional Beliefs of Taiwan). Edited and translated by Gao Xianzhi 高賢治 and Feng Zuomin 馮作民 (Taibei: Zhongwen Tu Gongsi).

TAI MINGZI 泰明子(1965) *Qimen Shenshu* 奇門神術 (Divine Art of the Unique Gate)(Taizhong: Chuanze Chuban She).

TAISHANG LINGBAO ZHENJI XUANKE 太上靈寶賑濟玄科 (n.d.) Taoist text, manuscript.

TAMBIAH, STANLEY J. (1970) *Buddhism and the Spirit Cults in Northeast Thailand* (Cambridge: Cambridge University Press).

THAXTON, RALPH (1982) 'Mao Zedong, Red *Miserables*, and the Moral Economy of Peasant Rebellion in Modern China' in Robert P. Weller and Scott Guggenheim (eds.), *Power and Protest in the Countryside* (Durham: Duke University Press).

THOMAS, KEITH V. (1971) *Religion and the Decline of Magic: Studies in Popular Beliefs in Sixteenth and Seventeenth Century England* (London: Weidenfeld & Nicolson).

THOMPSON, E. P. (1963) *The Making of the English Working Class* (New York: Vintage).

THOMPSON, LAURENCE G. (1975) 'Yu Ying Kung: The Cult of Bereaved Spirits in Taiwan' in L. Thompson (ed.), *Studia Asiatica: Essays in Felicitation of the Seventy-Fifth Birthday of Professor Chen Shou-yi* (San Francisco: China Materials Center).

TWFZ (1765) *Taiwan Fuzhi* 台灣府志 (Taiwan Prefecture Gazeteer), compiled by Yu Wenyi 余文儀 in *Taiwan Quanzhi* 台灣全誌 (Taibei: Taiwan Jingshi Xinbaoshe, 1922).

TWSZ (1980) *Taiwan Sheng Tongzhi* 台灣省通志 (Complete Gazeteer of Taiwan Province), compiled by the Taiwan Sheng Wenxian Weiyuanhui 台灣省文獻委員會 (Taibei: Zhongwen Tushu).

WAKEMAN, FREDERICK (1975) *The Fall of Imperial China* (New York: Free Press).

WANG SHI 王氏(1976) *Luojing Xiangjie* 羅經詳解 (Detailed Explanation of the Geomantic Compass)(Taizhong: Ruicheng Shuju).

WANG SHIH-CH'ING (1974) 'Religious Organization in the History of a Chinese Town' in Arthur P. Wolf (ed.), *Religion and Ritual in Chinese Society* (Stanford: Stanford University Press).

——王世慶(1976) 'Haishan Shihua (Shang)' 海山史話 (上)(History of Haishan, Part I) *Taibei Wenxian*, 37, pp. 49–131.

WANG DEXUN 王德薰(1968) *Shanshui Fawei* 山水發微 (Subtleties of Geomancy)(Taipei: Wenwu).

WANG TIANCONG 王天從 (1967) *Sanxia Diqu Yiwei Kangri Shiliao* 三峽地區乙未抗日史料 (Historical Materials on the Yi-wei Resistance to Japan in the Sanxia Area) (Sanxia: Wang Tianzong).

WATSON, RUBIE (1981) 'Class Differences and Affinal Relations in South China', *Man*, 16, pp. 593–615.

WEBER, MAX (1951) *The Religion of China* (Glencoe, Ill.: Free Press).

—— (1968) *Economy and Society*, edited by Guenther Roth and Claus Wittich (New York: Bedminster).

WELCH, HOLMES (1967) *The Practice of Chinese Buddhism, 1900–1950* (Cambridge: Harvard University Press).

WELLER, ROBERT P. (1981) 'Affines, Ambiguity, and Meaning in Hokkien Kin Terms', *Ethnology*, 20, pp. 15–29.

—— (1982) 'Sectarian Religion and Political Action in China', *Modern China*, 8, pp. 463–83.

—— (1984) 'Affinal Contradiction and Symbolic Resolution in Chinese Kinship', *Ethnology*, 23, pp. 249–60.

WICKBERG, EDGAR (1981) 'Continuities in Land Tenure, 1900–1940' in Emily Martin Ahern and Hill Gates (eds), *The Anthropology of Taiwanese Society* (Stanford: Stanford University Press).

WIEGER, LEO (1913) *Moral Tenets and Customs in China* (Peking: Catholic Mission Press).

WILLIAMS, RAYMOND (1977) *Marxism and Literature* (Oxford: Oxford University Press).

WOLF, ARTHUR P. (1970) 'Chinese Kinship and Mourning Dress' in Maurice Freedman (ed.), *Family and Kinship in Chinese Society* (Stanford: Stanford University Press).

—— (1974a) 'Introduction' in Arthur P. Wolf (ed.), *Religion and Ritual in Chinese Society* (Stanford: Stanford University Press).

—— (1974b) 'Gods, Ghosts, and Ancestors' in Arthur P. Wolf (ed.), *Religion and Ritual in Chinese Society* (Stanford: Stanford University Press).

—— (1976) 'Aspects of Ancestor Worship in Northern Taiwan' in William Newell (ed.), *Ancestors* (The Hague: Mouton).

—— and CHIEH-SHAN HUANG (1980) *Marriage and Adoption in China, 1845–1945* (Stanford: Stanford University Press).

WOLF, MARGERY (1972) *Women and the Family in Rural Taiwan* (Stanford: Stanford University Press).

—— (1975) 'Women and Suicide in China' in Margery Wolf and Roxanne Witke (eds), *Women in Chinese Society* (Stanford: Stanford University Press).

WU YINGTAO 吳瀛濤 (1975) *Taiwan Minsu* 台灣民俗 (Folk Customs of Taiwan) (Taibei: Zhongwen Shuju).

XSB. *Xin Sheng Bao* 新生報 (Taiwan newspaper).

YANG, C. K. (1961) *Religion in Chinese Society* (Berkeley: University of California Press).

YAO MENG-CHIA and LINCOLN KAYE (1976) 'Grappling with Ghosts', *Echo of Things Chinese*, 6(2), pp. 13–18, 60.

YAO YING 姚瑩 (1957[1832]) *Dongcha Jilue* 東槎紀略 (Sketch of My Assignment to Taiwan)(Taibei: Taiwan Yinhang).

YQYK (n.d.) *Yuqie Yankou* 瑜伽燄口 (Yogacara Feeding of the Fiery Mouths) (Buddhist sutra).

YE JIUSHENG 葉九升(1973) *Shanfa Quanshu* 山法全書(Complete Book of the Mountain Method)(Taizhong: Ruicheng Shuju).

YOSHIOKA YOSHITORO 吉岡義豐(1959) *Dokyo to Bukkyō* 道教全佛教 (Taoism and Buddhism) vol. I (Tokyo: Nihon Gakujutsu Shinkosha).

_____ (1979) 'Taoist Monastic Life' in Holmes Welch and Anna Seidel (eds.), *Facets of Taoism* (New Haven: Yale University Press).

ZHANG YAOWEN 張耀文 (1977) *Wushu Zhanbu Quanshu* 五術占卜全書(Complete Book of Divination and the Five Arts), vol. 2 (Tainan: Wangjia Chuban She).

ZHUHONG 袾宏 (1976) *Yuqie Yankou Shishi Yaoji Xiangzhu* 瑜伽焰口施食要集詳註 (Detailed Annotation to the Yogacara Feeding of the Fiery Mouths)(Taibei: Fojiao Chuban She).

Index

Aborigines, 69, 78, 138
Acupuncture, 173
Administrative units, 192n.9
Adoption, 27, 99
Aesthetics, 64–5
Affines, 29, 31, 33, 35–6
Age: and frequency of worship, 27, 29; of sample, 196n.51. *See also* Old age
Ahern, Emily Martin, 52, 197n.57
Altars, 18; Buddhist, 163; domestic, 25–6, 31, 72, 147; for neglected spirits, 136; for state cult, 131–2; for temple founders, 45; for Universal Salvation festival, 15, 19, 41, 43, 57, 91–2; Taoist, 101
Amoy, 77
Ananda, 119
Ancestors, 24–37; and geomancy, 153; in Buddhism, 46, 116; in Catholicism, 196n.43; relation to social world, 22, 28; tablets for, 27, 27, 31; worship of, 16, 151
Ancestral halls, 27
Ang Kong, 55
Anxi County, 12, 39, 51, 53, 77
Azure Dragon, 148–9, 154

Bandits, 62, 70, 79, 80, 98. *See also* Ghosts: as marginal gods
Barnett, Steve, 192n.5
Beggars, 62, 67. *See also* Ghosts: as marginal ancestors
Bei Di, 92
Bernstein, Basil, 9, 10
Betrothal, 34, 84
Big Dipper, 154, 174
Birthday celebrations: for Kuan Kong, 45. *See also* Co Su Kong: birthday celebration for
Black-headed priests, 91, 194n.18; and Universal Salvation ritual, 18
Bloch, Maurice, 198n.62
Bodhisattvas, 113; Kshitigarba, 193n.12; Protectors of the Dharma, 1, 18, 164
Bridewealth, 35
Brothers: tensions between, 26, 152
Buddha Patriarch. *See* Hut Co

Buddhas, 1, 113–14
Buddhism, 9, 87, 90, 111–17, 140, 160, 161, 162; and community, 112–13, 168; and equality, 113, 170; and kinship, 116–17, 167–8; and politics, 12, 113–15, 135, 165, 168; clergy, 13, 45–6; schools of, 46, 112, 121, 166, 196n.42, 196n.47; social organization of, 13, 111, 195n.40
Buddhist texts, 18, 19. *See also* Ritual texts
Bureaucratic order: possibility of questioning, 49, 113–15
Bureaucrats: at rituals, 14, 131, 133; behavior toward, 48–9; low-ranking, 72–3, 137
Burials, 138, 150, 152. *See also* Geomancy
Businessmen: and feasts, 16, 55; as temple founders, 45; periodic worship by, 30
Butchers, 193n.14

Camphor, 78–9
Capitalism: discussed by Weber, 10
Carvings, 40, 64
Caste, 191n.1, 192n.5
Cau Kun. *See* Stove God
Celibacy, 116
Chai tng, 38, 45–6; and ties to local community, 46, 112; Universal Salvation festival in, 194n.17
Chan Buddhism, 46
Charms, 107–8; as receipts for payment, 43; for exorcism, 71; for protection of temple, 18; on ancestral altars, 26; Taoist, 95
Chia: sin, 93
Chiu: ko. See Robbing the lonely ghosts
Christian, William, 4
Christianity, 52, 135, 147, 161, 193n.10, 196n.43
Ciou, 42, 57–8, 91, 99, 123, 146, 195n.29
City God, 131, 133, 136, 137–8; and ghost ritual, 193n.12; bureaucratic iconography of, 48

208

214 *Index*